AF261145

The Facts of Life is about life, about us and the world we're living in. The language is symbolic. But where pictogram language uses stereotype to attempt direct unequivocal meaning in a controlled environment, Facts of Life is perverting the "banal" to destabilize the comfort of generalization, to ask the awkward questions and to propose the awkward answers. The truth emerges from the process of deciphering — from the construction of ones own interpretation, form appropriation.

I lay awake nights trying to pull the Facts of Life out of my ceiling. Sometimes they were good and I could build on them, they meant something, they came to life and flew on their own - the others were dead-enders. It was hard to recognize the good ones before wasting time on the duds. Making an almost self-evident image is very difficult. There is no method, the process isn't rational – I just worked at it until it either worked or I got fed up.

Facts of Life as a language is open ended, unorganized and structureless. It is ambiguous, imprecise and impartial. Each symbol is intentionally created to lack descriptive detail, thus to avoid codifying reality. They are non-linear indivisible wholes to be read from any direction and in any order. There are no prescribed meanings - they are only catalysts to provoke interpretation. Facts of Life is not optimistic or pessimistic. It is critical, even brutal at times. There is no invention of an aesthetic - I want Facts of Life to be anti-style, anti-decoration.

This Fat Facts of Life book is a selection of pictograms published over 20 years ago. Times have changed but the problems are much the same: what is hypocrisy, what is the fallout of our dependency on technology, how is it that democracy is deteriorating, what do we do now that we have destroyed the earth, what is love in the techno virtual world, what is alienation...

The last images in this volume, from a series of books that were never published, are mutants of our pictograms in another world after ours but with much the same problems.

Pippo Lionni, Paris 03.01.20

…….“!”………….“!”……“!”……“!

“?”“?”“!”“?”“?”“?”“!”…….“!”

.“!”?”….“?”“?”…“!”………“?”

“!”; “!”,“!”:“!”;“!”,“!”;“!”,“!”:“

“!”…“!”..“!”“?”“!”…“?”“!”….

“?”…“?”………“?”…“?”..“?”.

..“!”…..“!”……“!”………“!”…. : . .

. : “!”…“?”“!”…. : ….“!”……,“!”.

……., …..“?”“?”“!”…..“?”….“!”..

…………“?”…“?”..“?”…………“?”.

“!”…….“!”…………“!”… : …“?”….“

"!" "!" "!". "?" .... "?" "?" "?" ,.. "?"

, ... "!" .... "!" "?" ... "?" ...:.... "!" ..

"?" ... "?" "!" .... "!" .... "!" . ...

"?" .... "!" .... "?" "!" ...... "?" .

.... "?" "!" "?" "!" . "!" "!" "!" .. "!"

.. "?" .. "!" .... "!" .. "?" . "?" . "?"

.. "!" .... "?" .. "?" .... "!" ..

" ... "!" .... "?" ... "!" "!" ... "!" "?"

"!" "?" "!" . "!" "!" "!" . "?" ... "?" ..

.... "!" .. "?" . "?" ... "!" ....

.... "?" ... "?" .. "?" ....

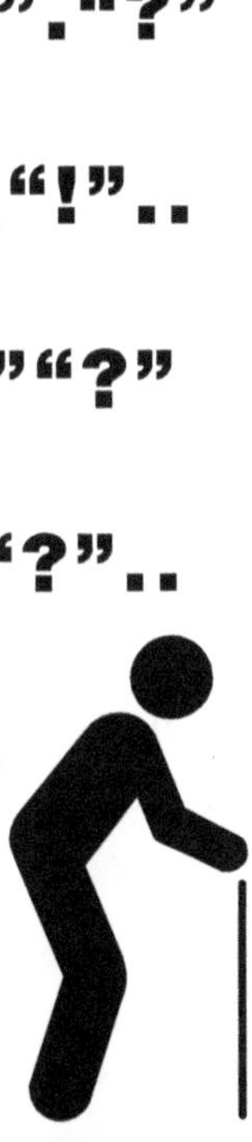

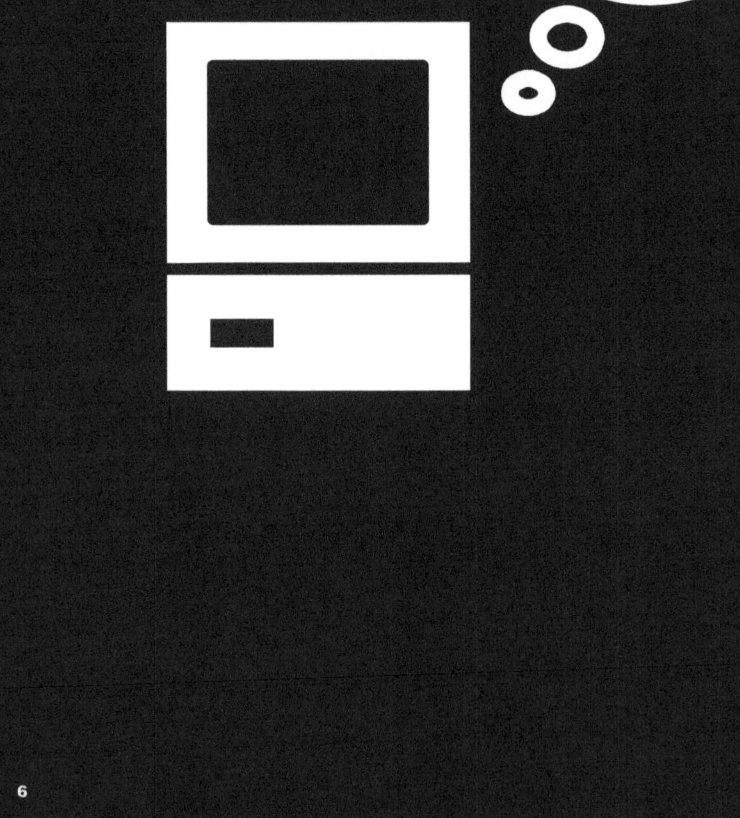

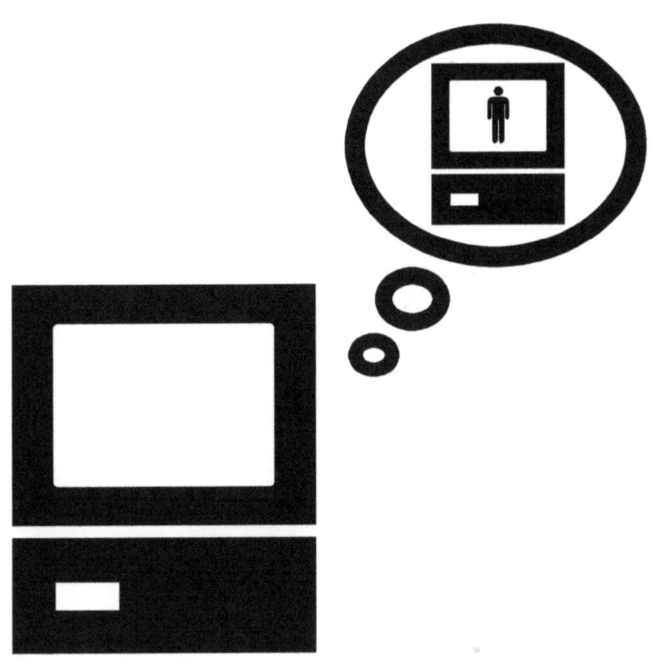

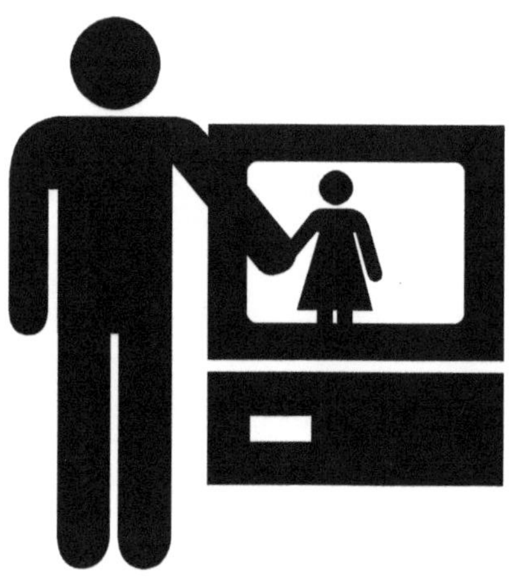

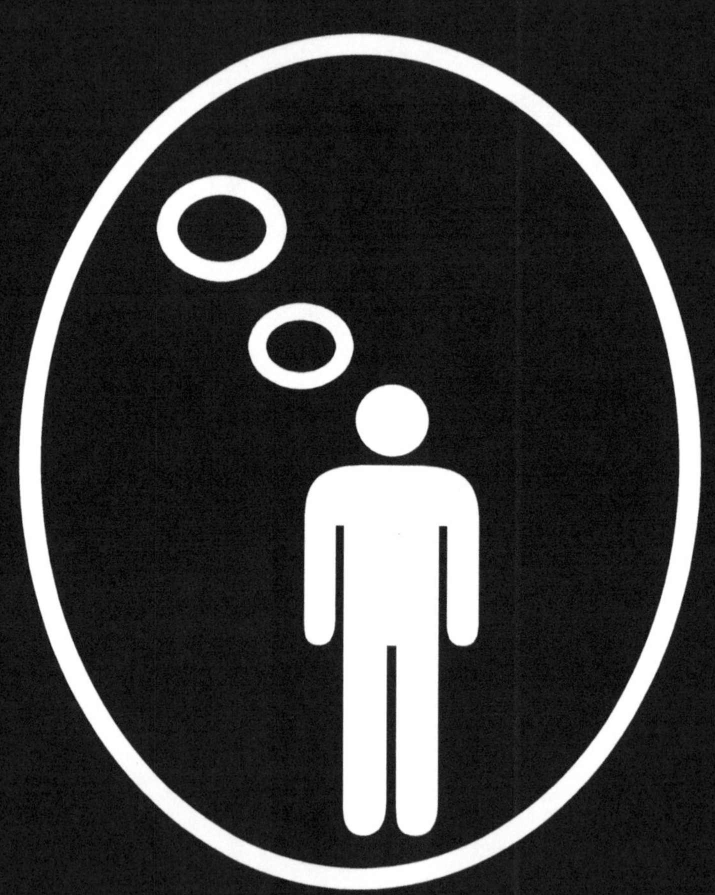

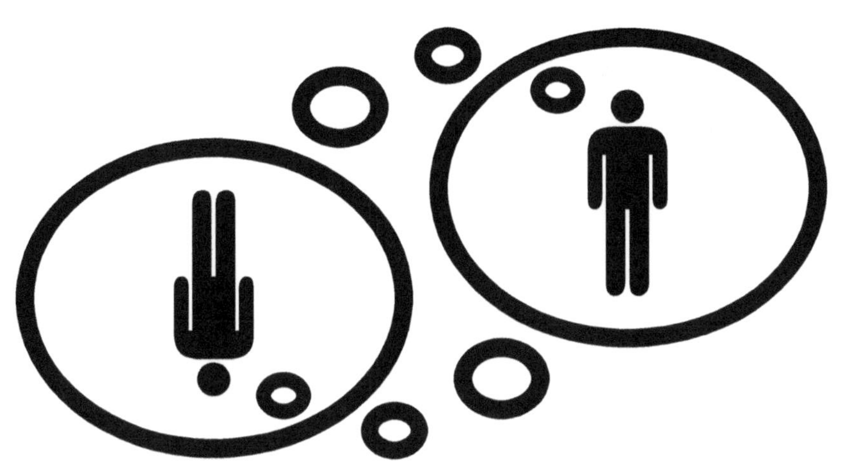

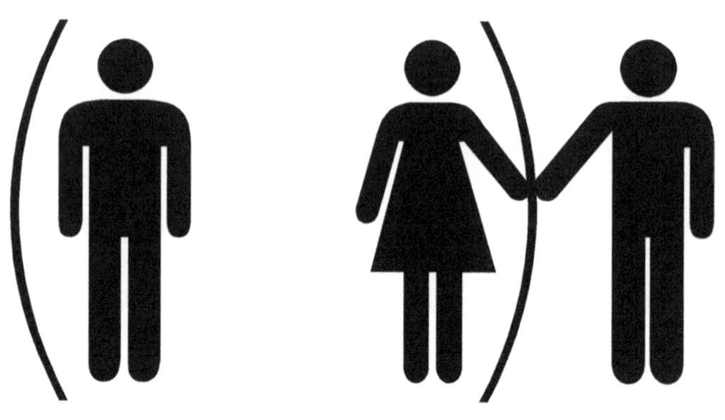

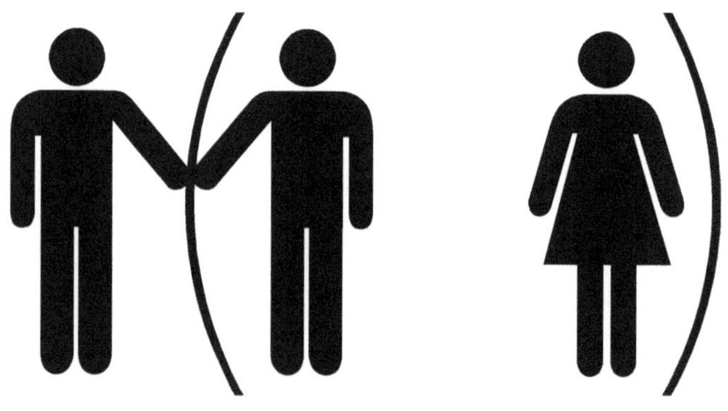

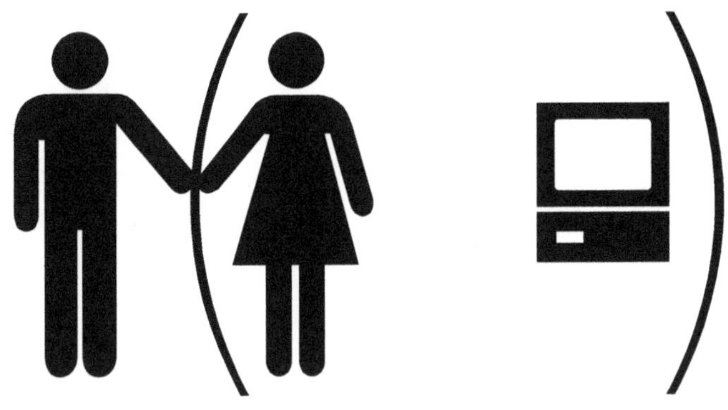

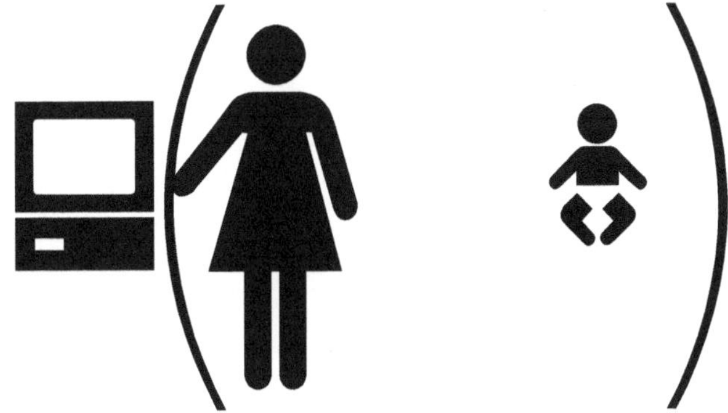

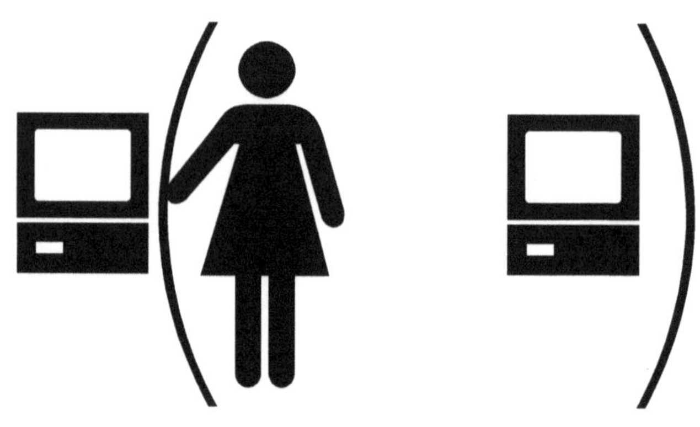

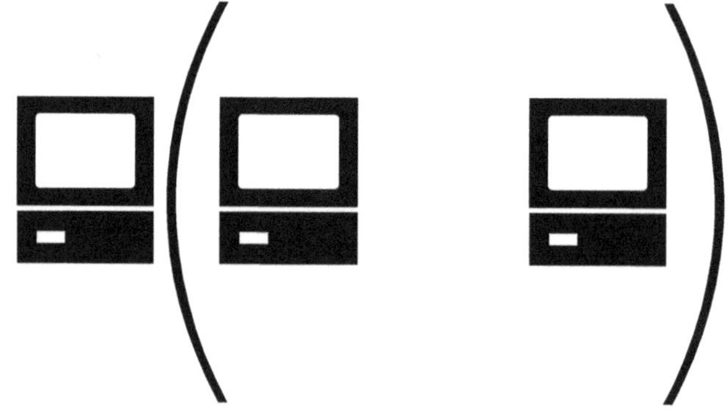

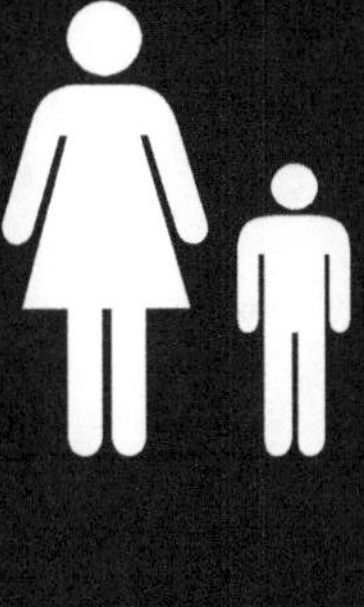

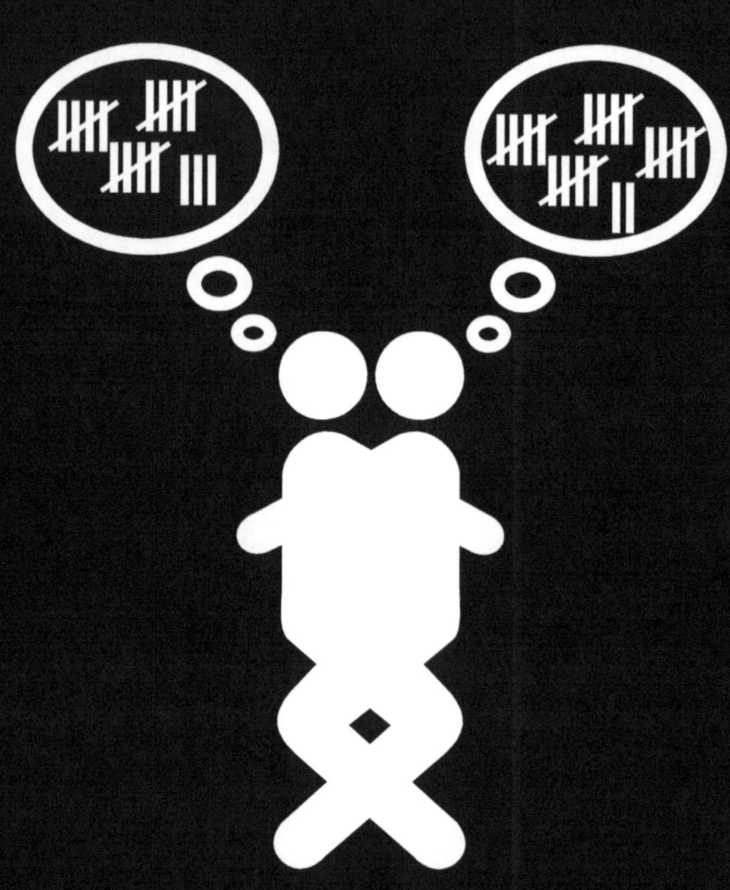

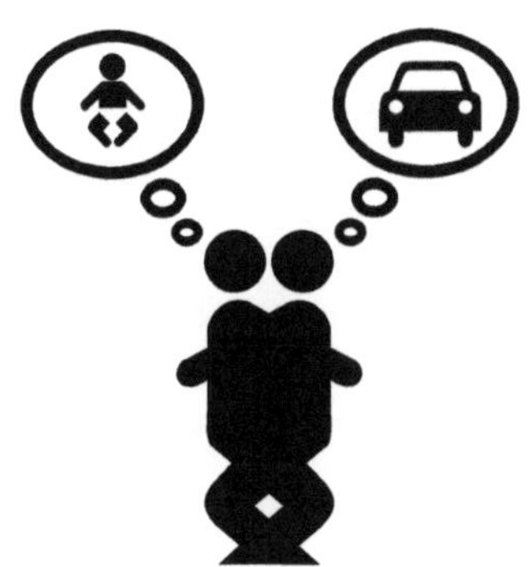

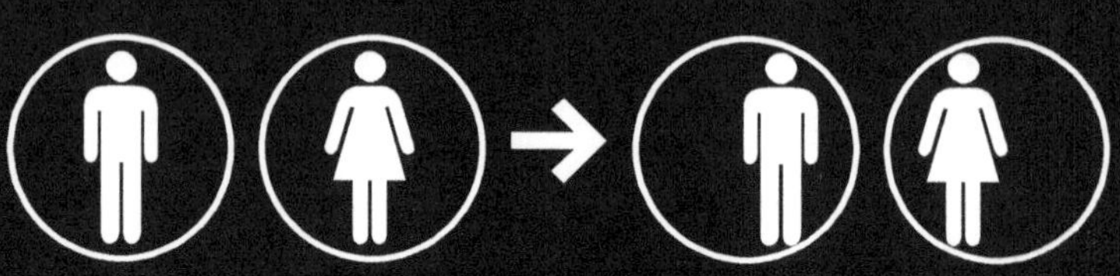

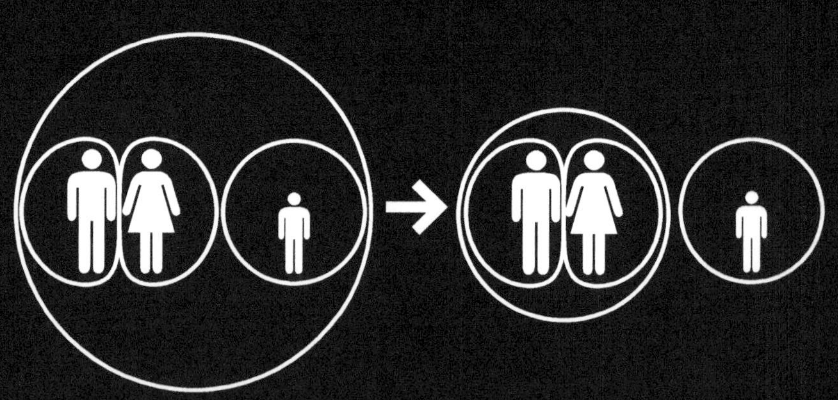

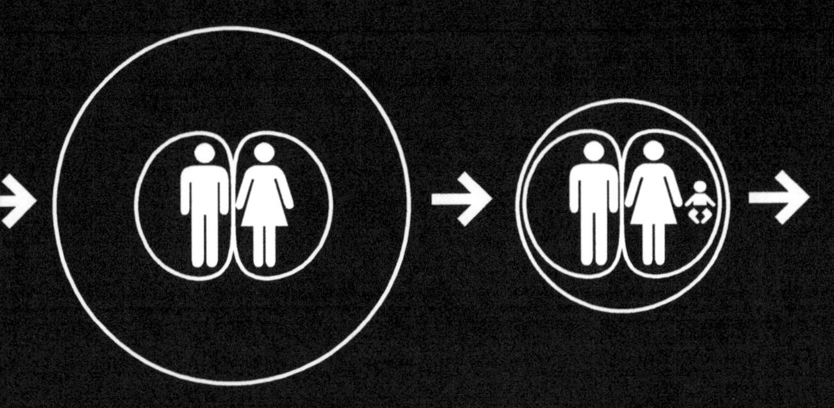

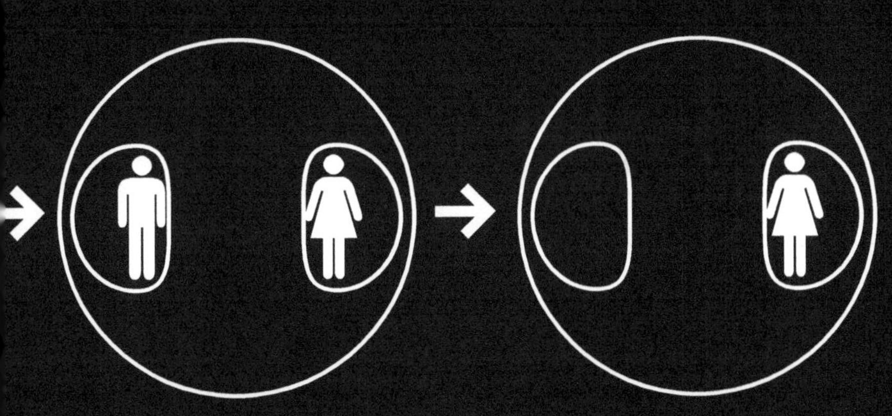

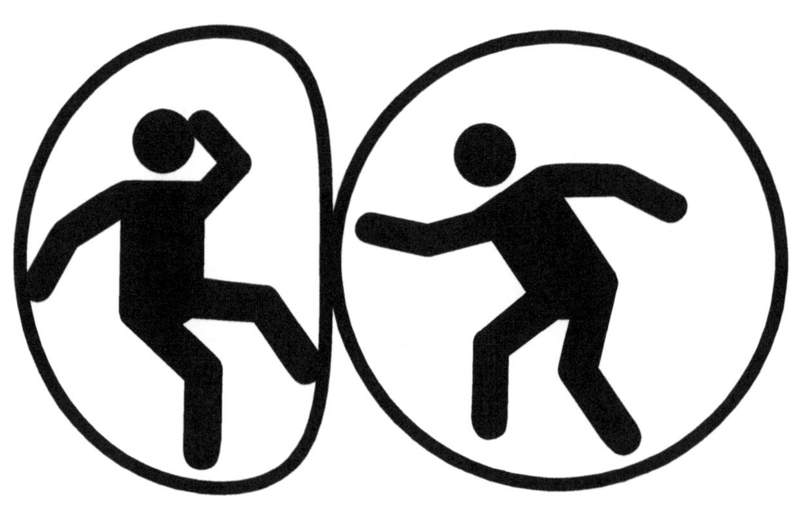

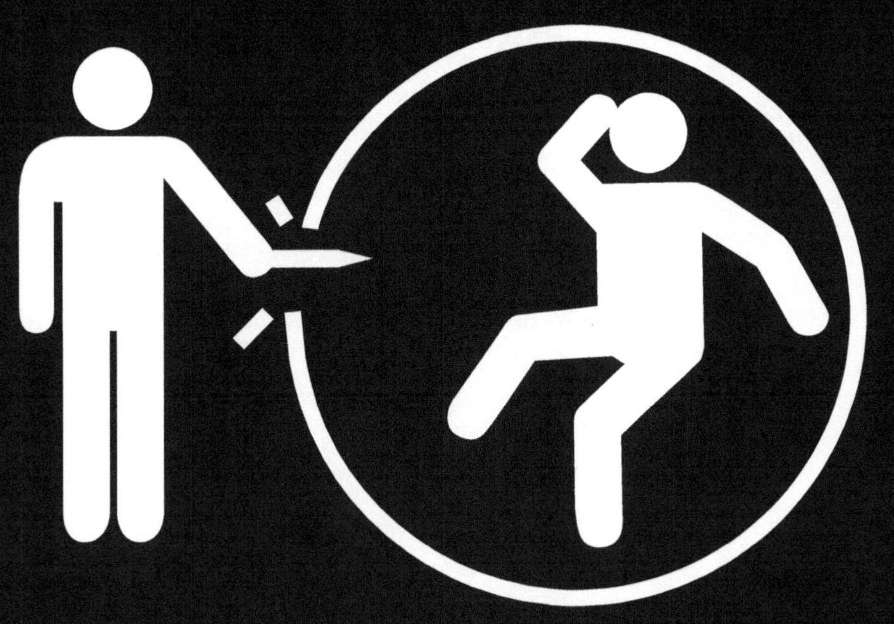

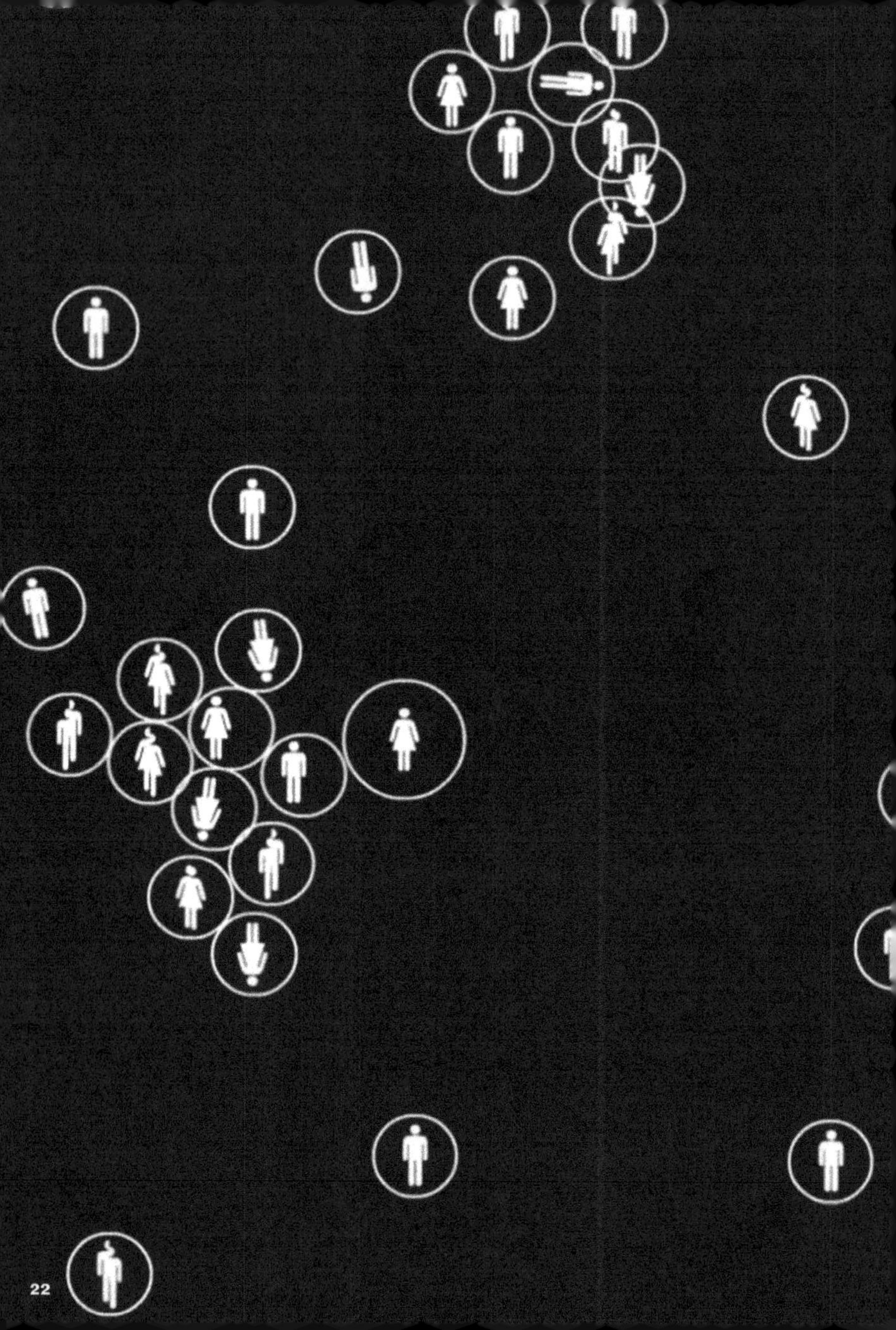

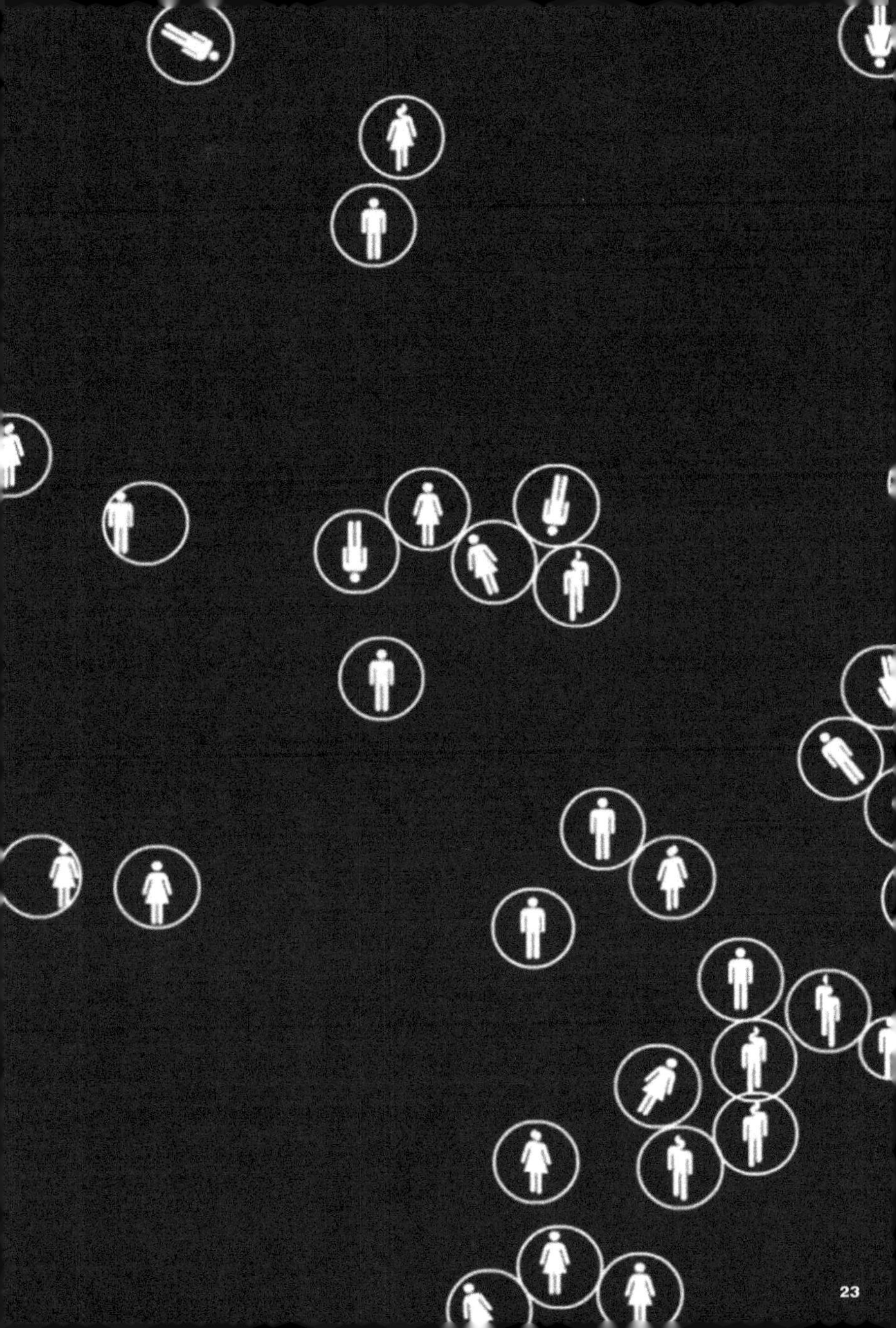

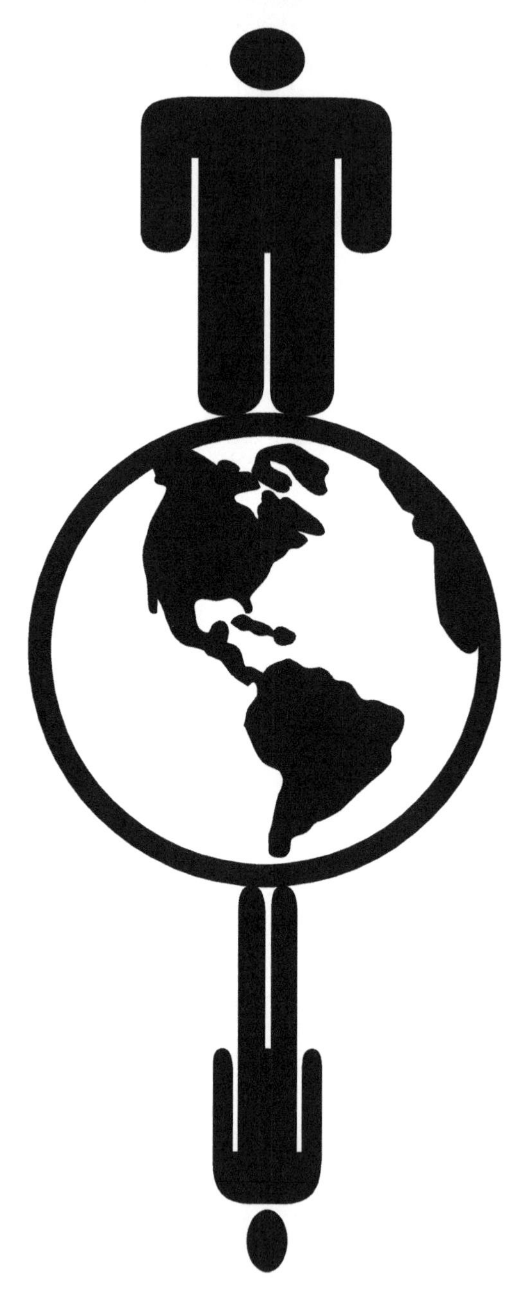

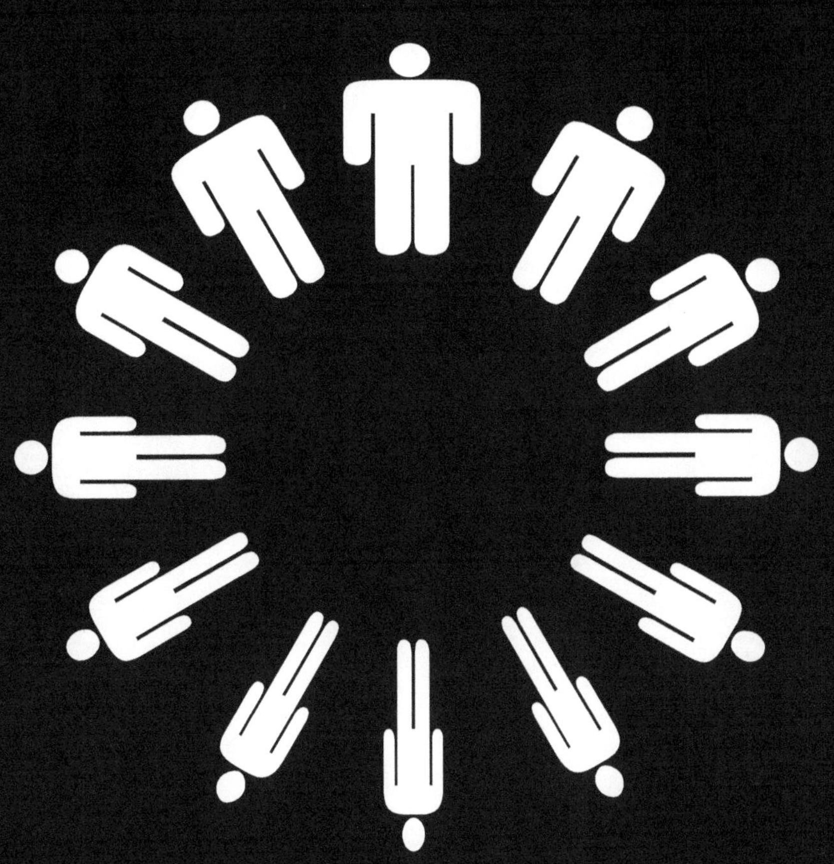

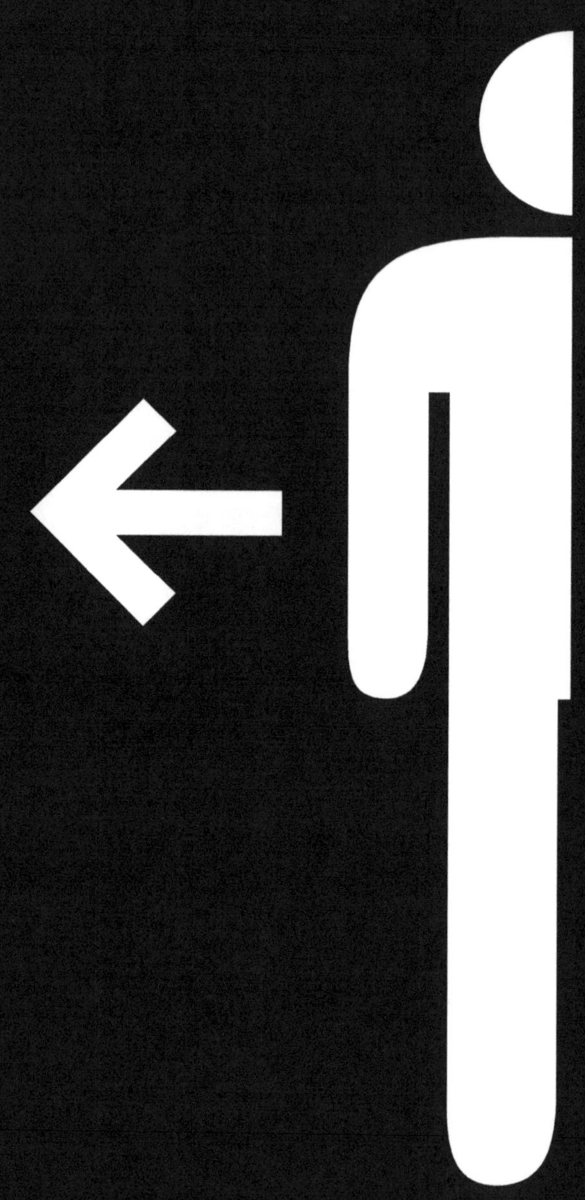

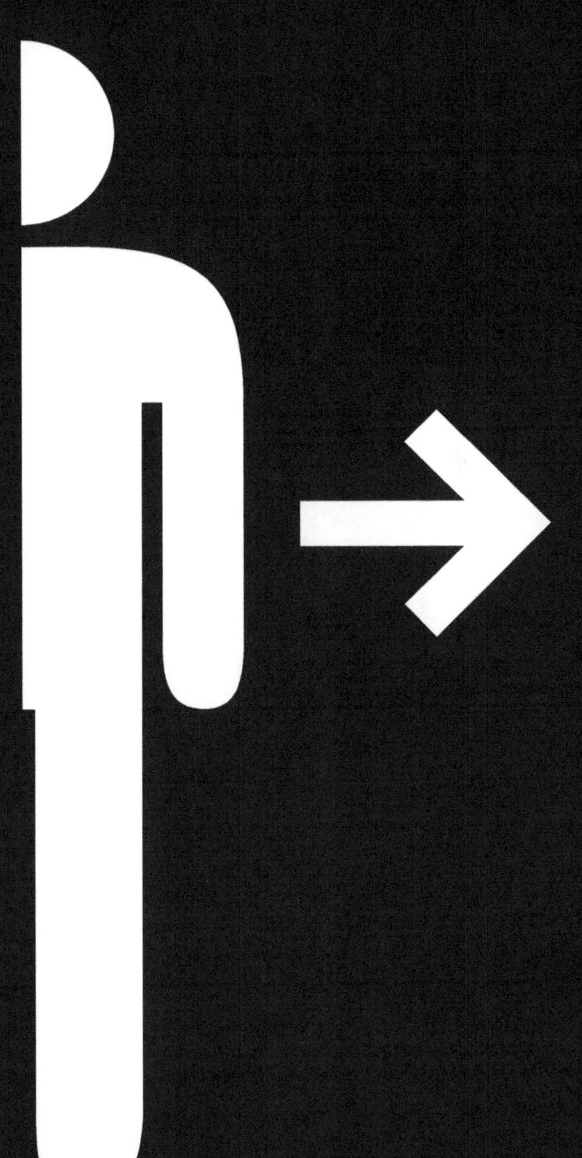

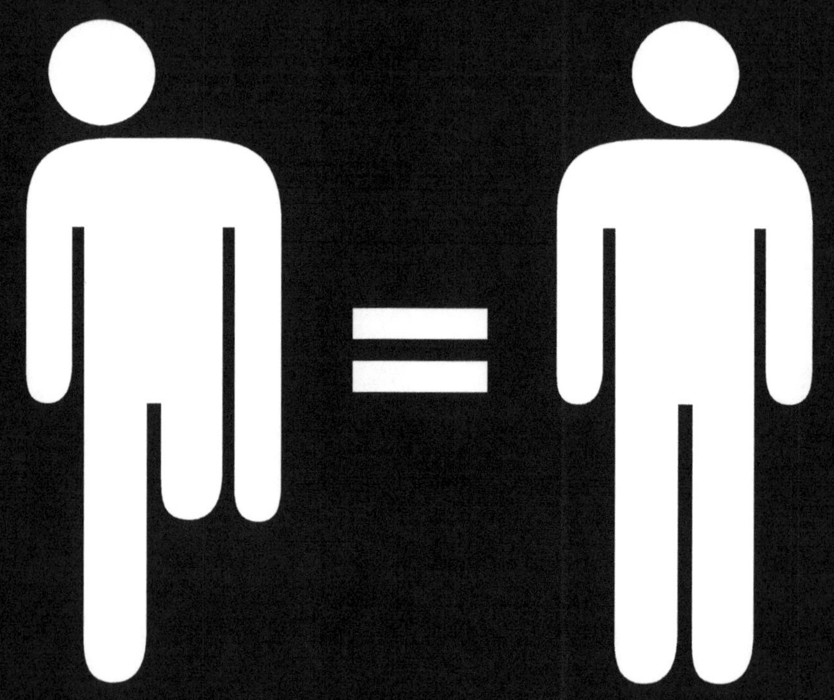

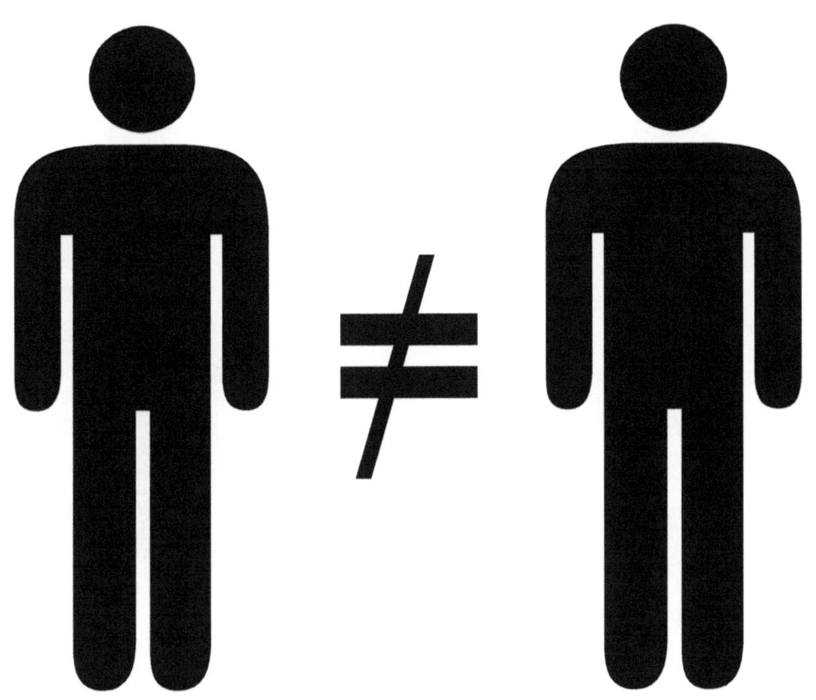

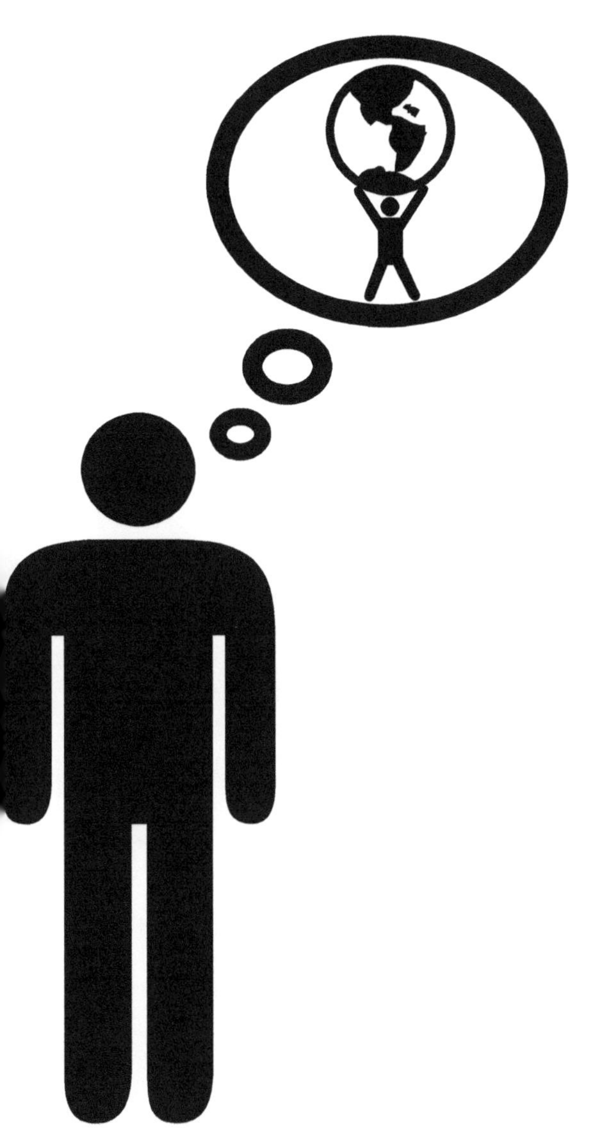

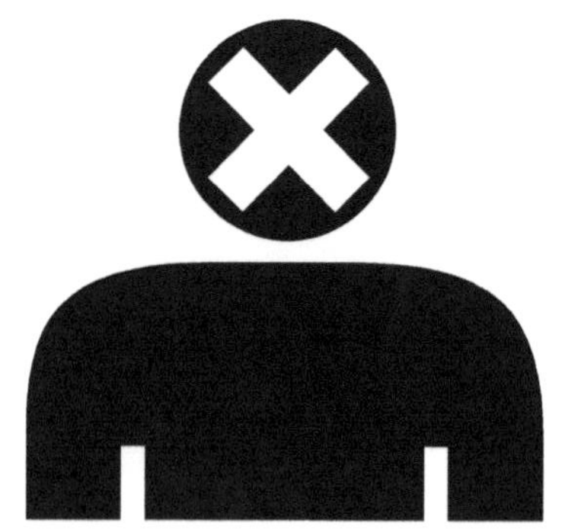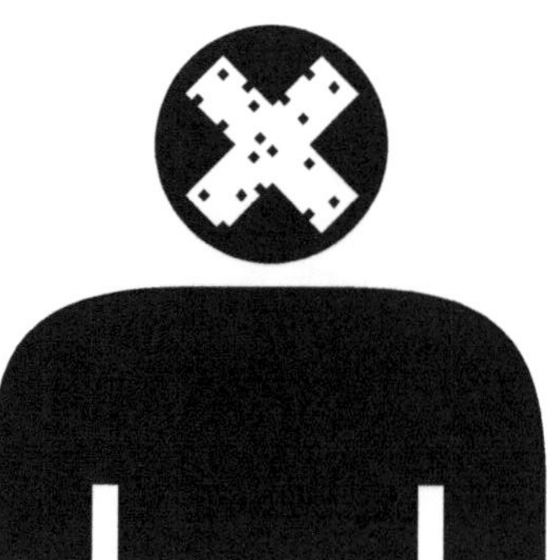

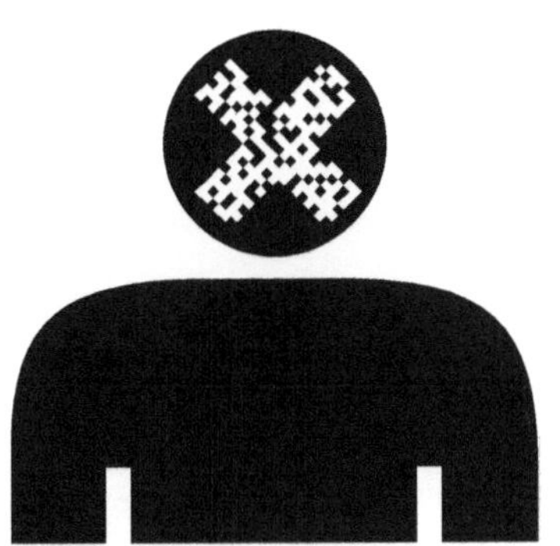 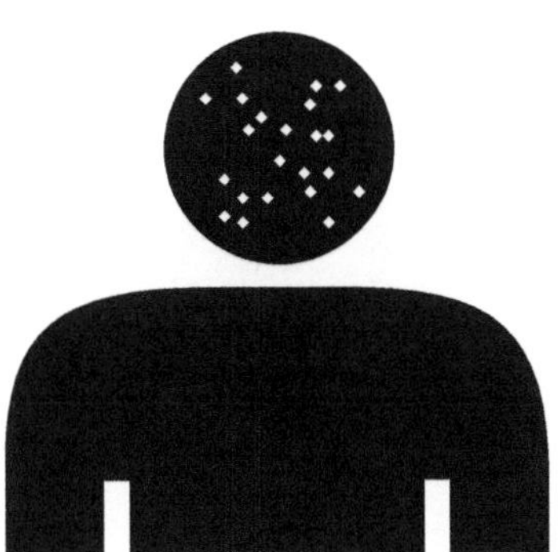

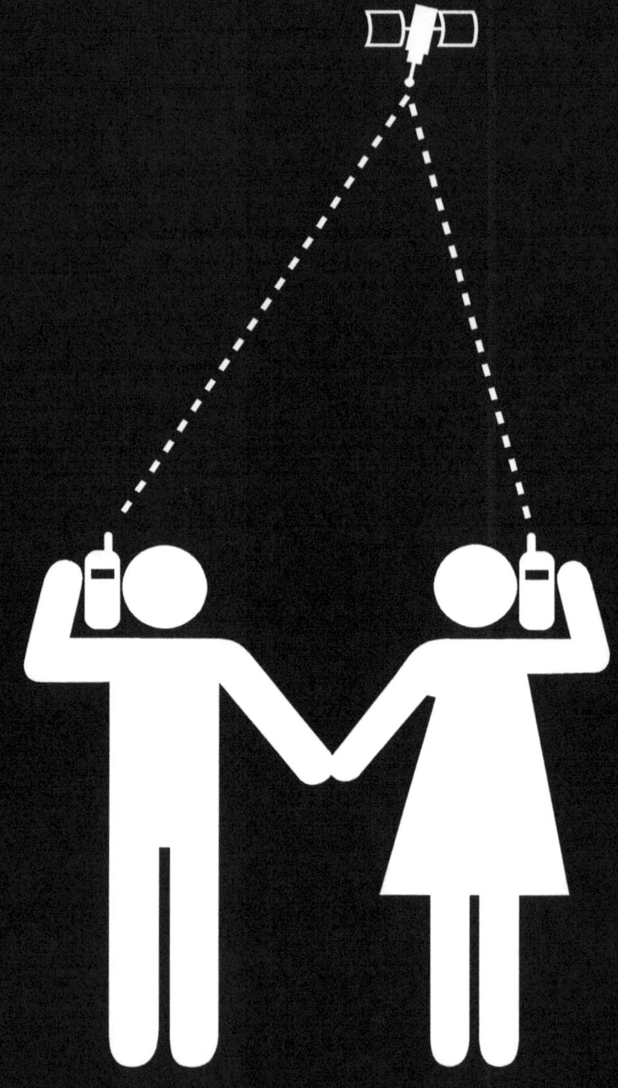

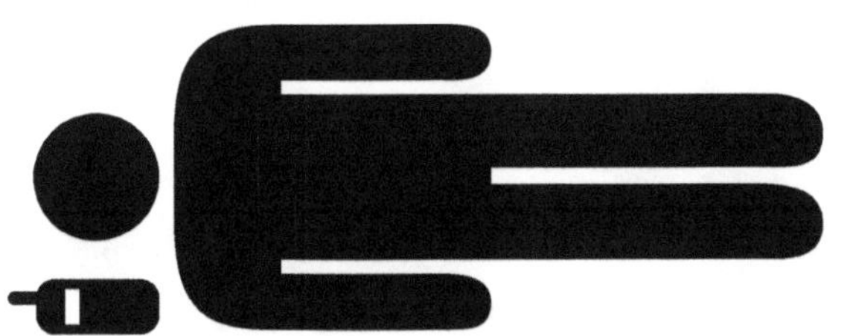

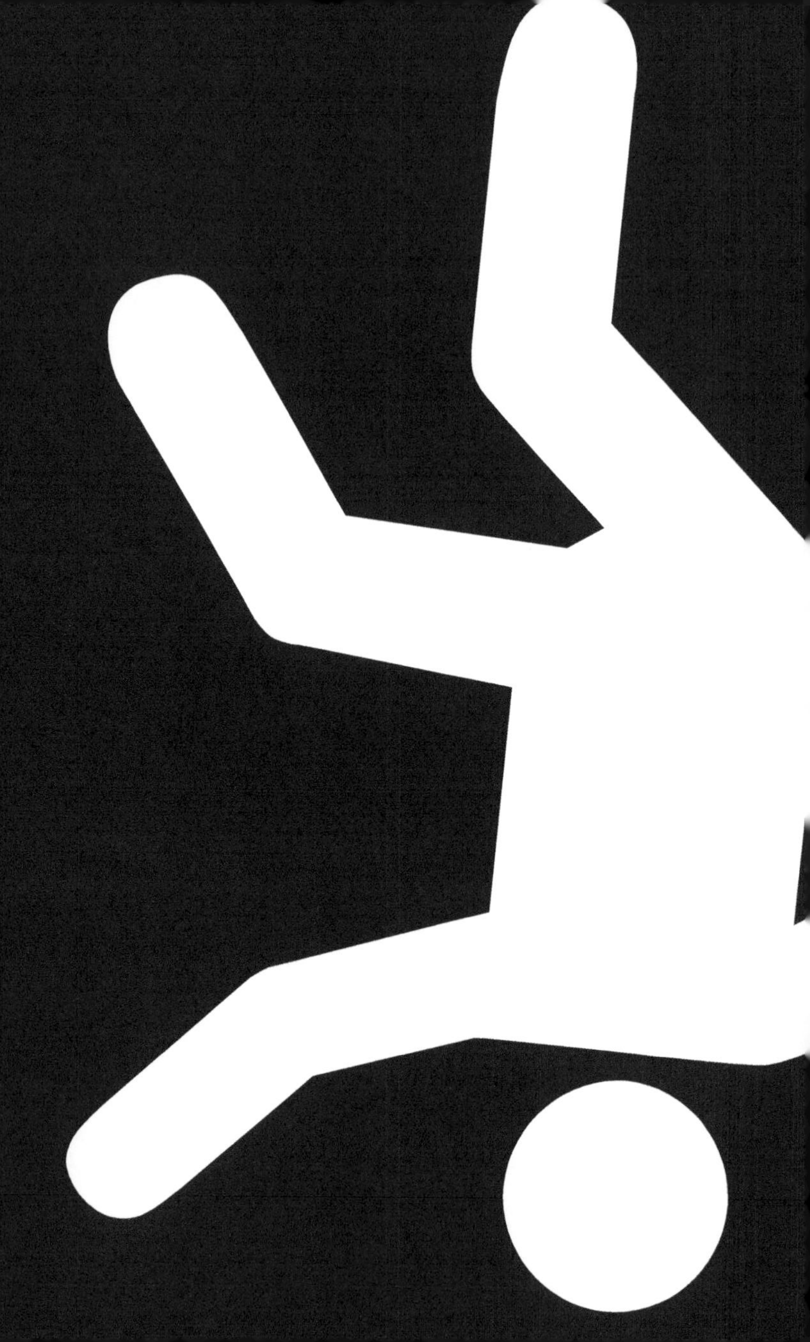

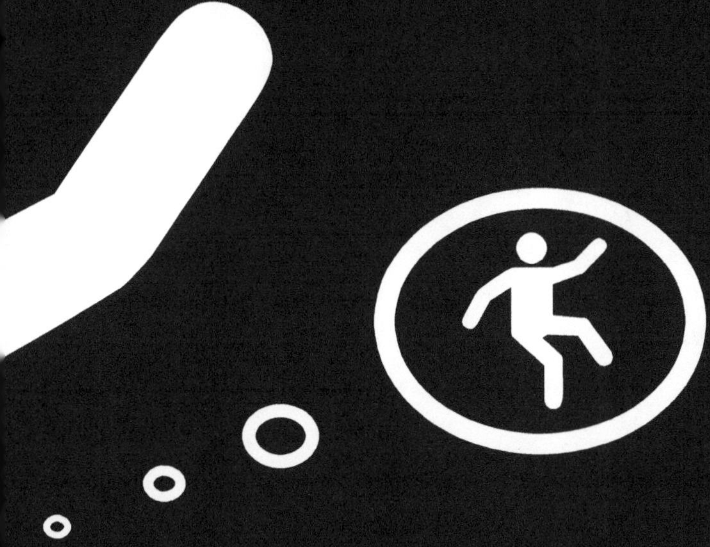

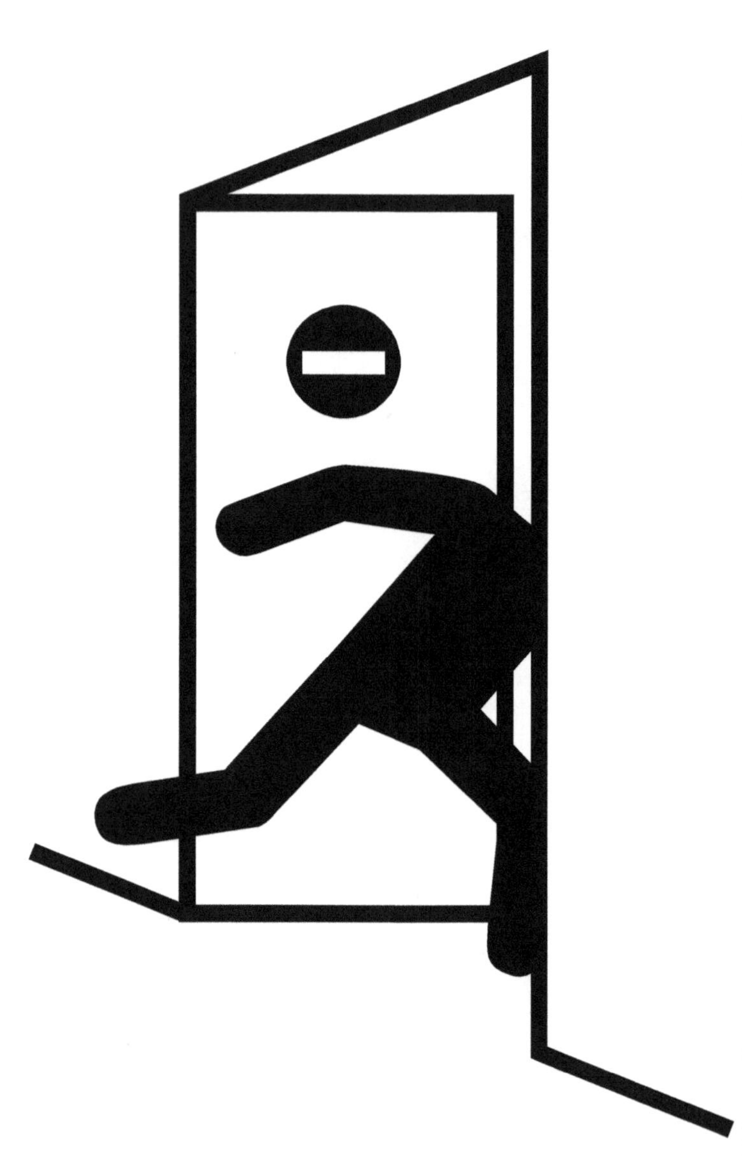

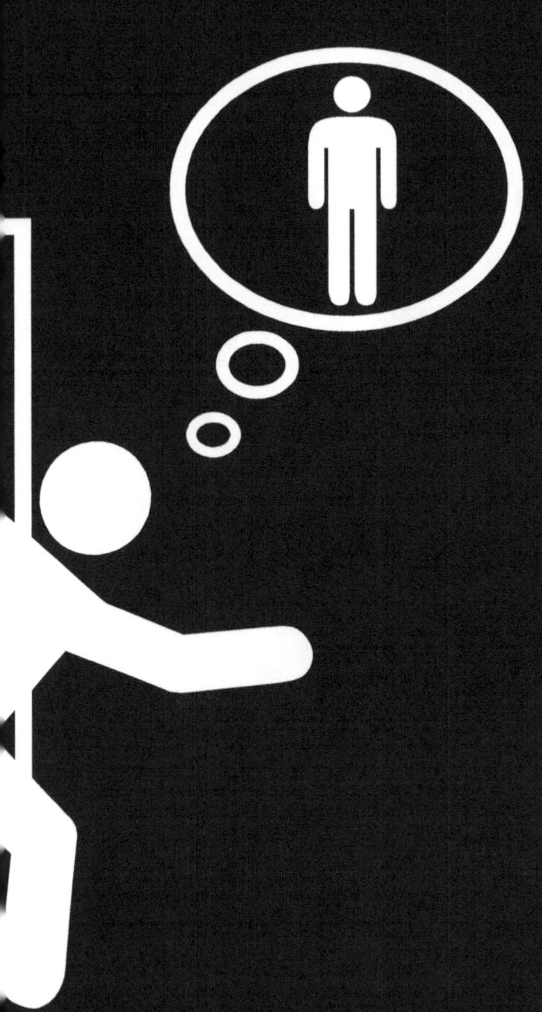

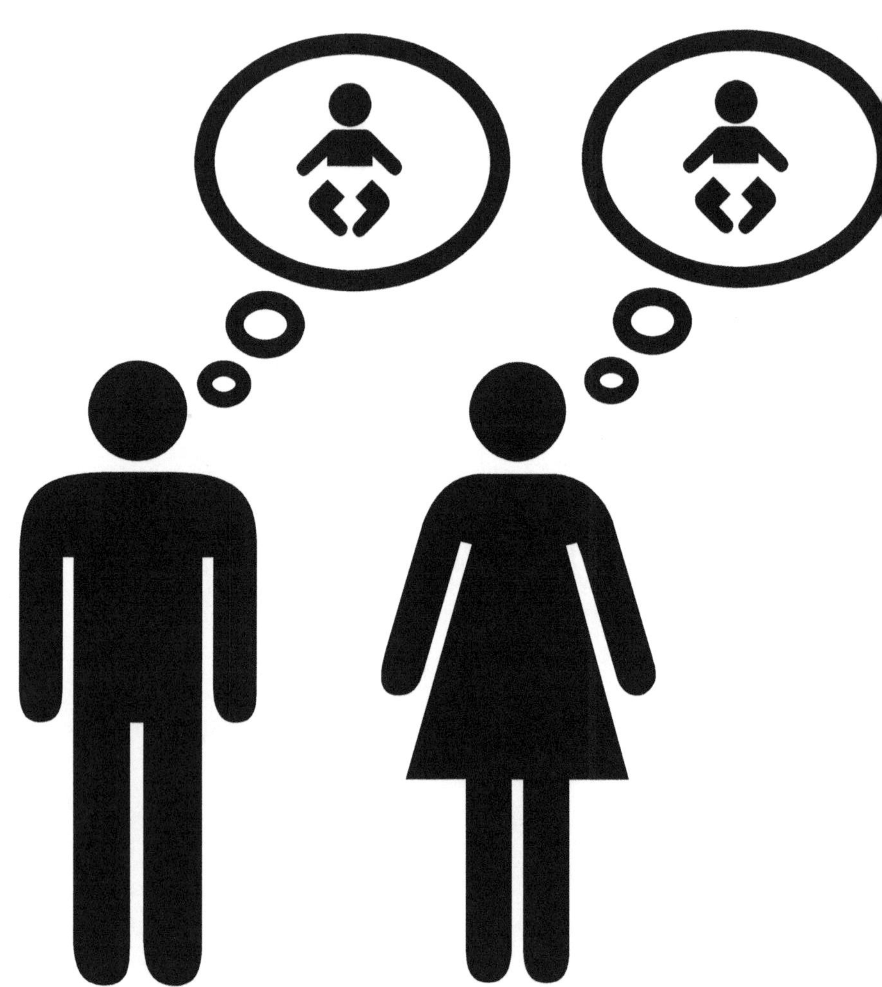

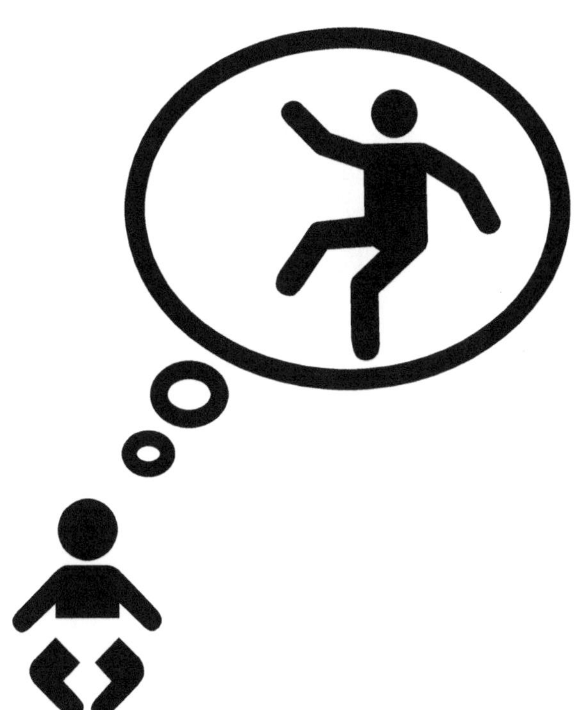

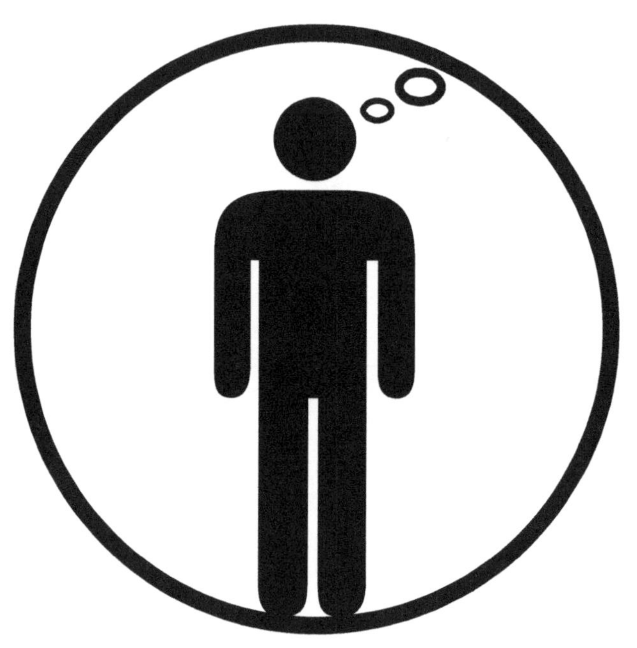

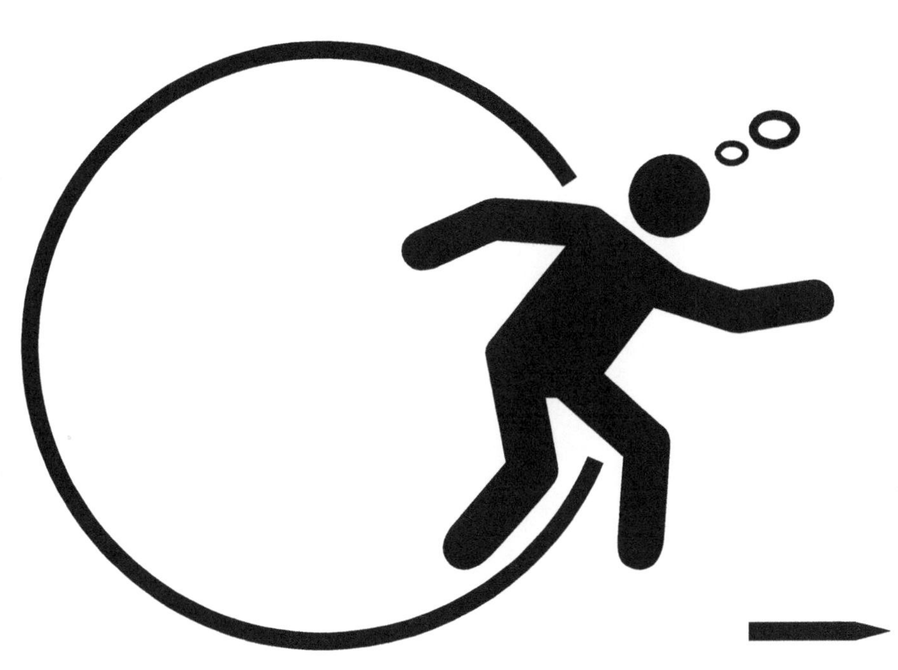

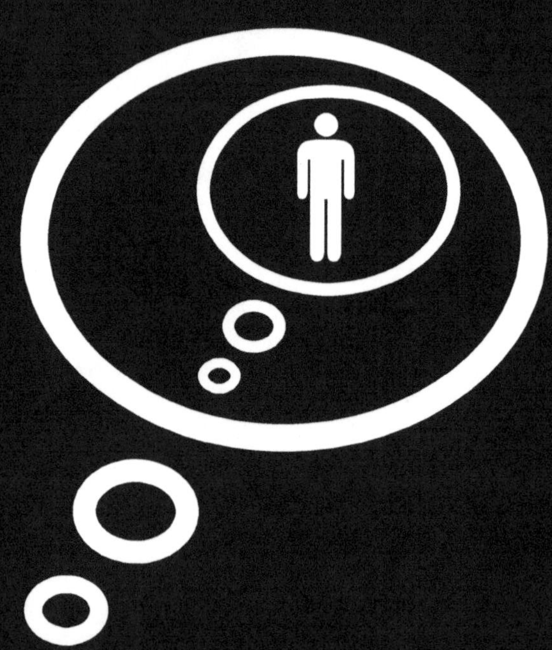

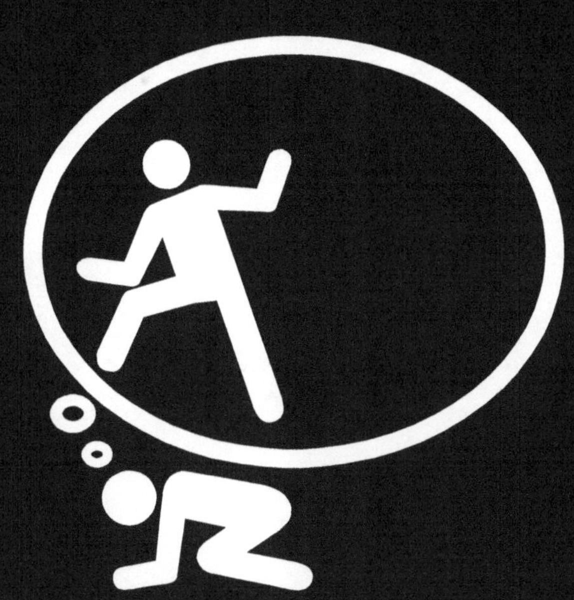

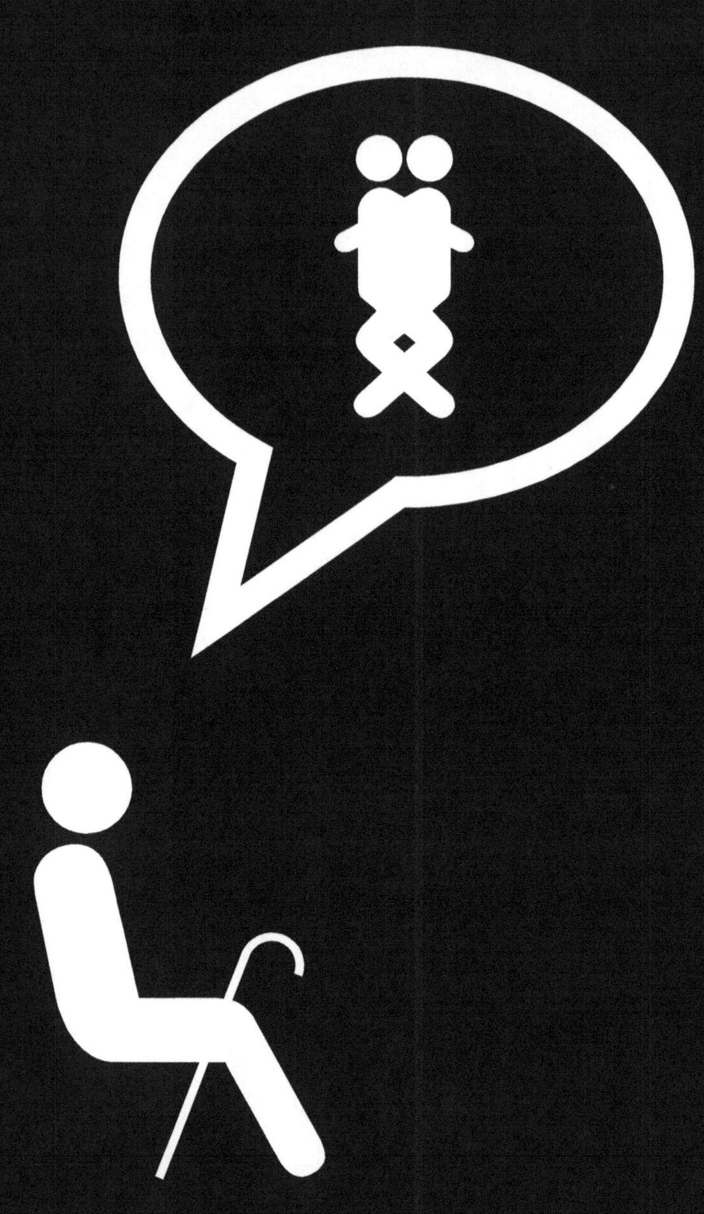

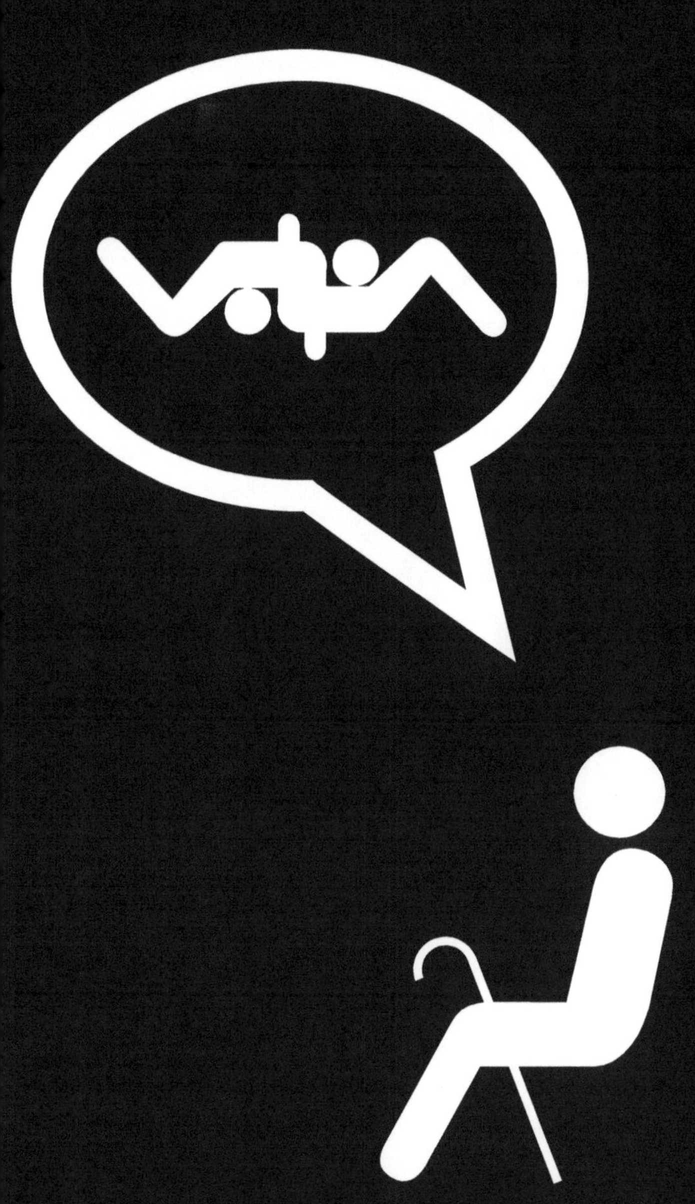

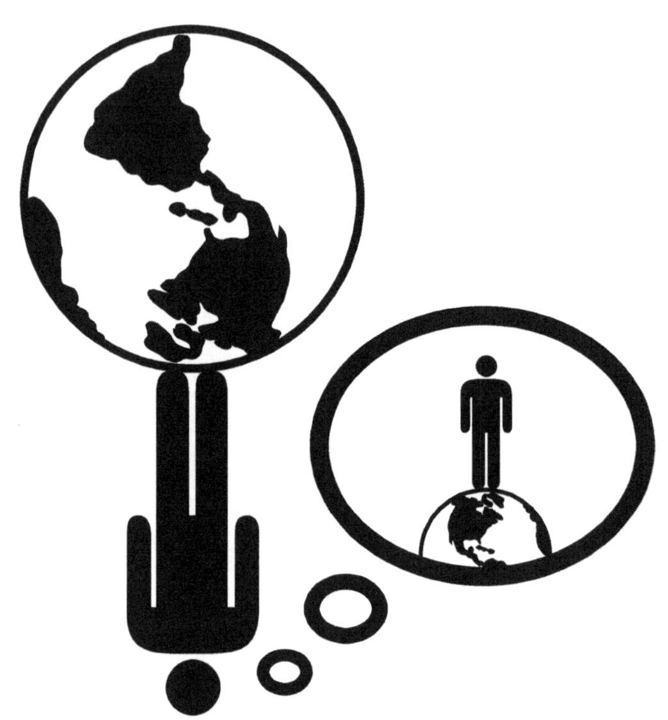

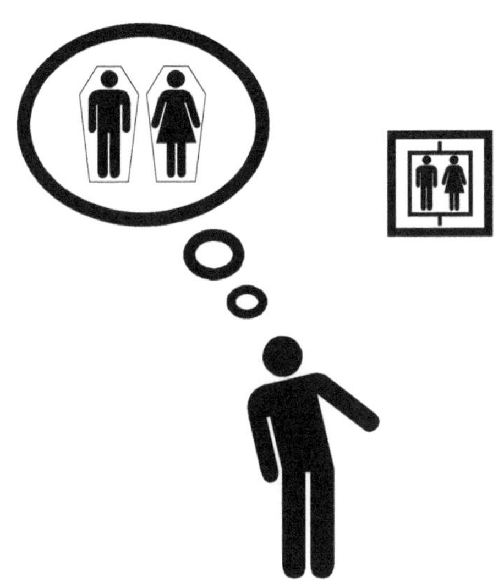

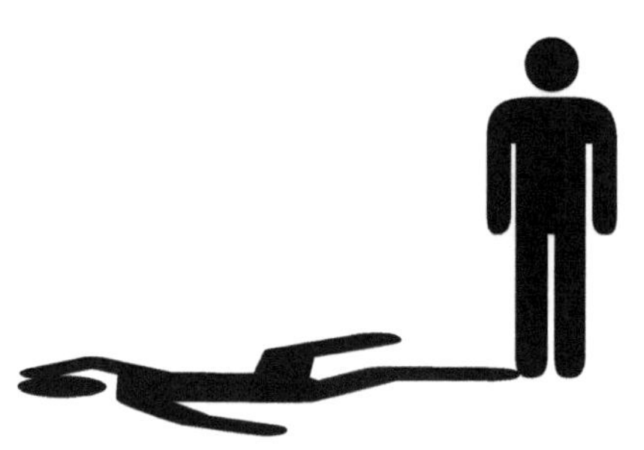

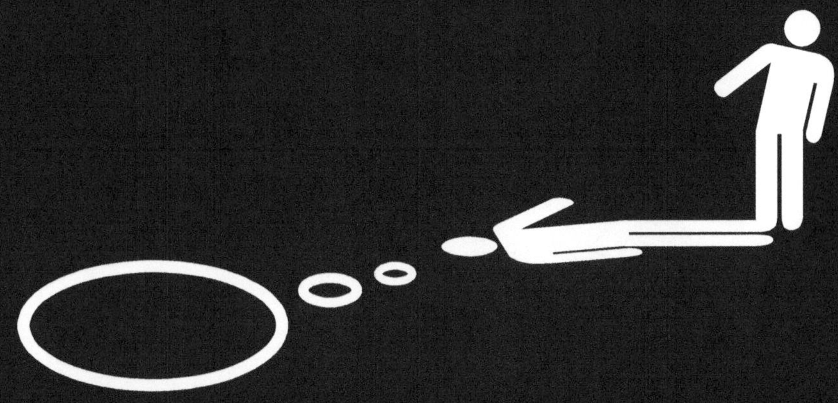

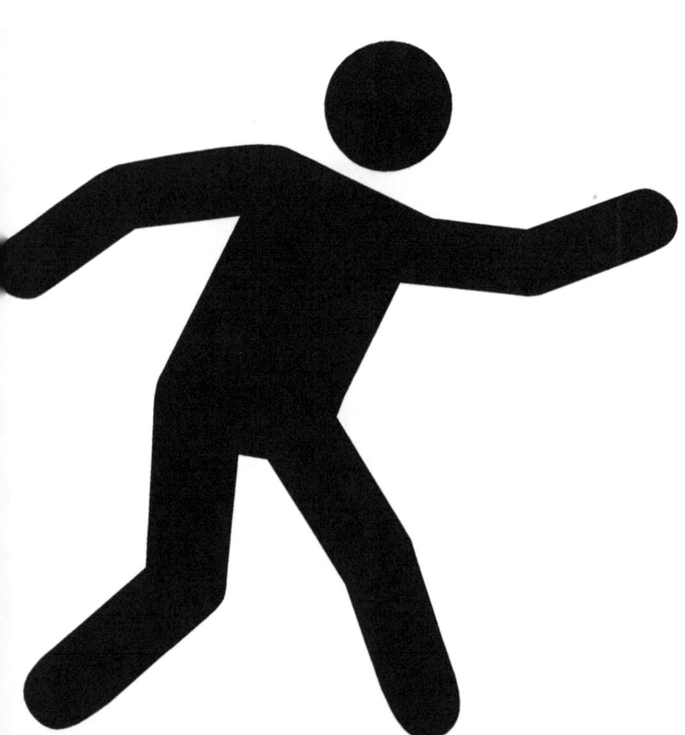

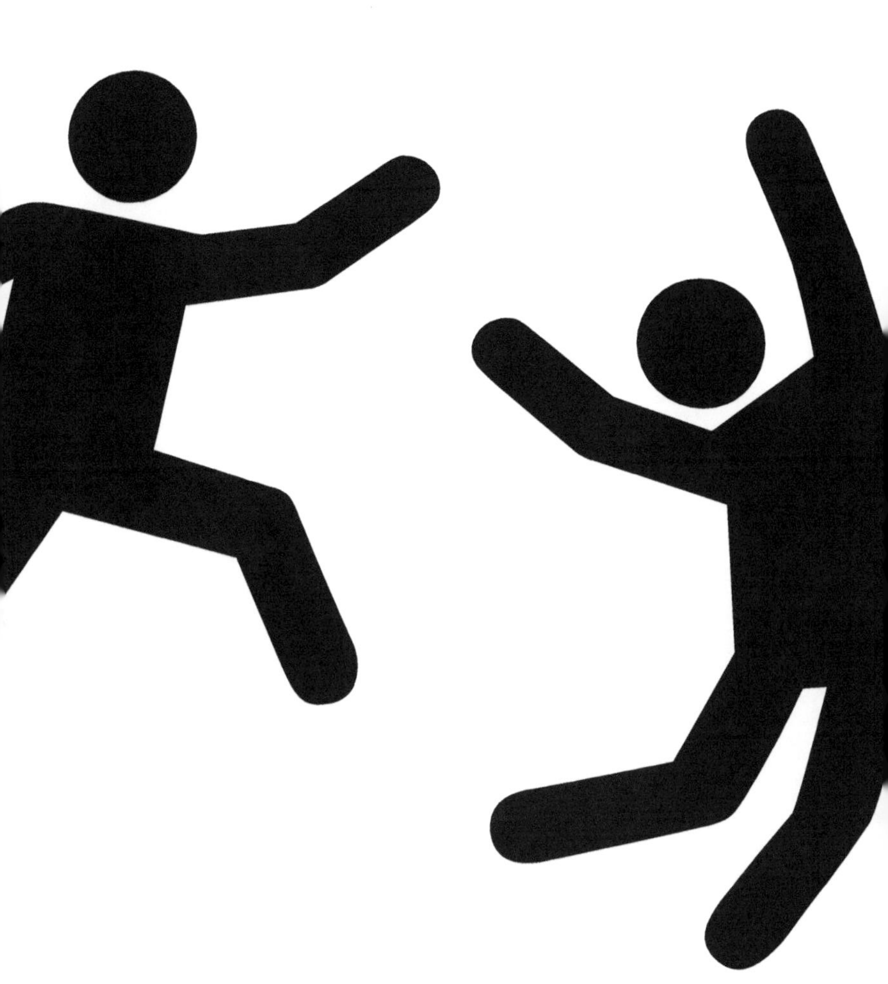

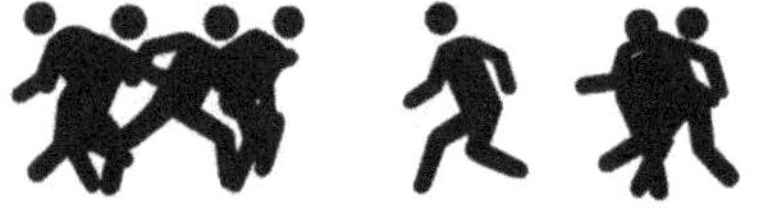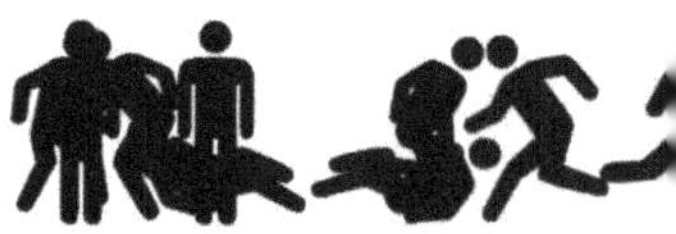

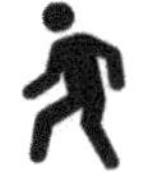
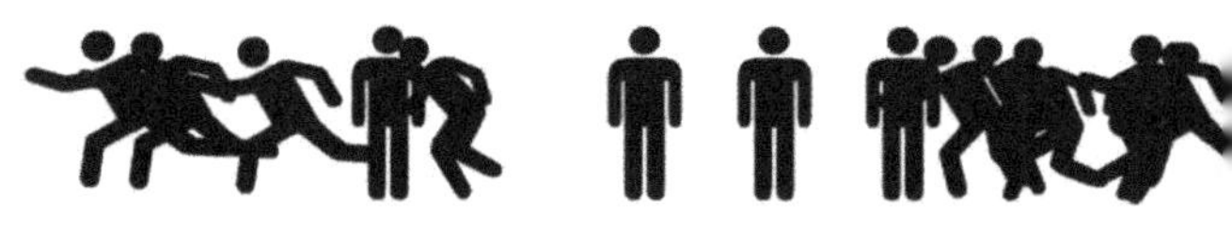

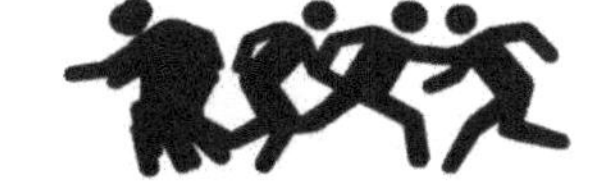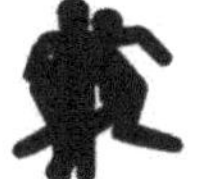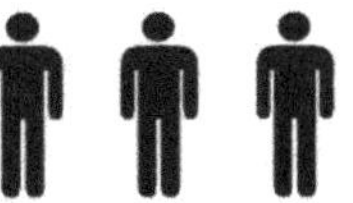

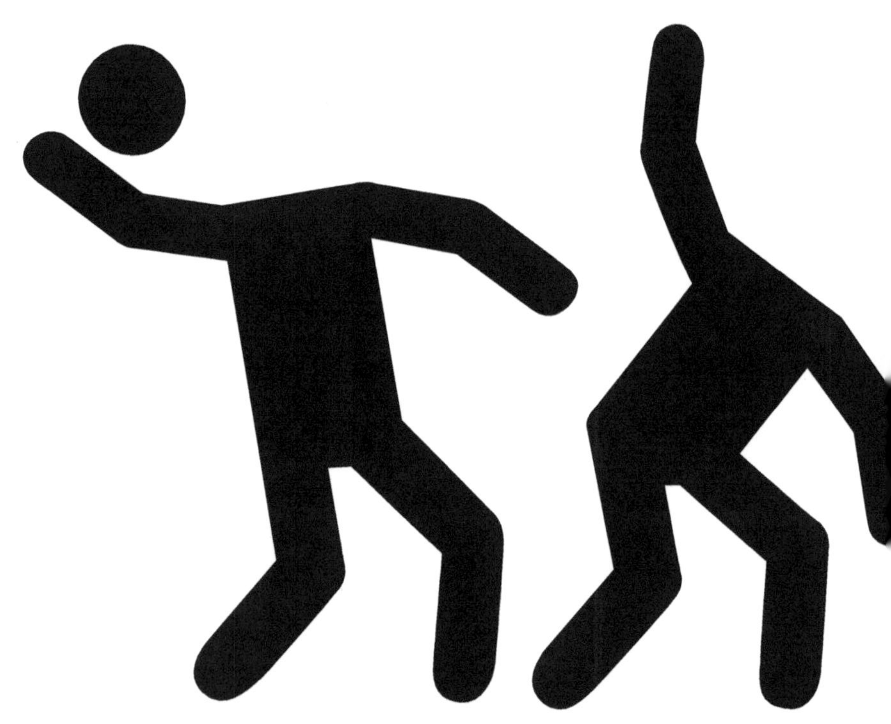

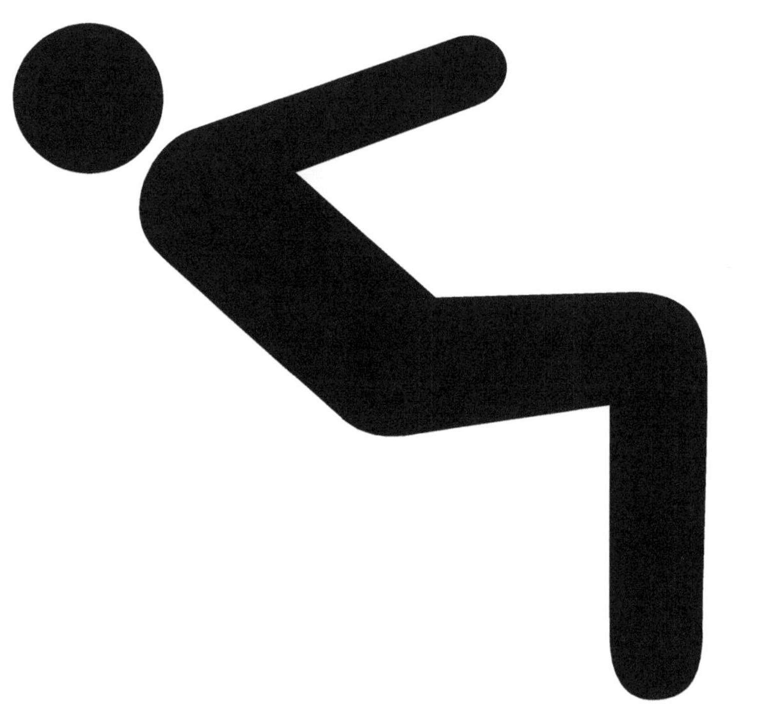

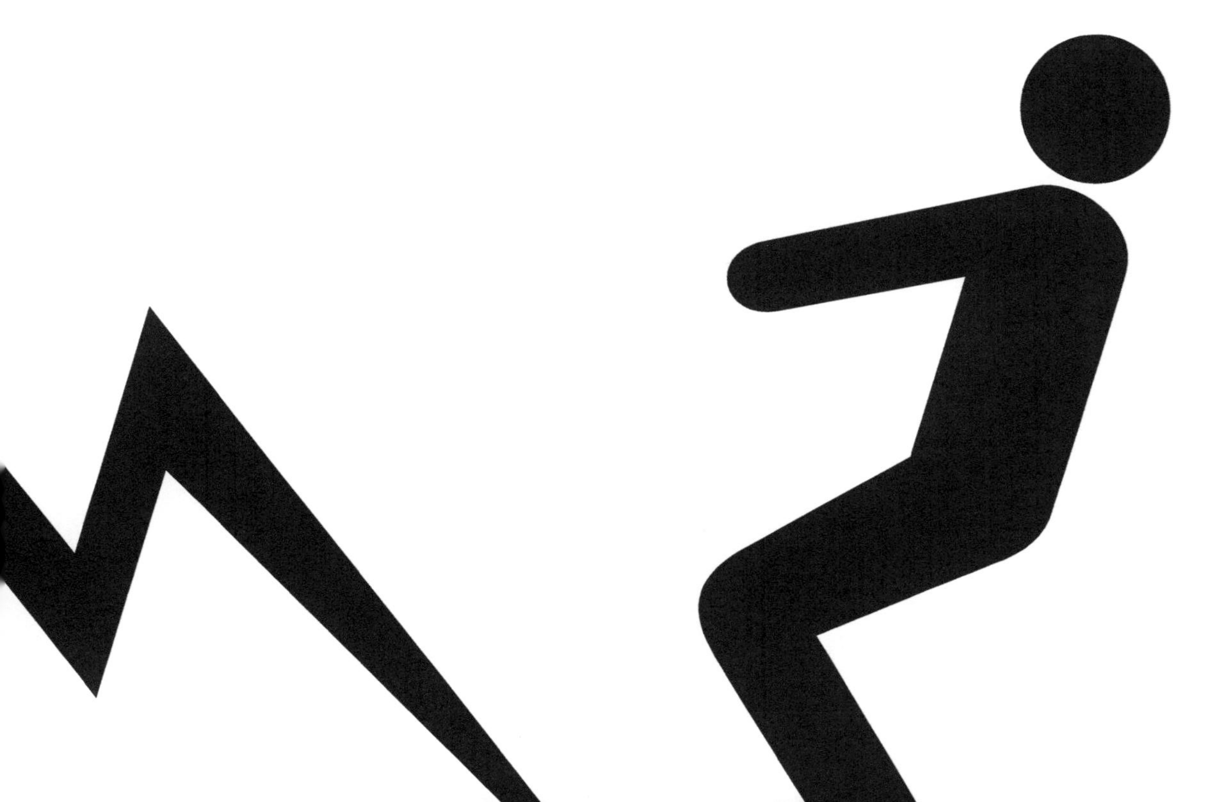

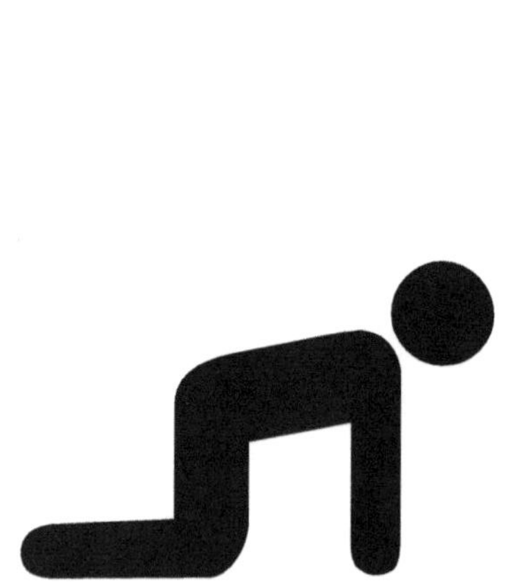

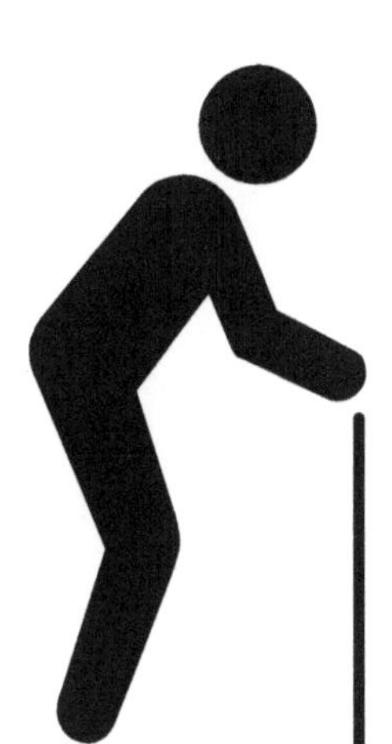

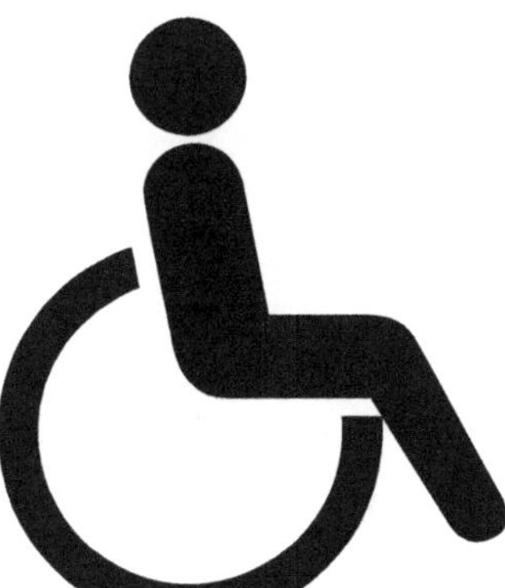

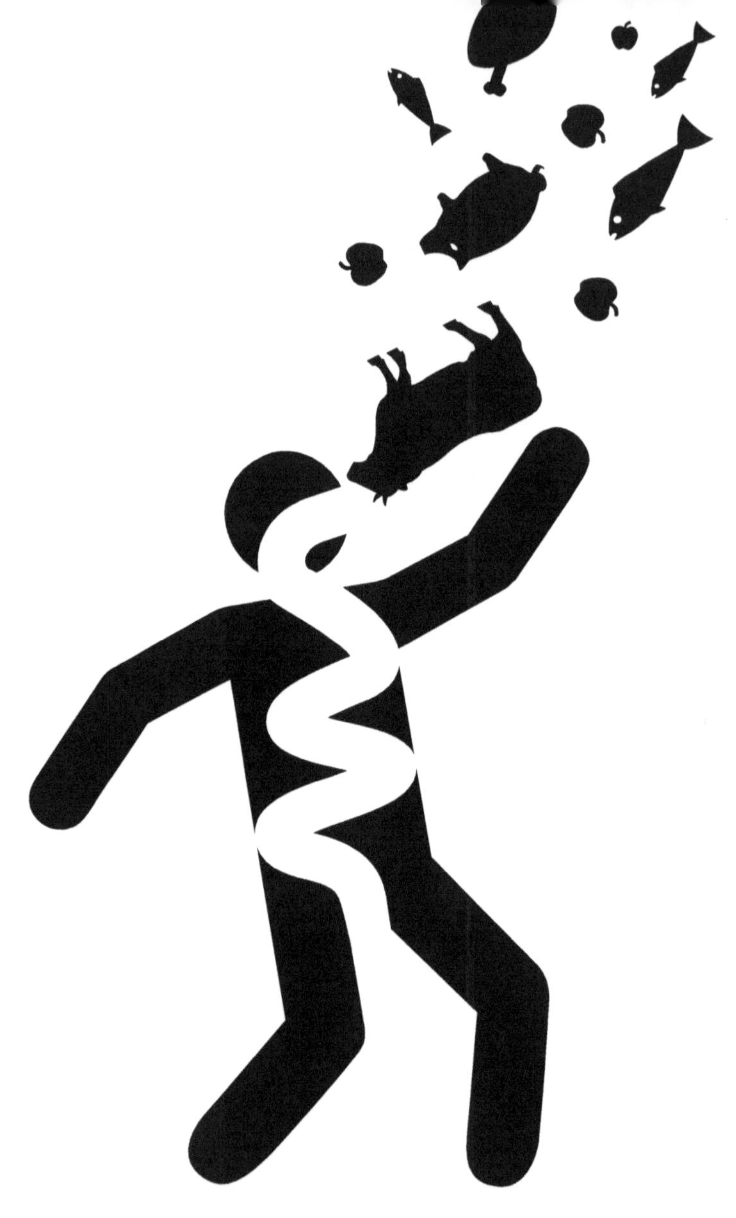

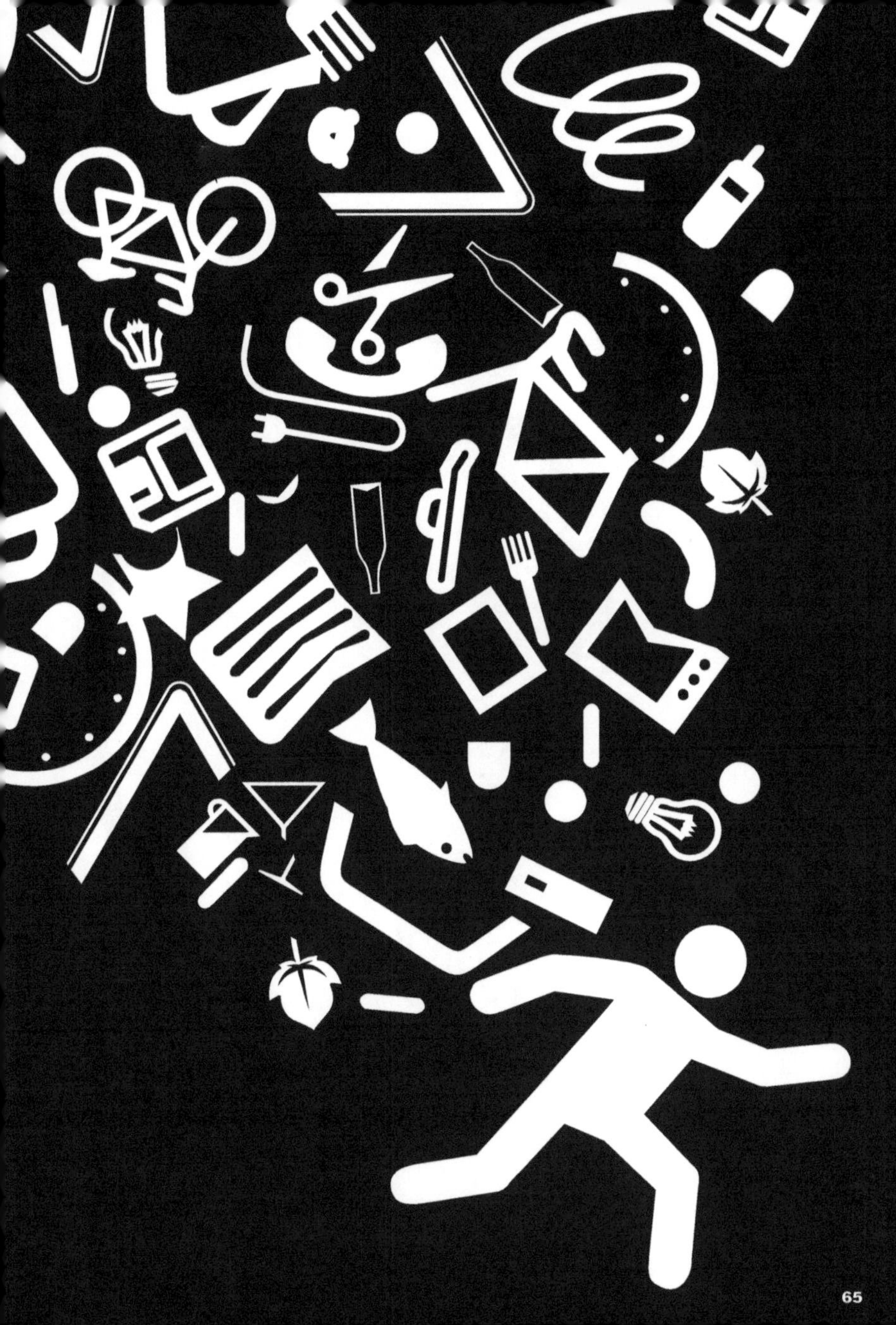

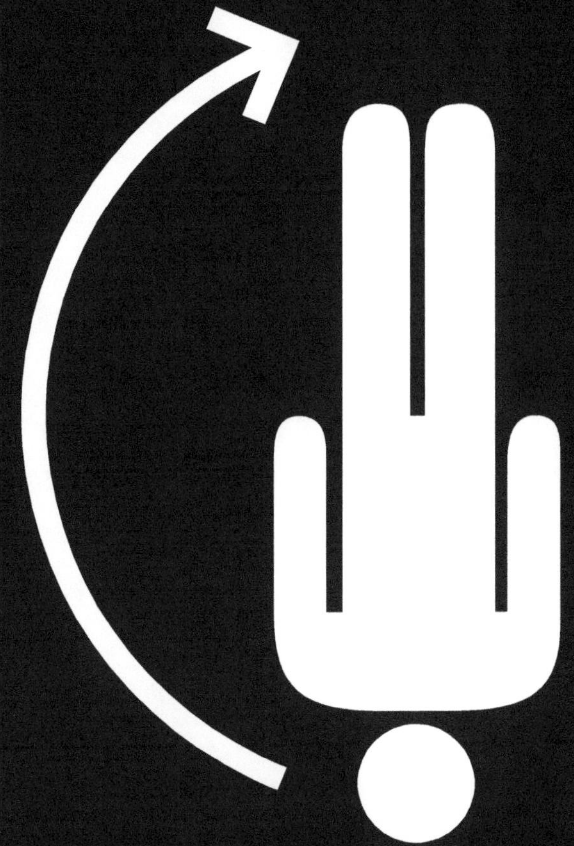

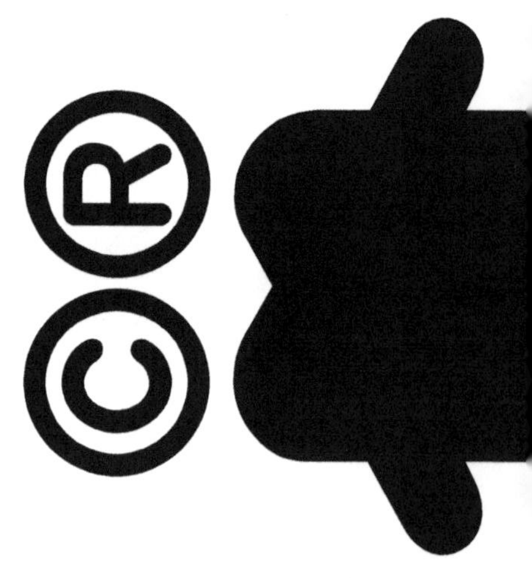

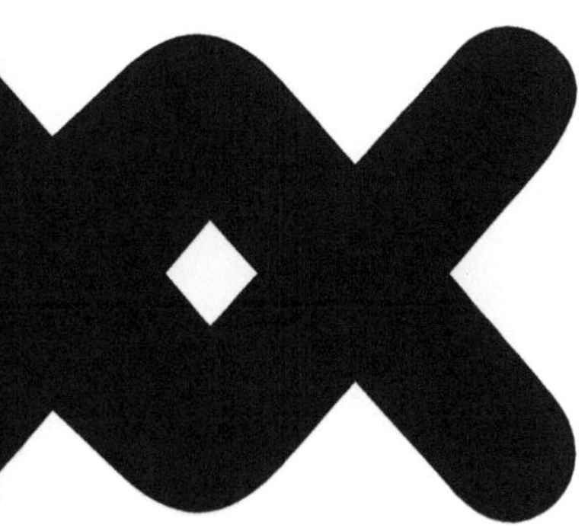

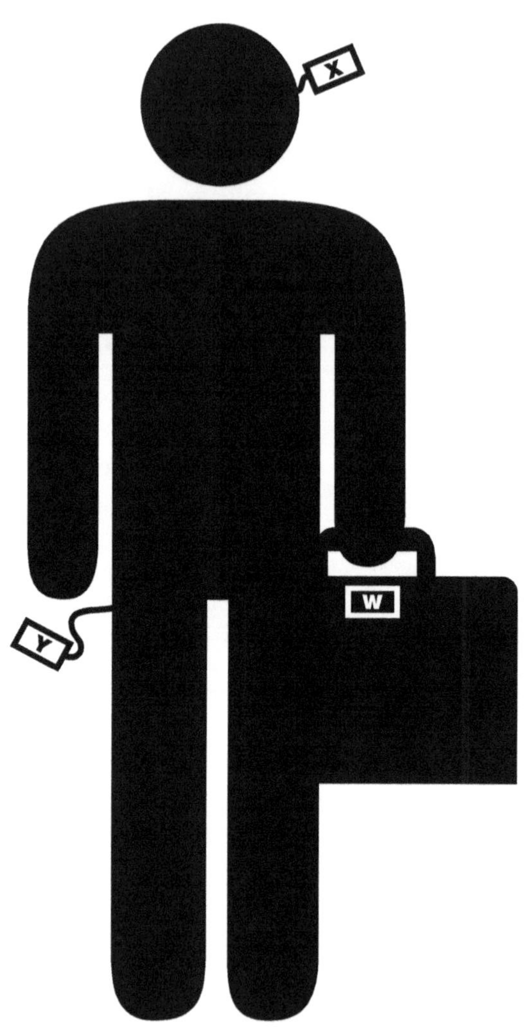

X
Y
W

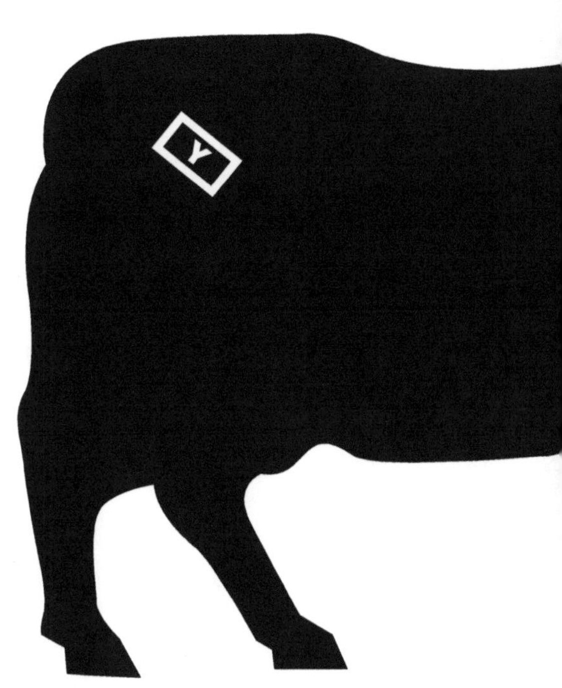Y

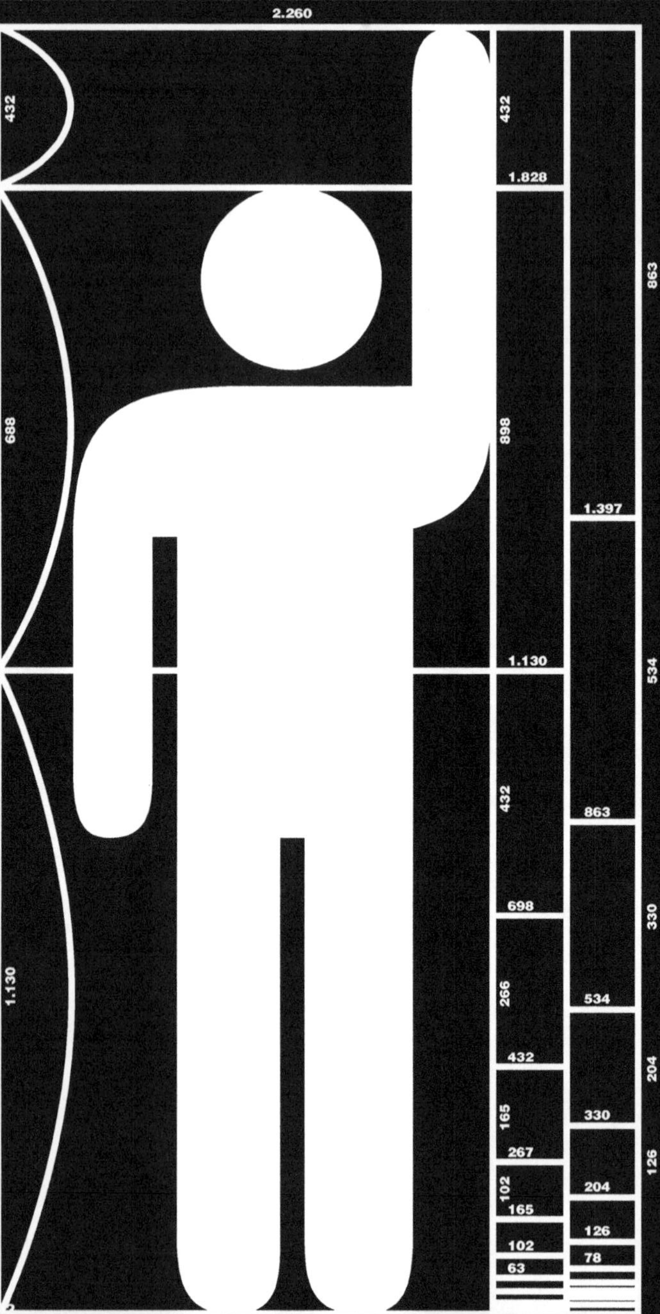

1536359

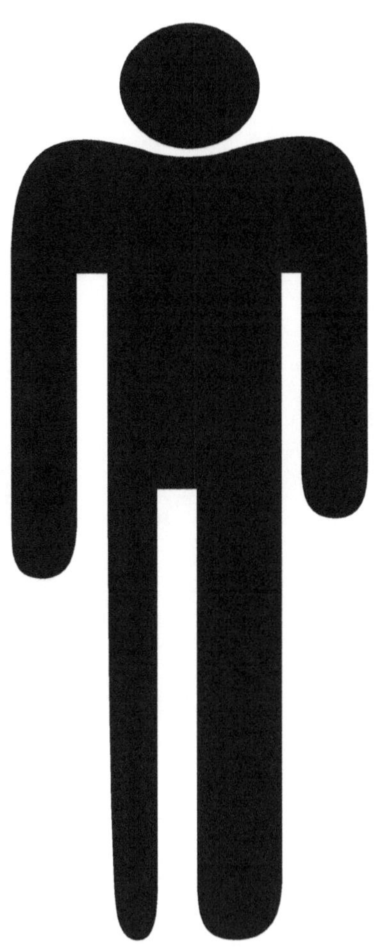

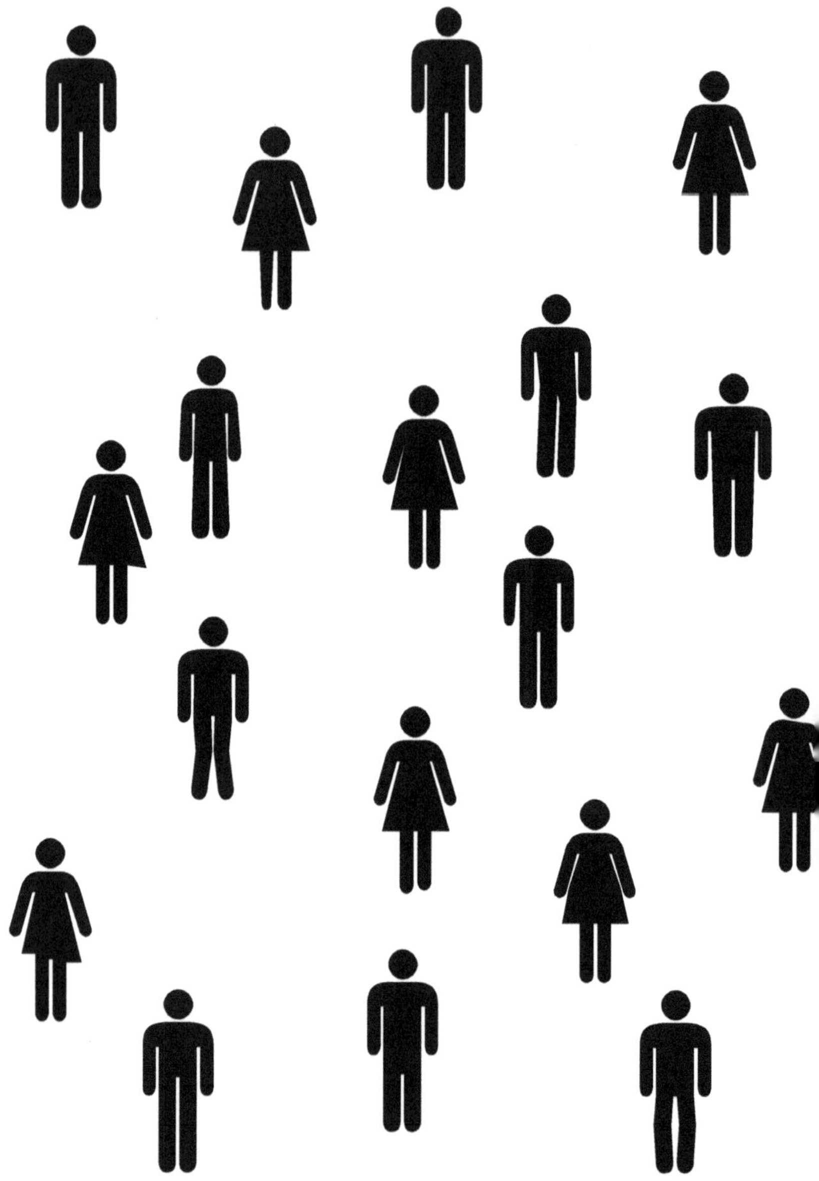

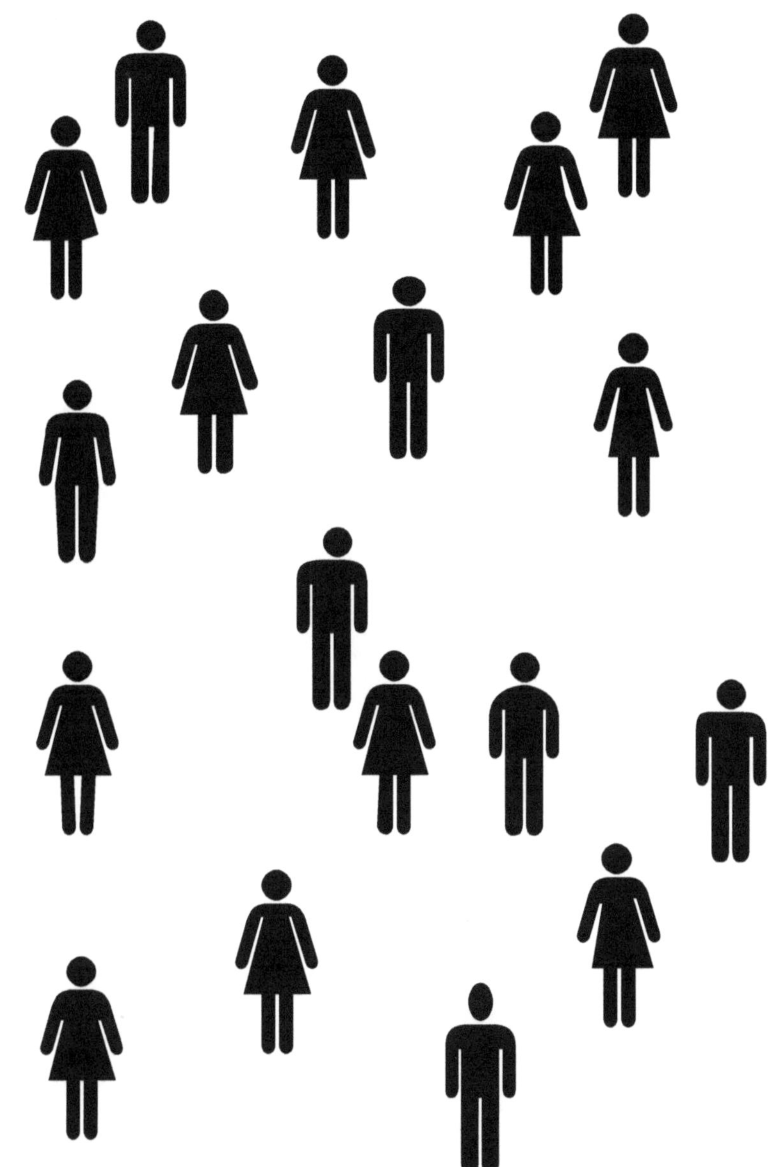

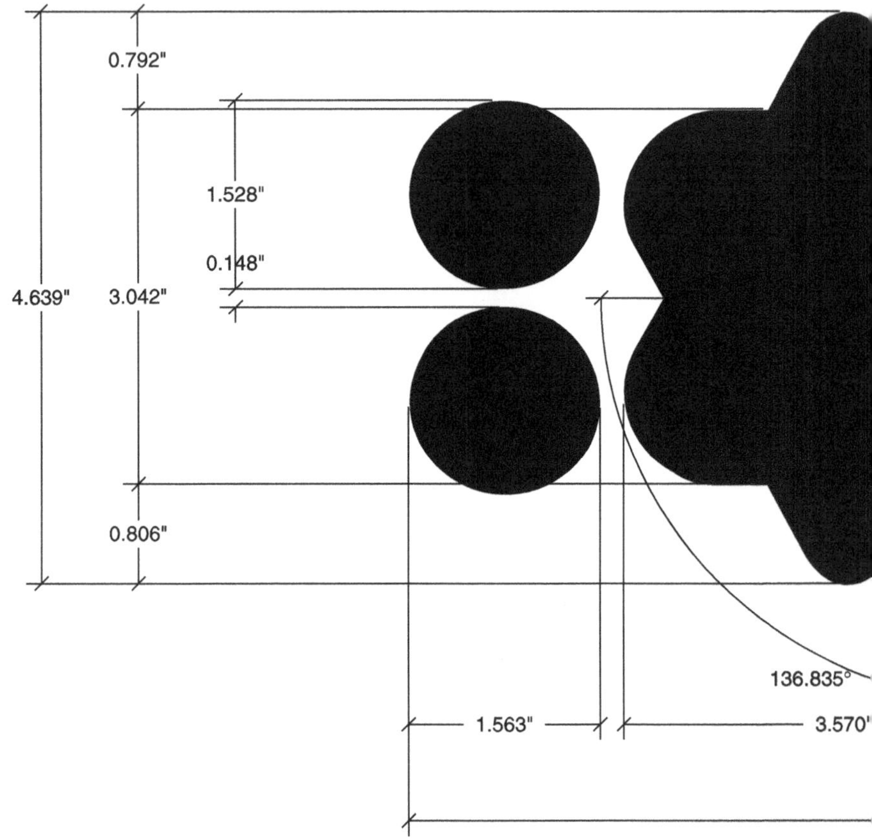

0.792"
1.528"
0.148"
4.639"
3.042"
0.806"
136.835°
1.563"
3.570"

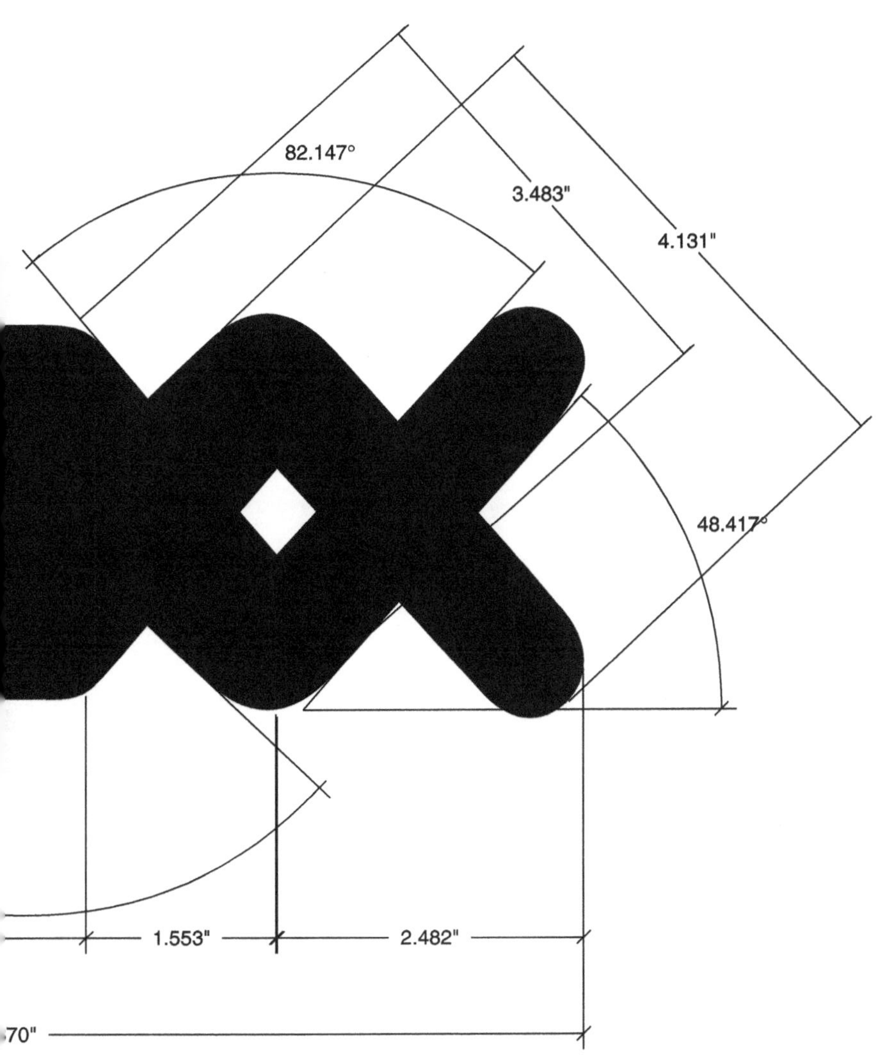

82.147°
3.483"
4.131"
48.417°
1.553"
2.482"
70"

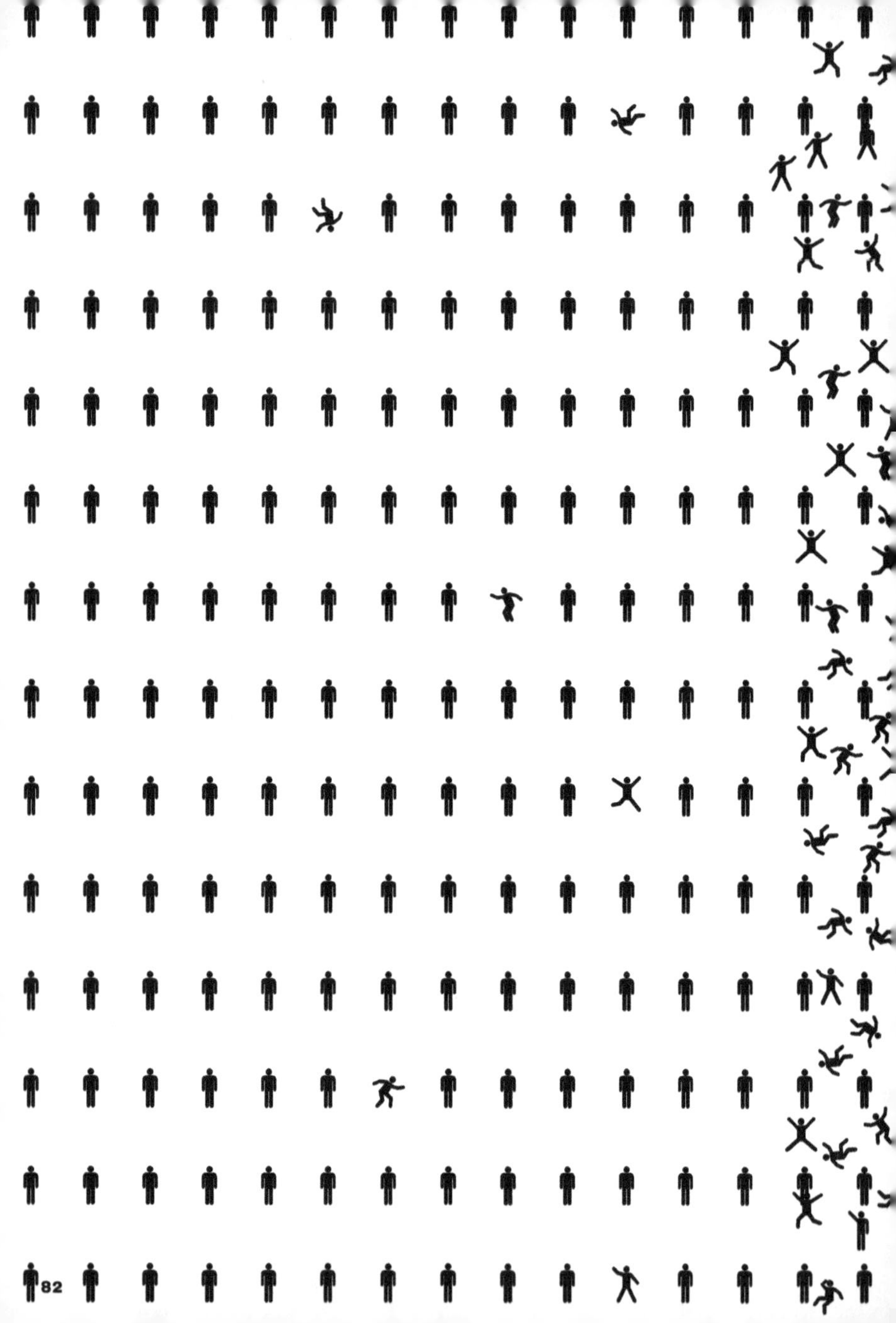

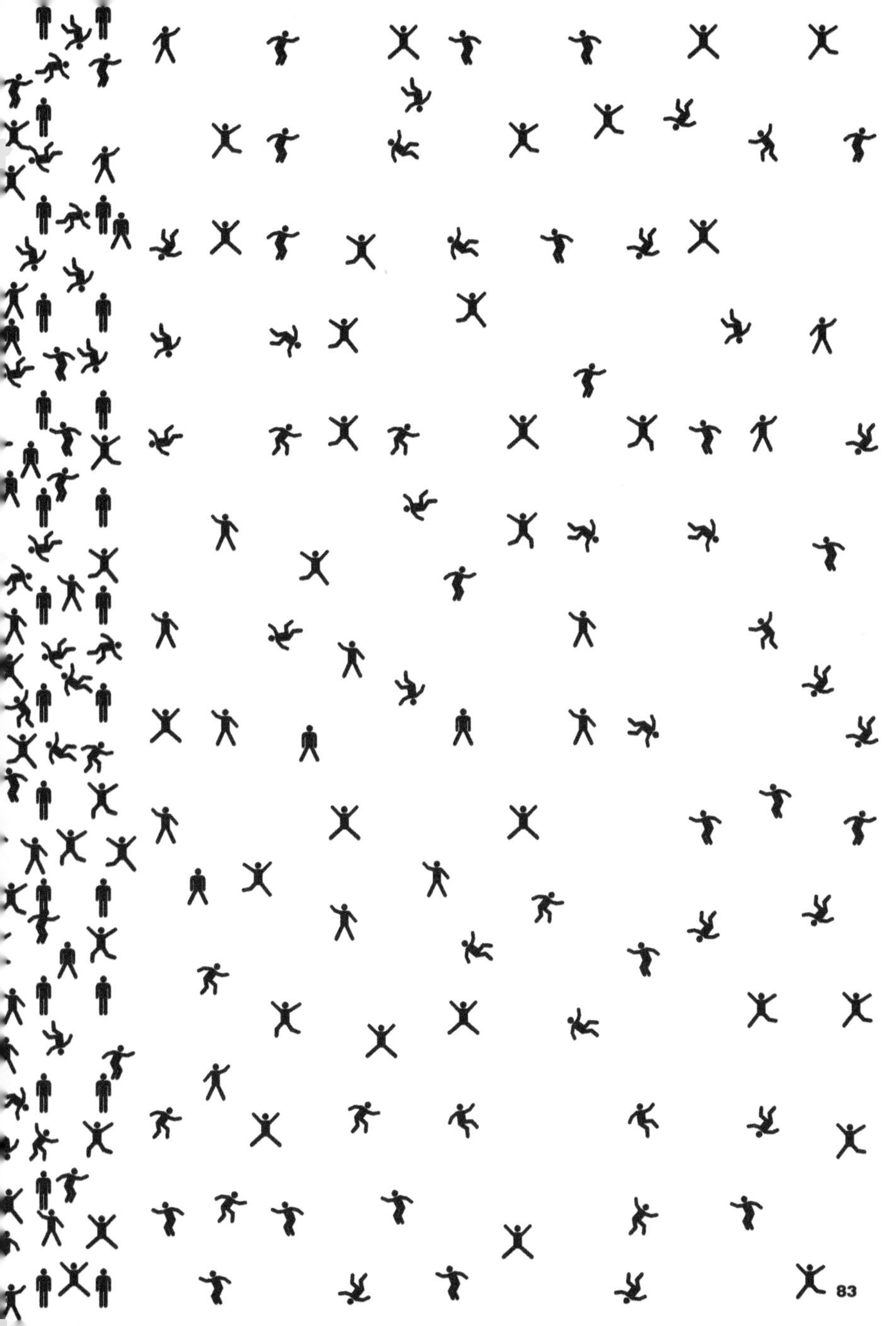

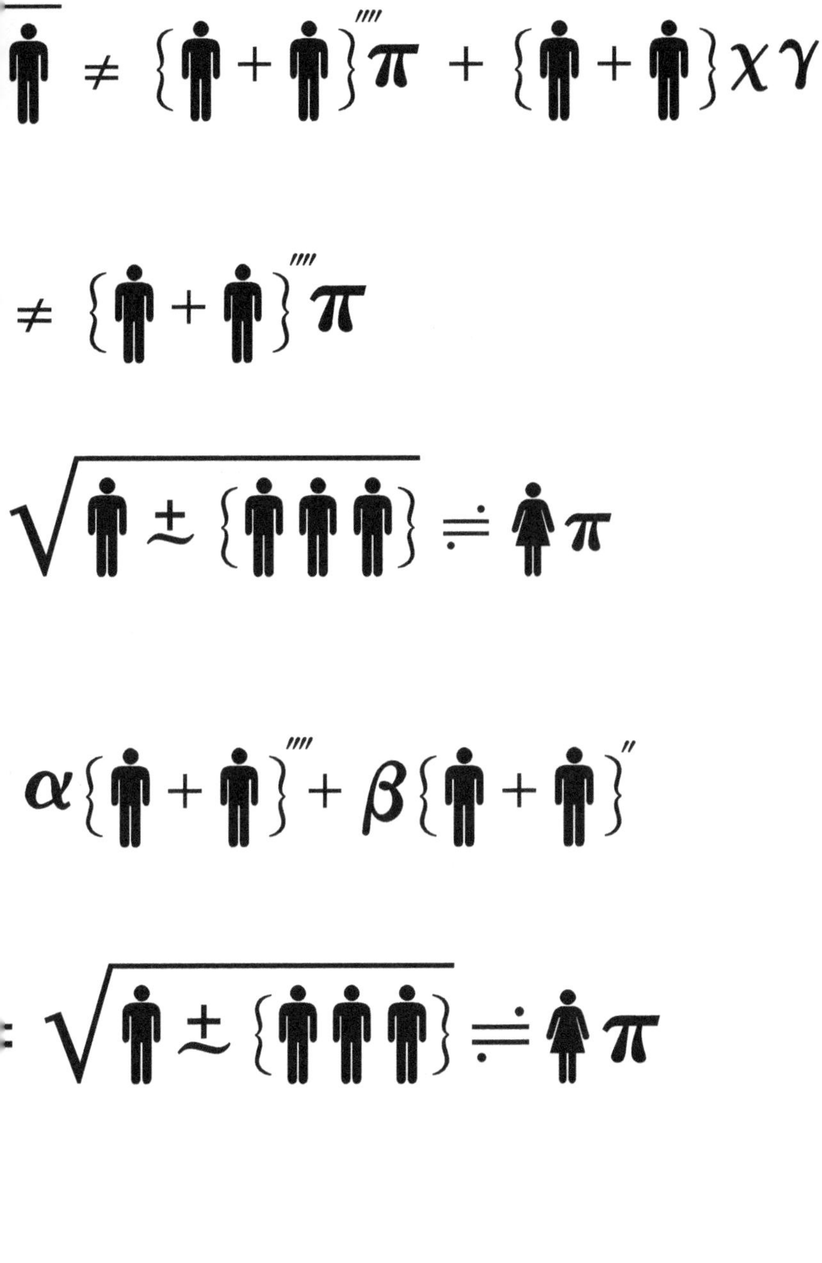

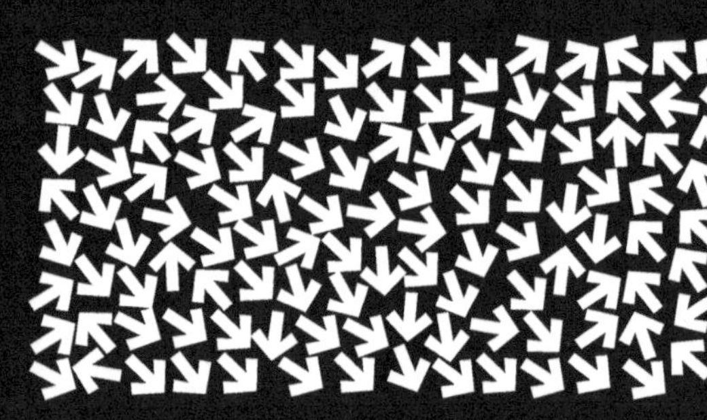

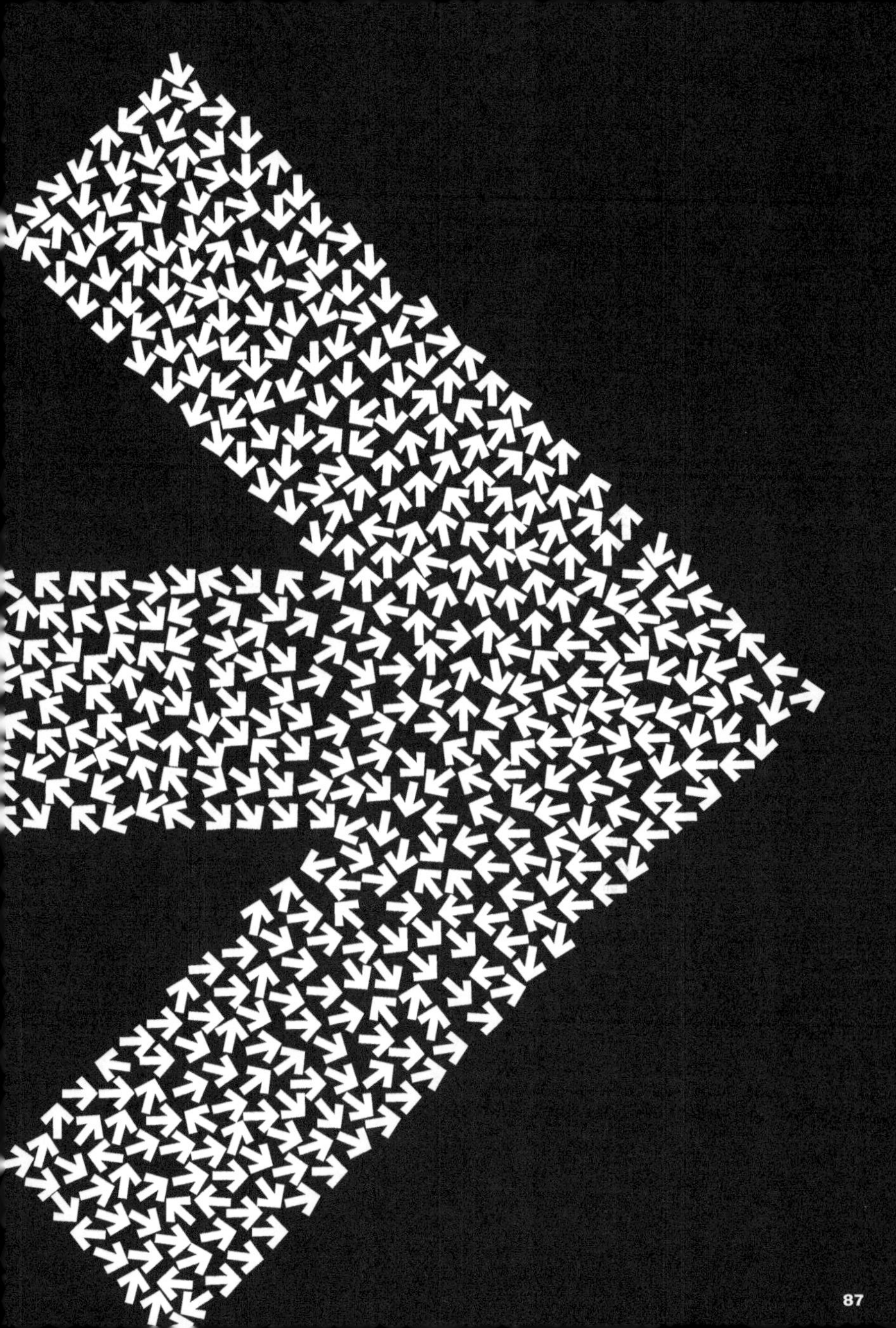

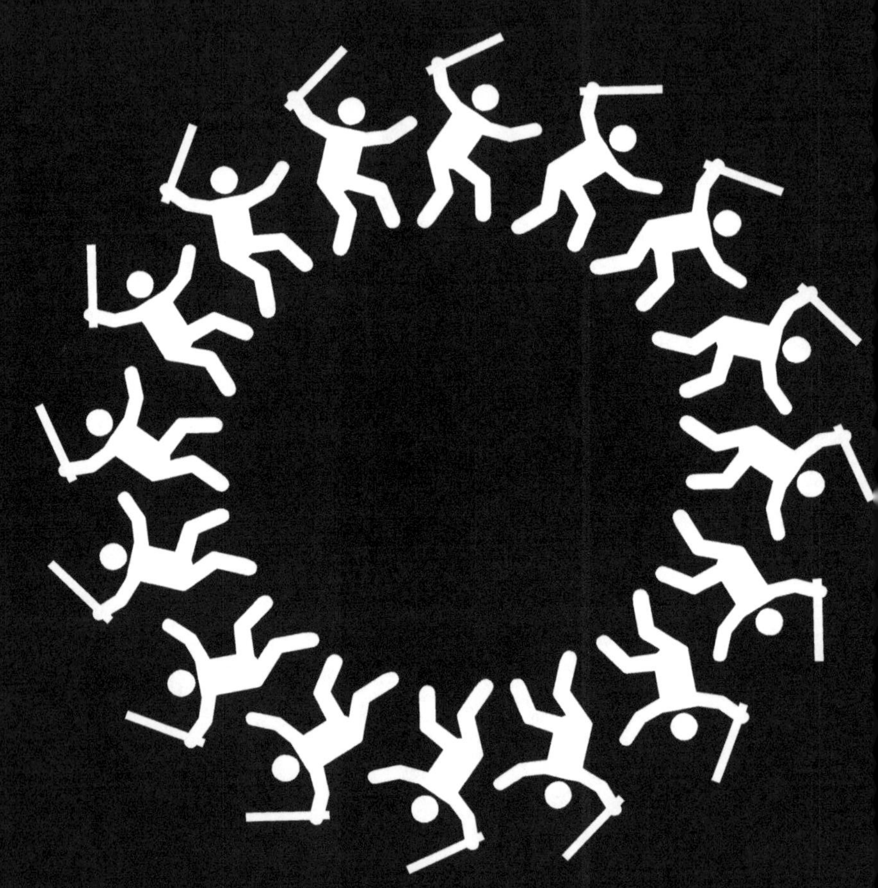

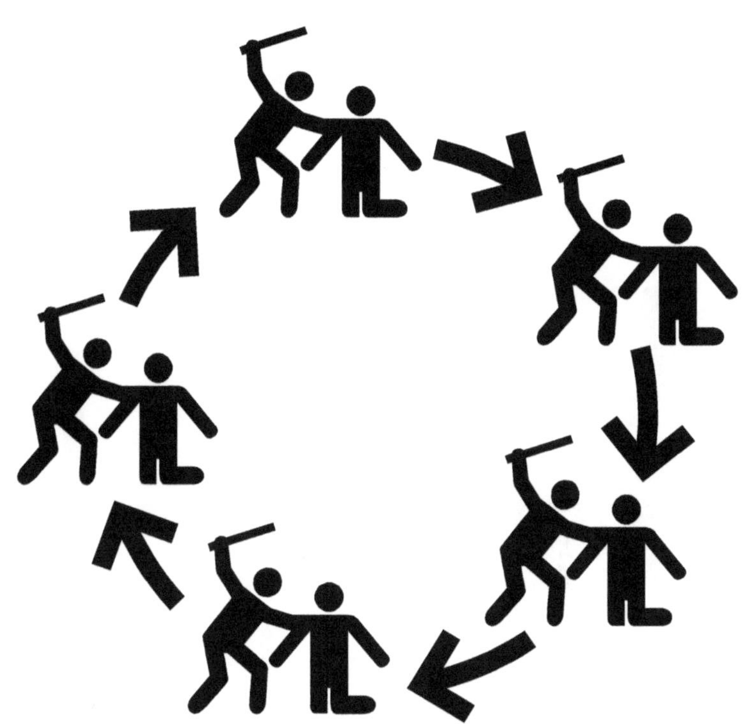

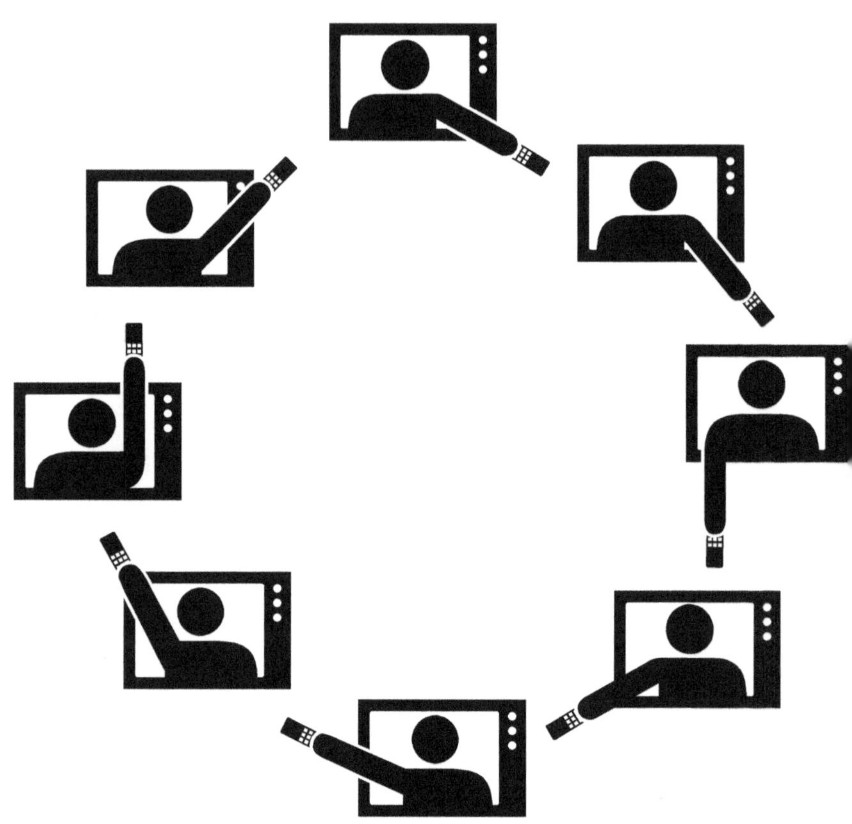

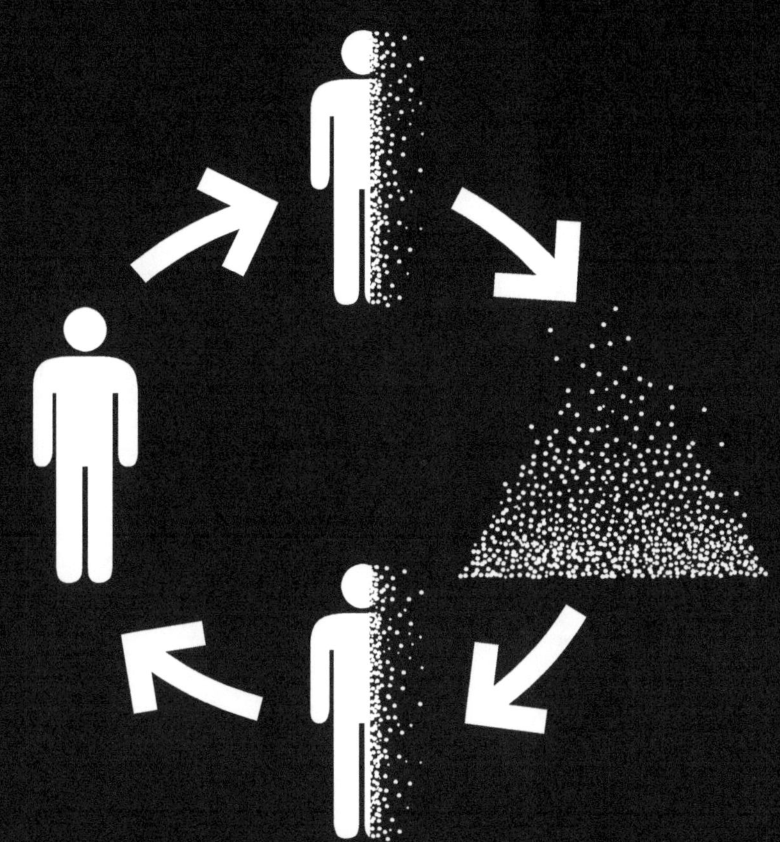

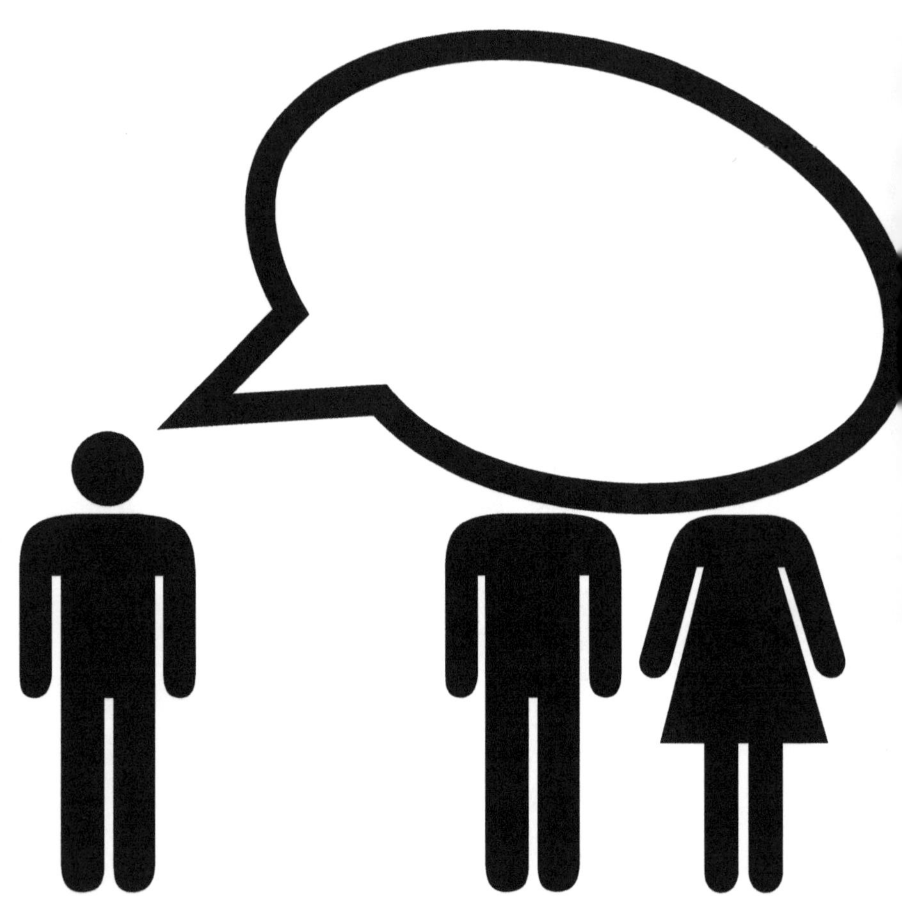

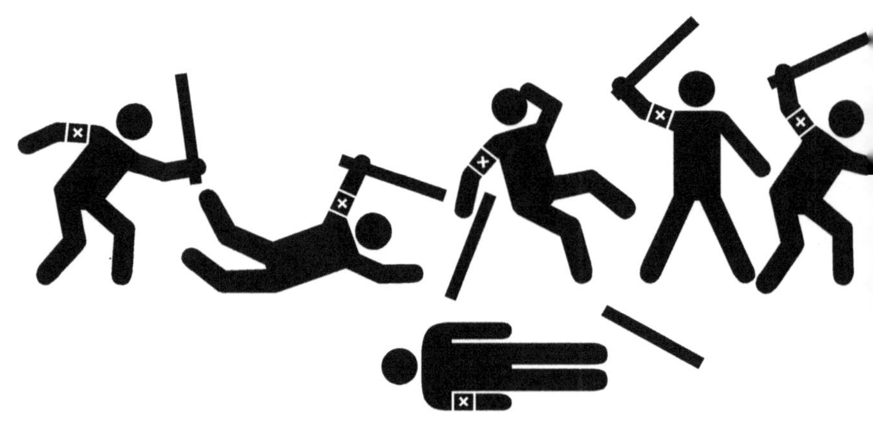

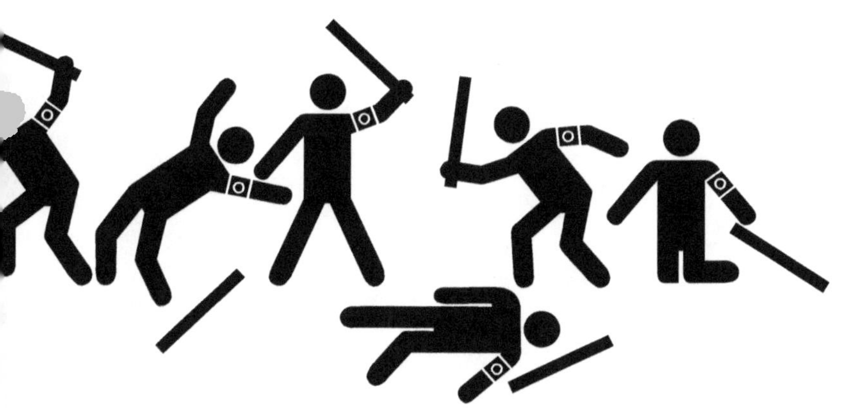

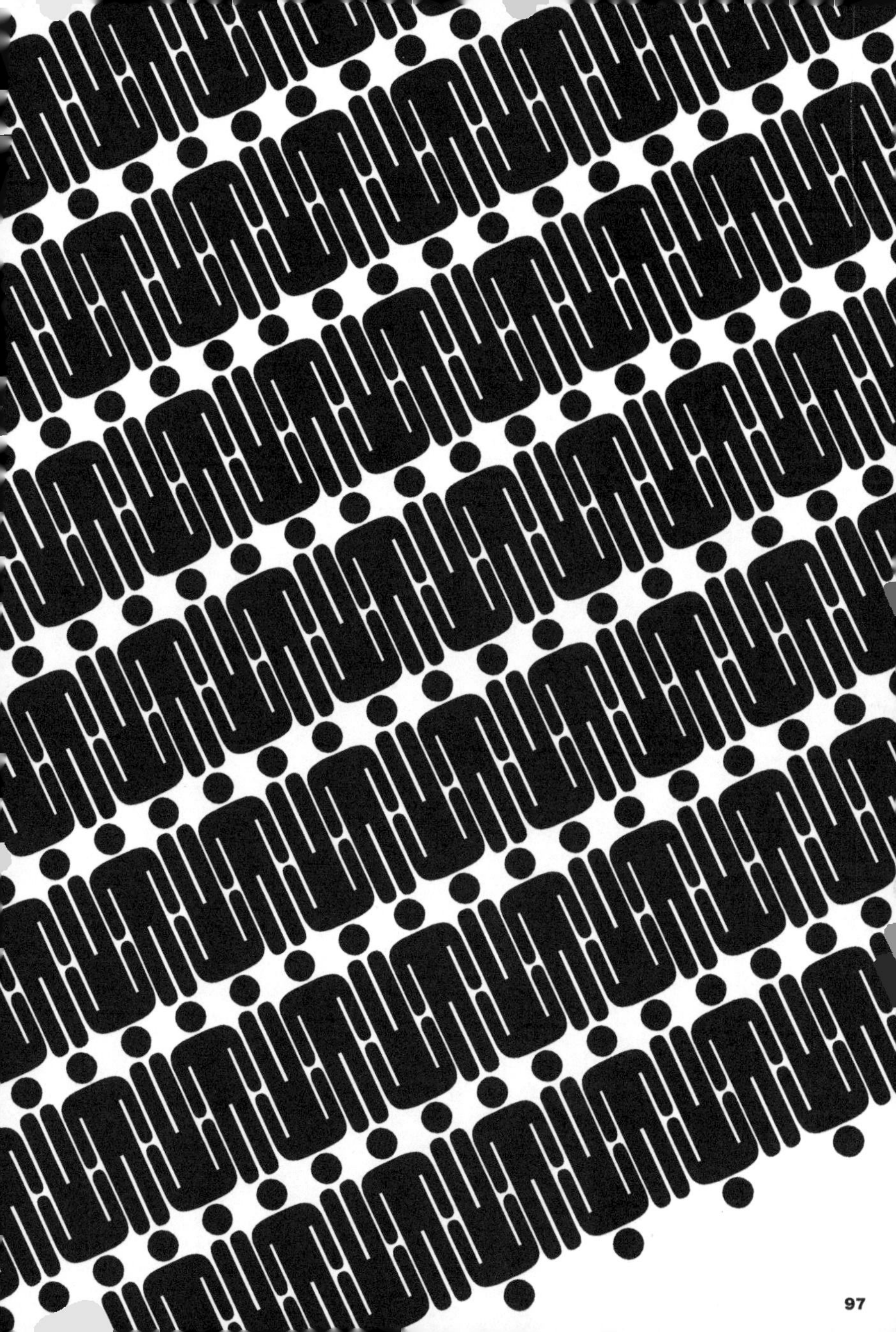

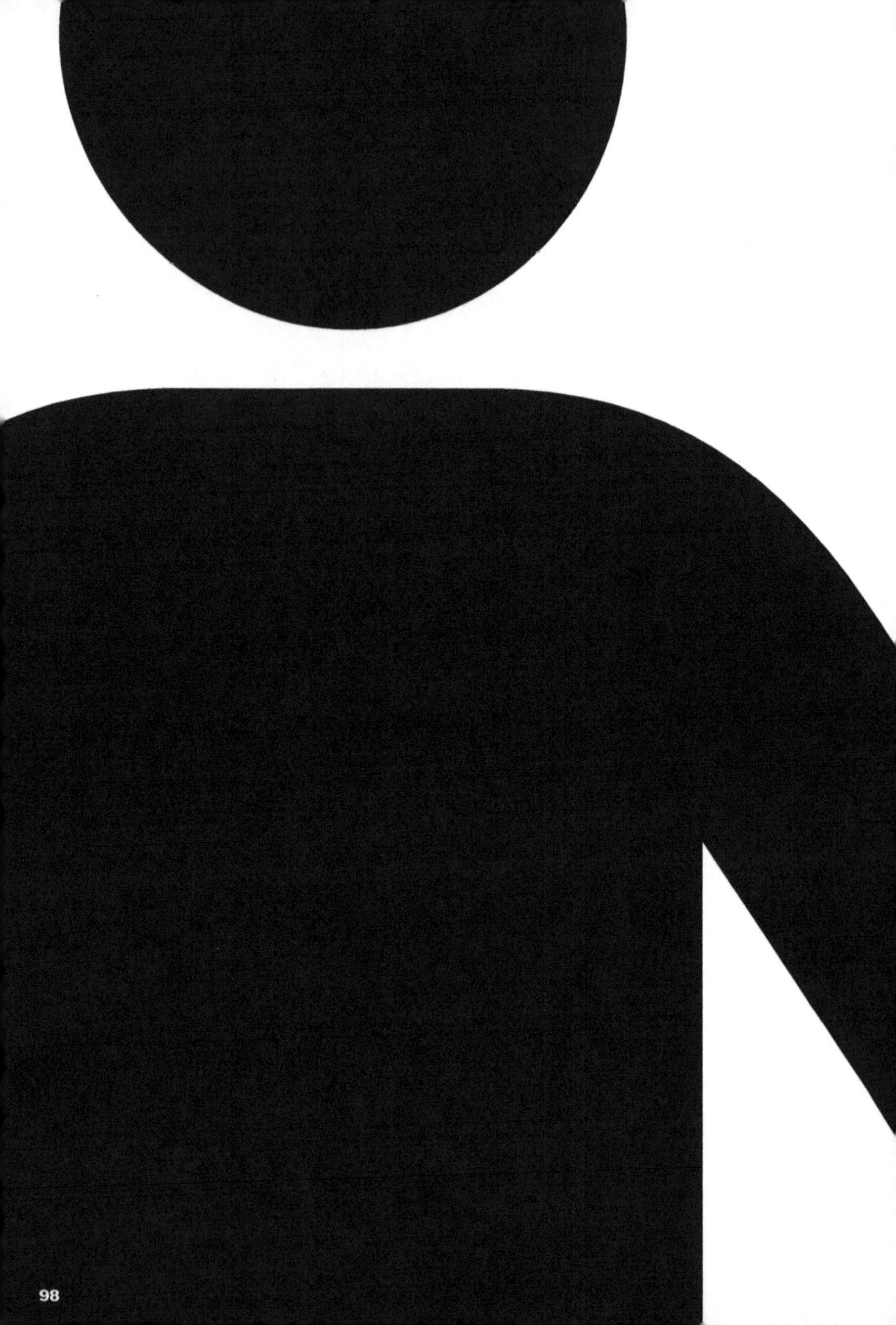

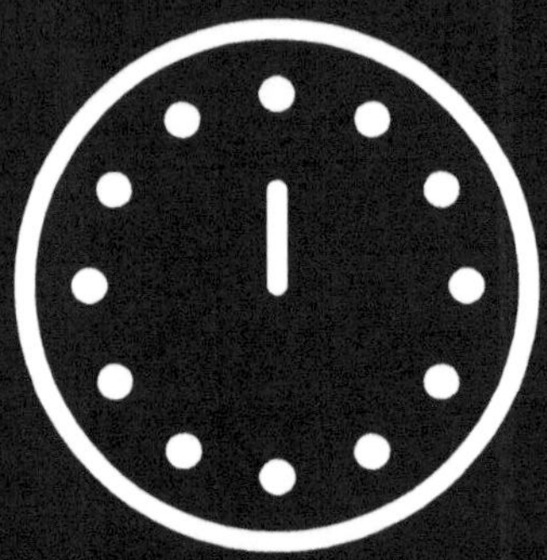

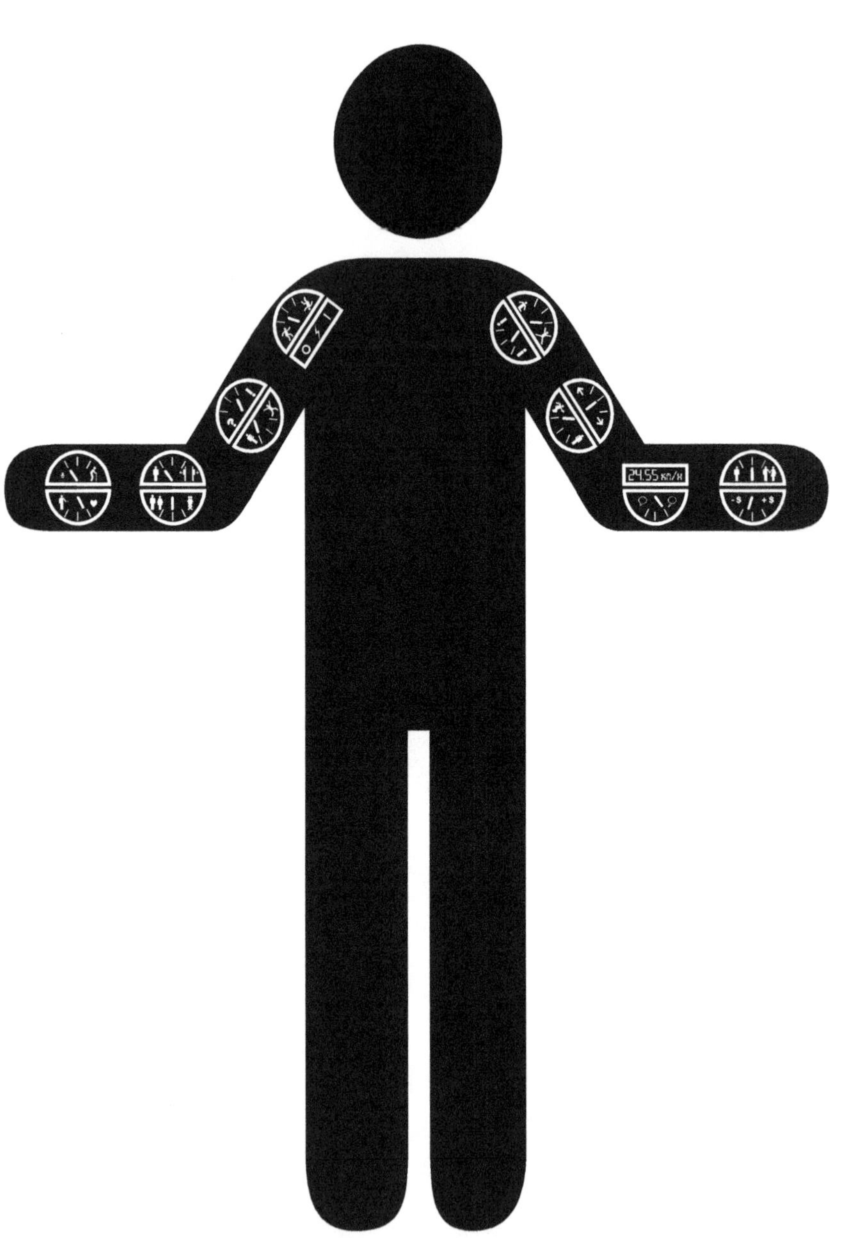

24.55 км/ч
-s / +s

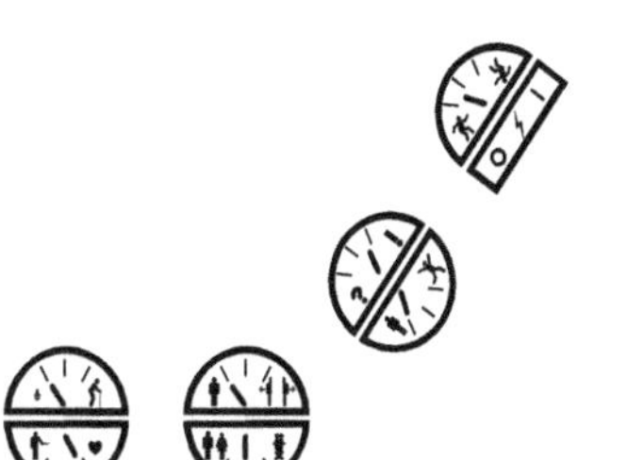

24.55 км/ч

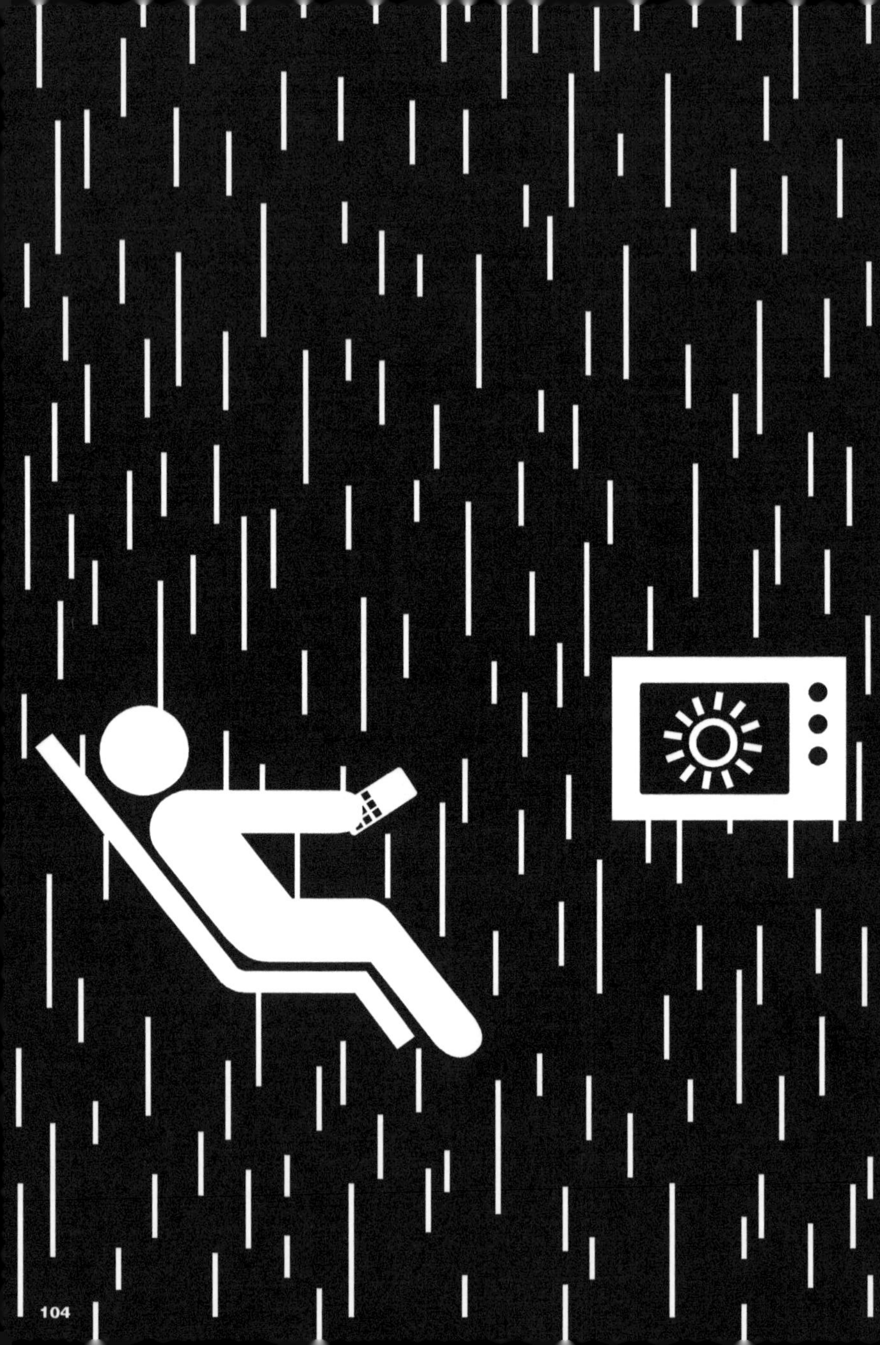

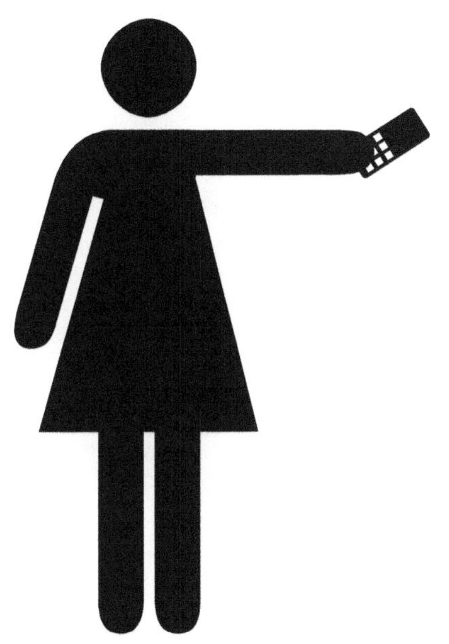
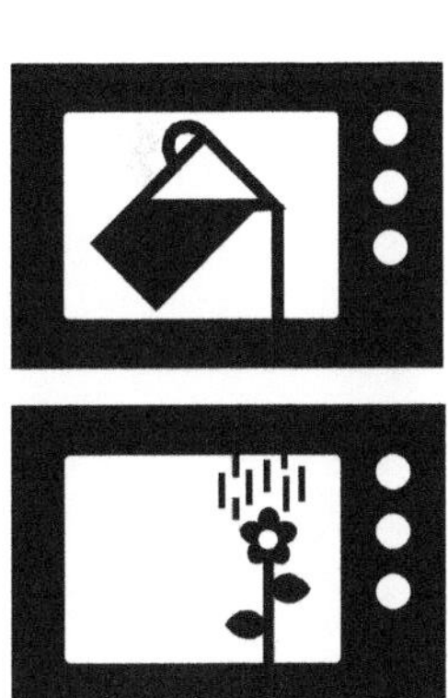

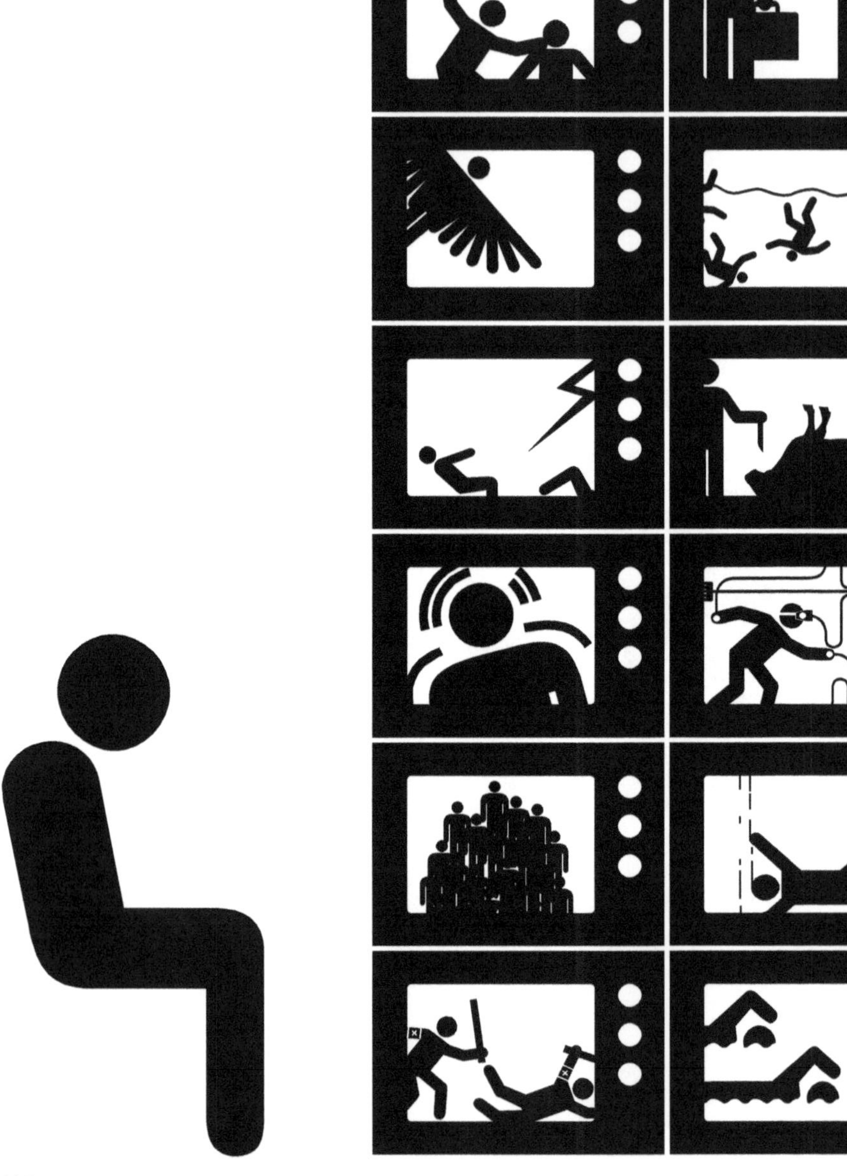

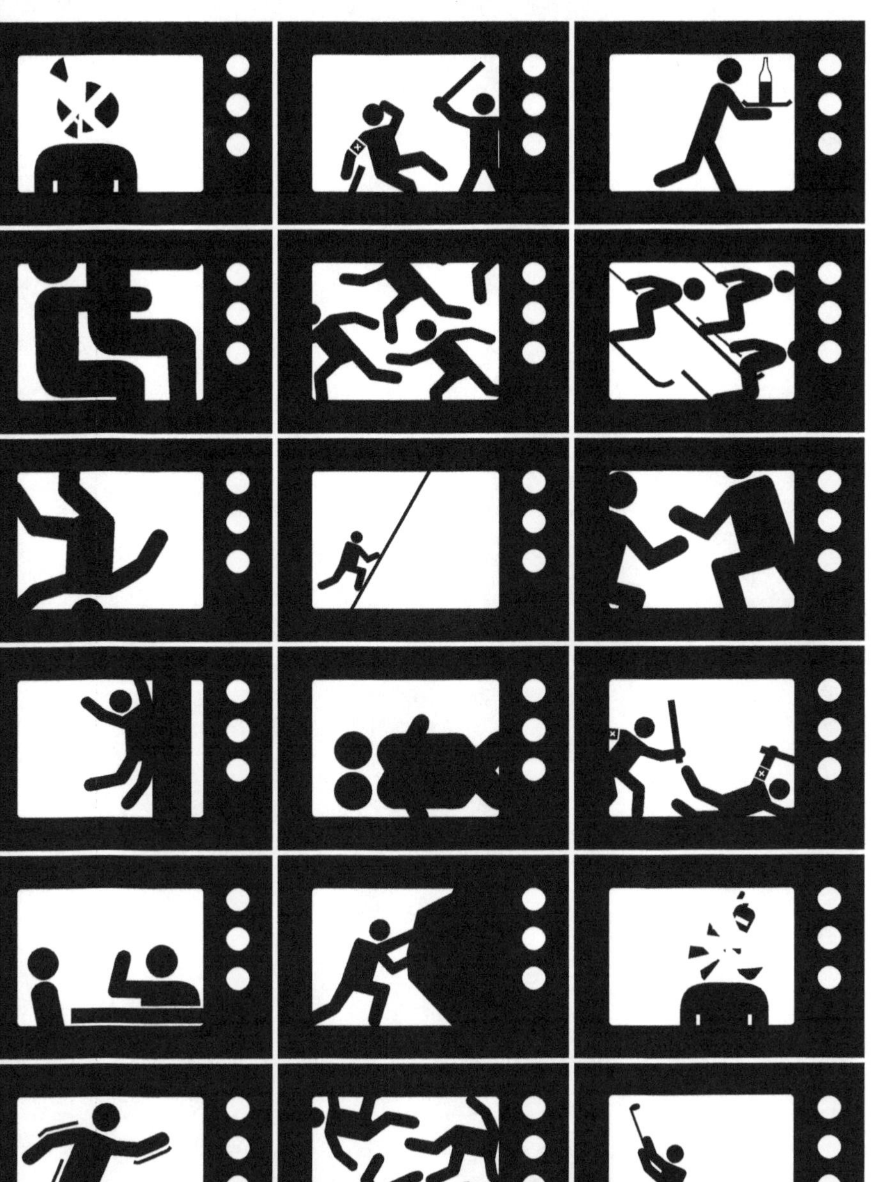

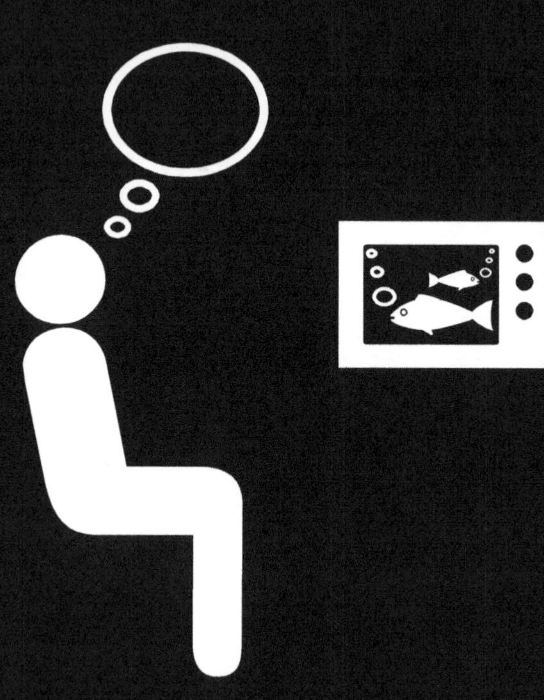

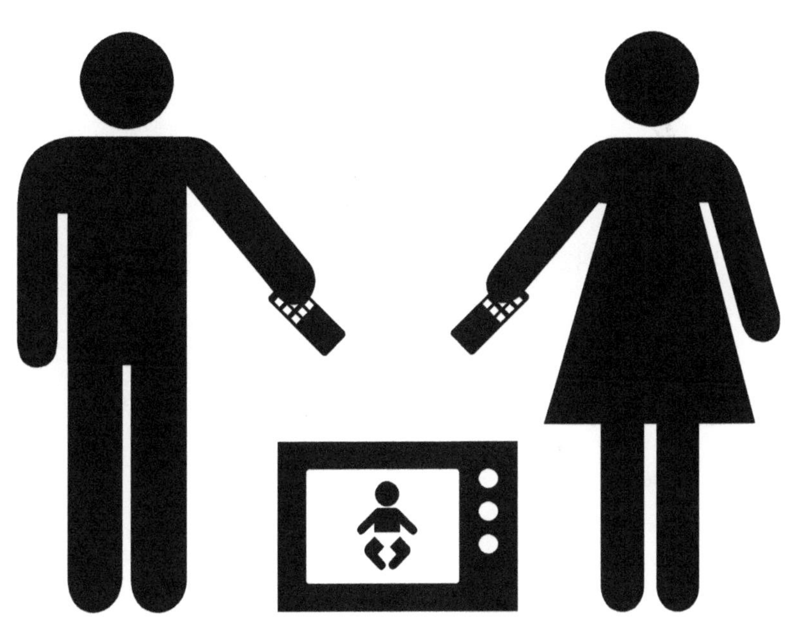

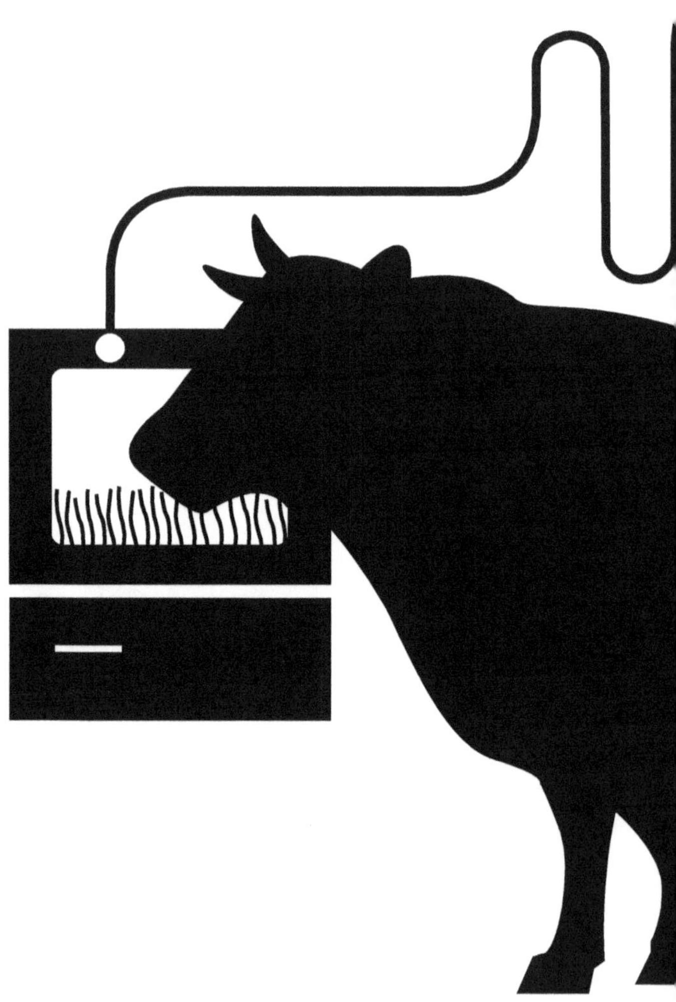

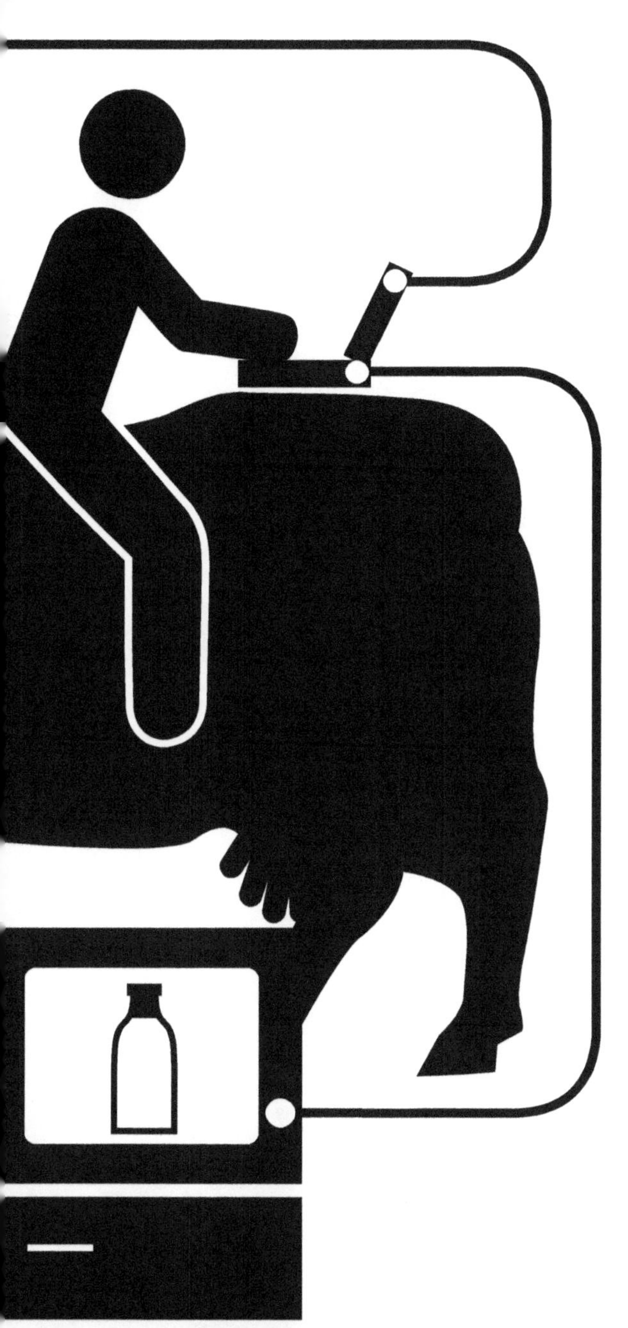

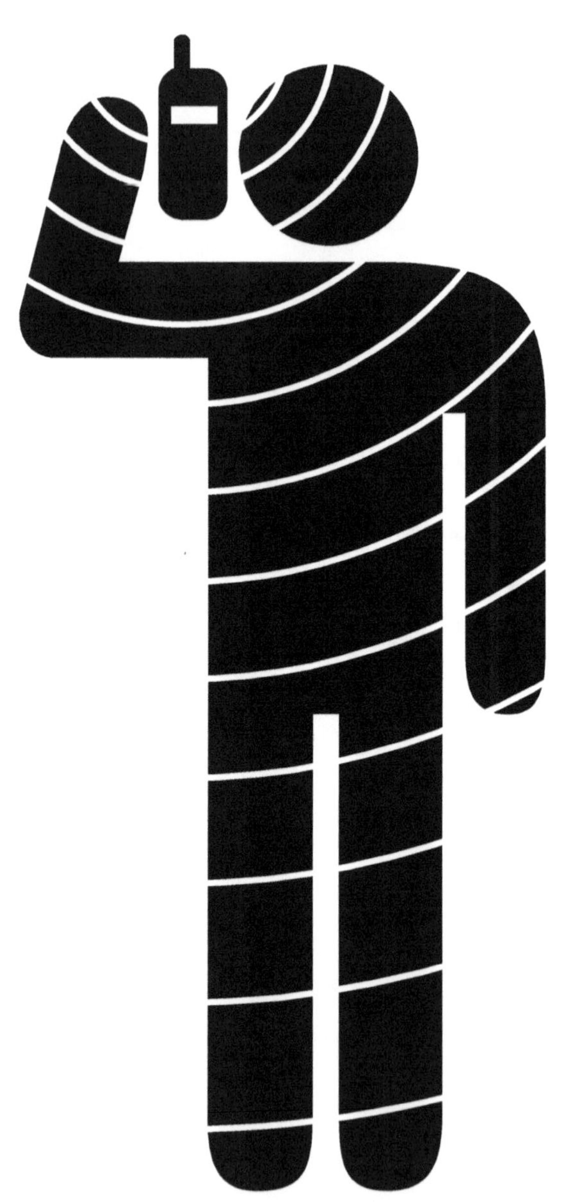

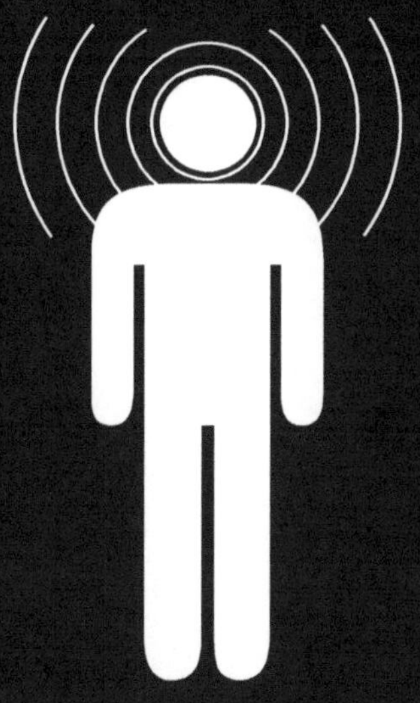

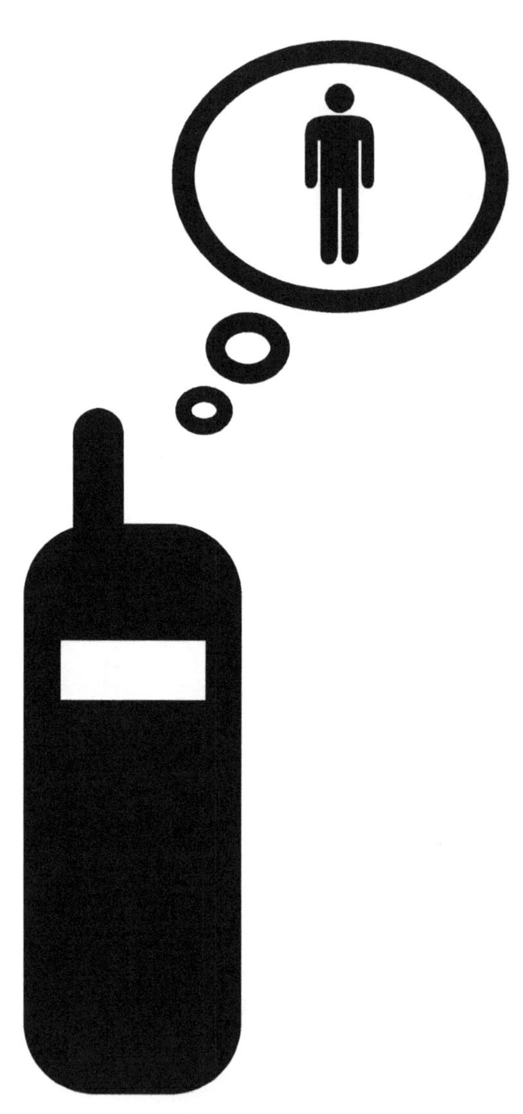

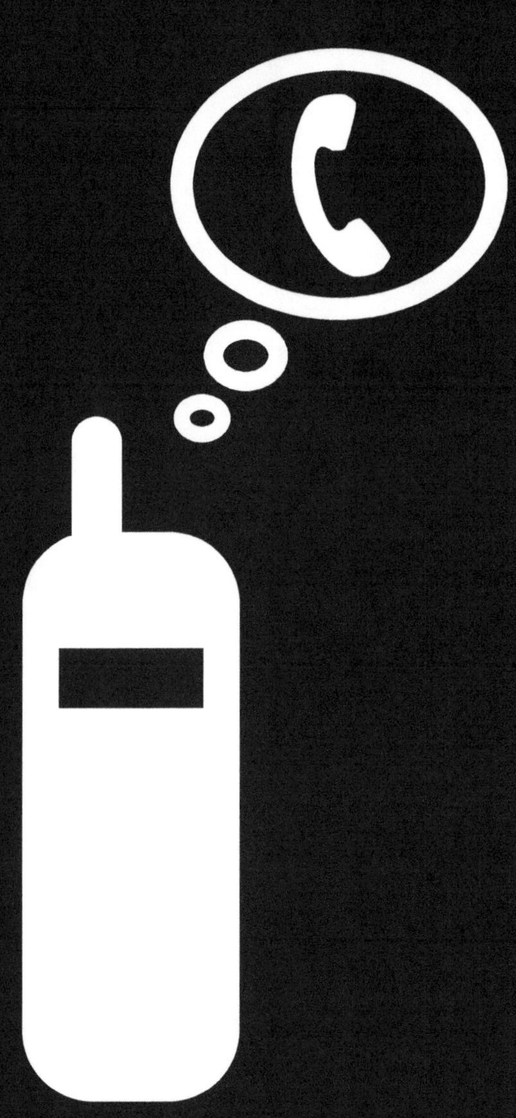

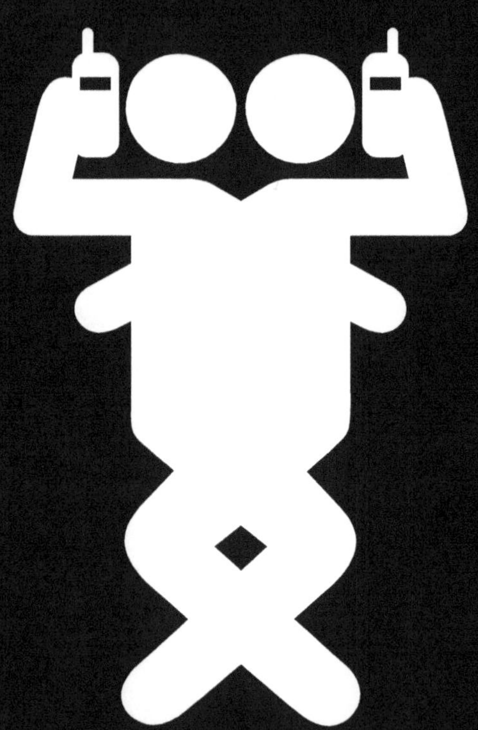

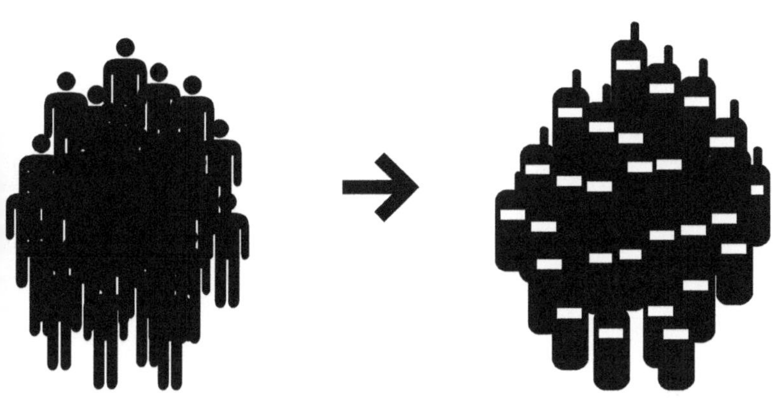

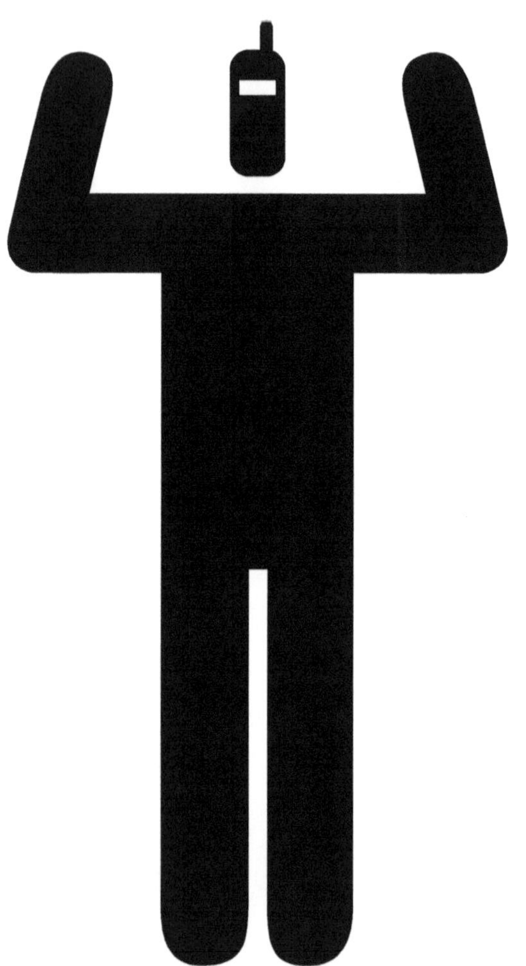

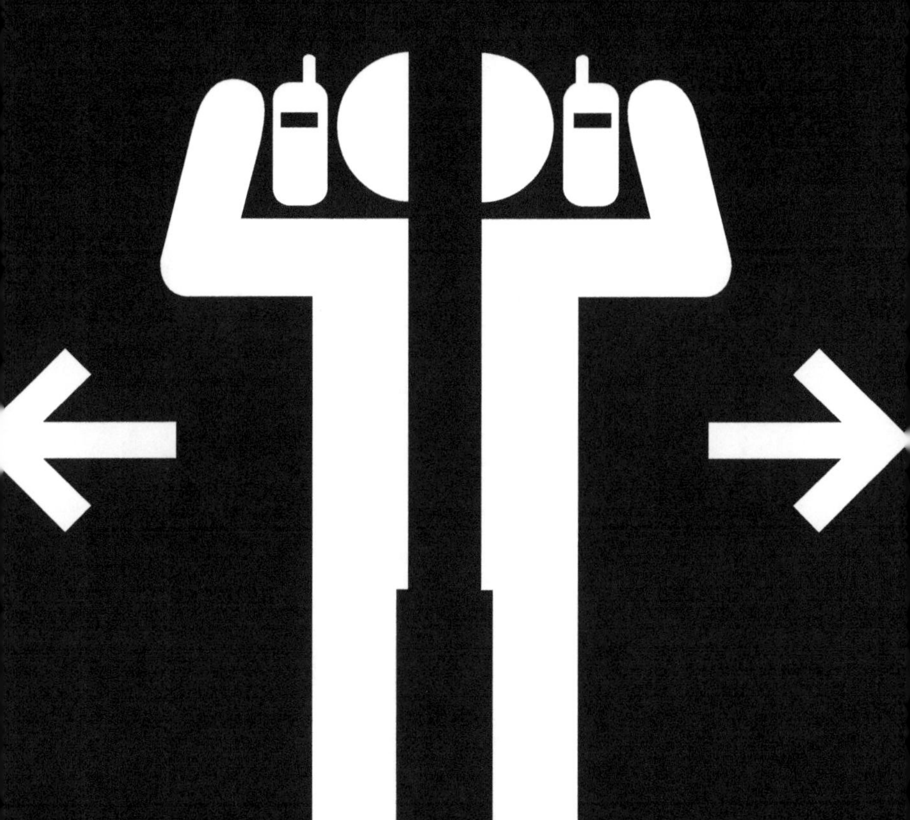

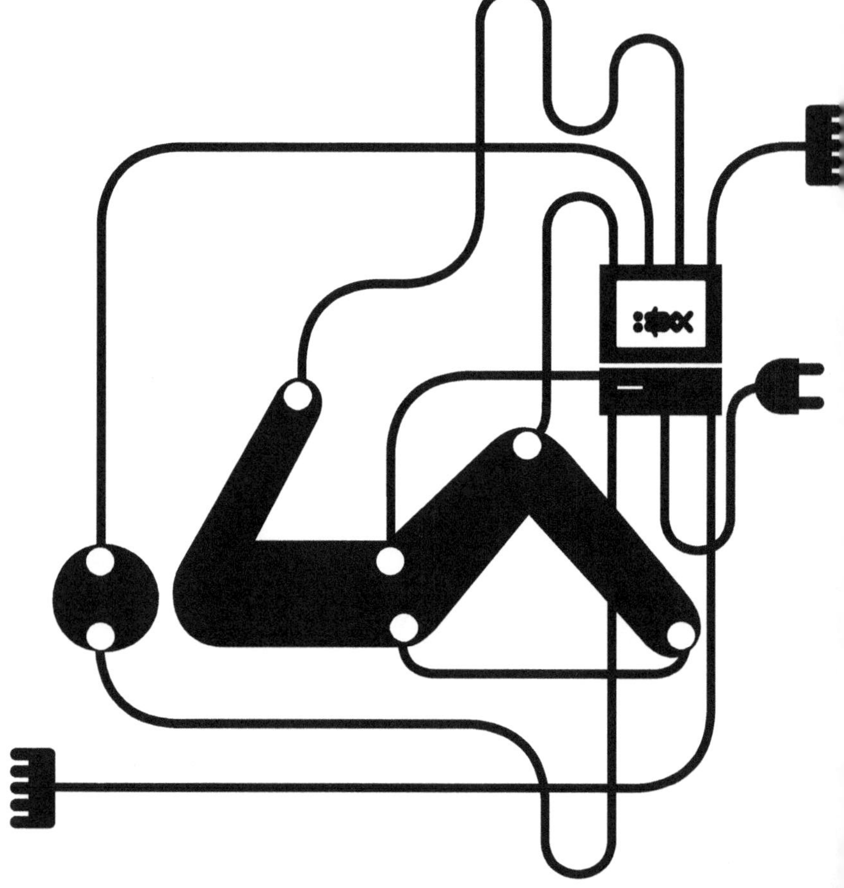

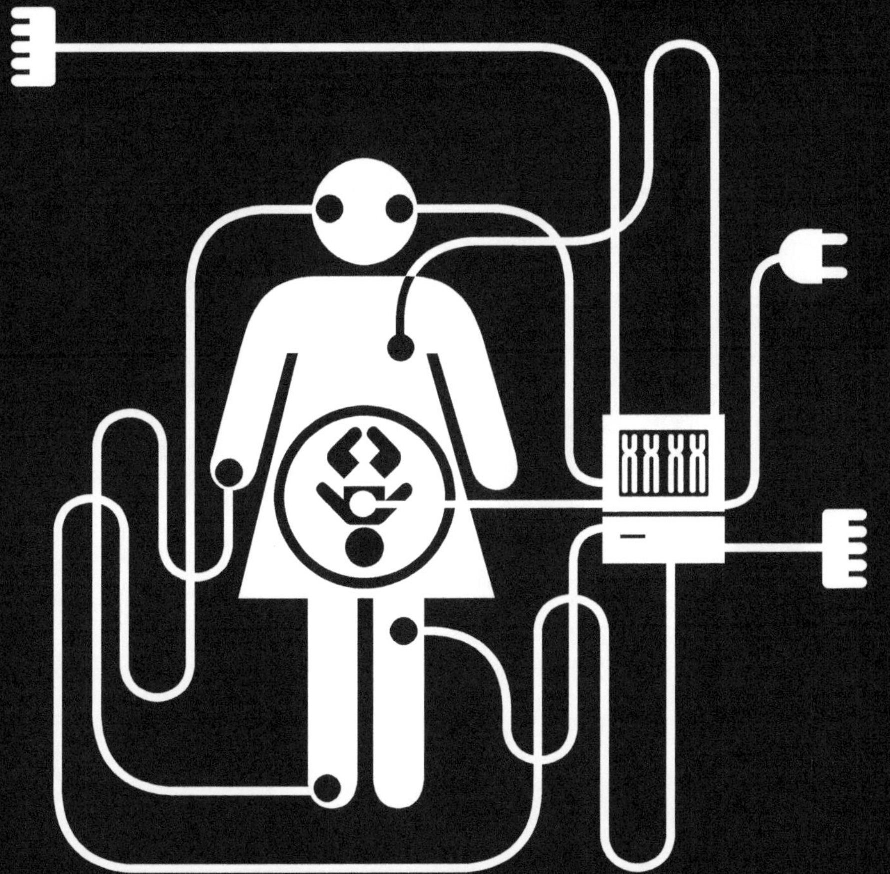

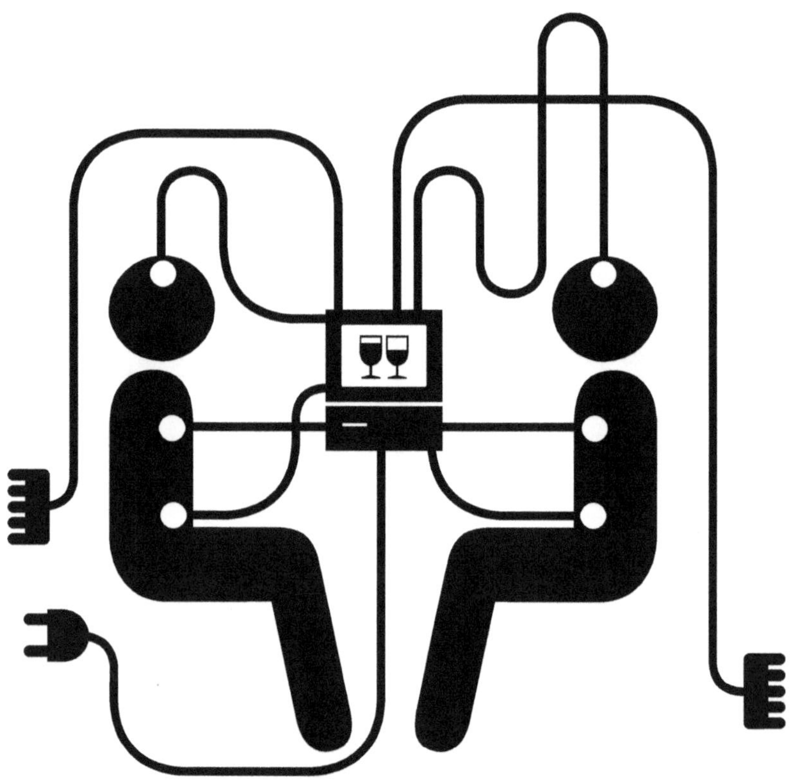

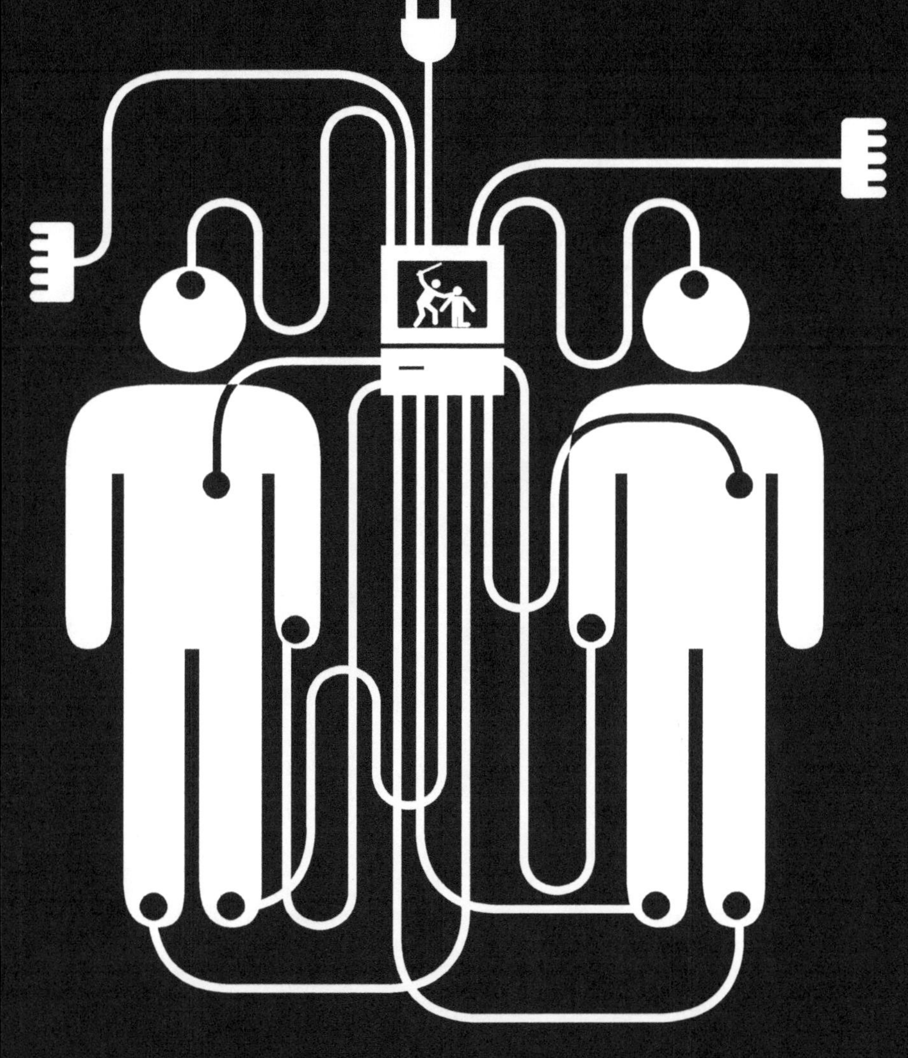

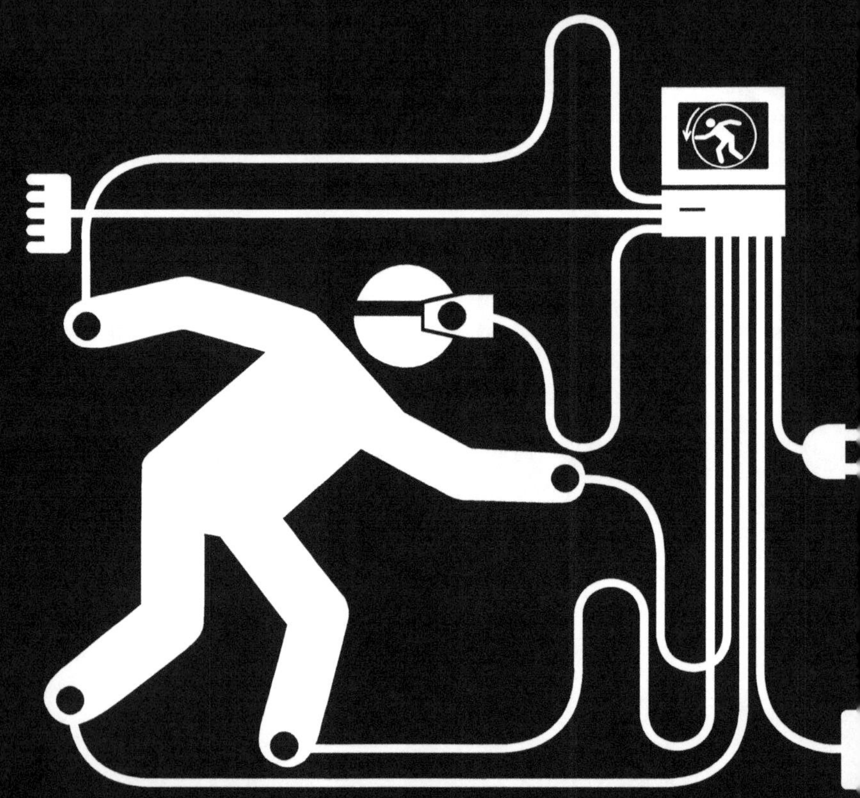

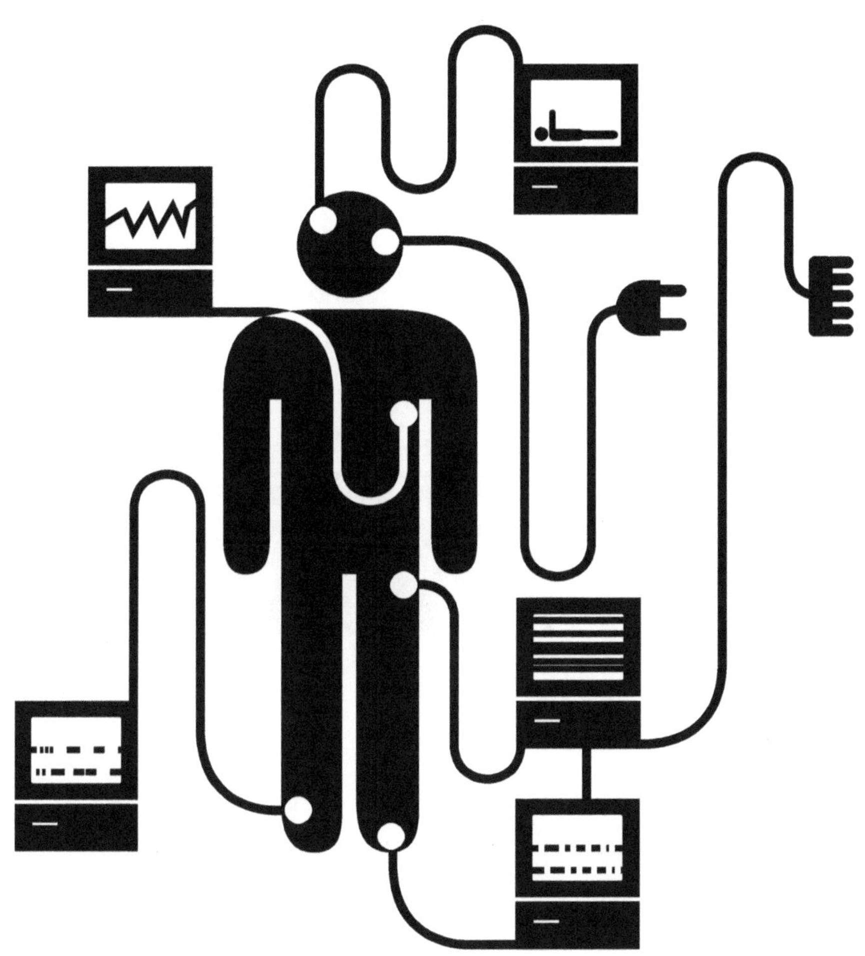

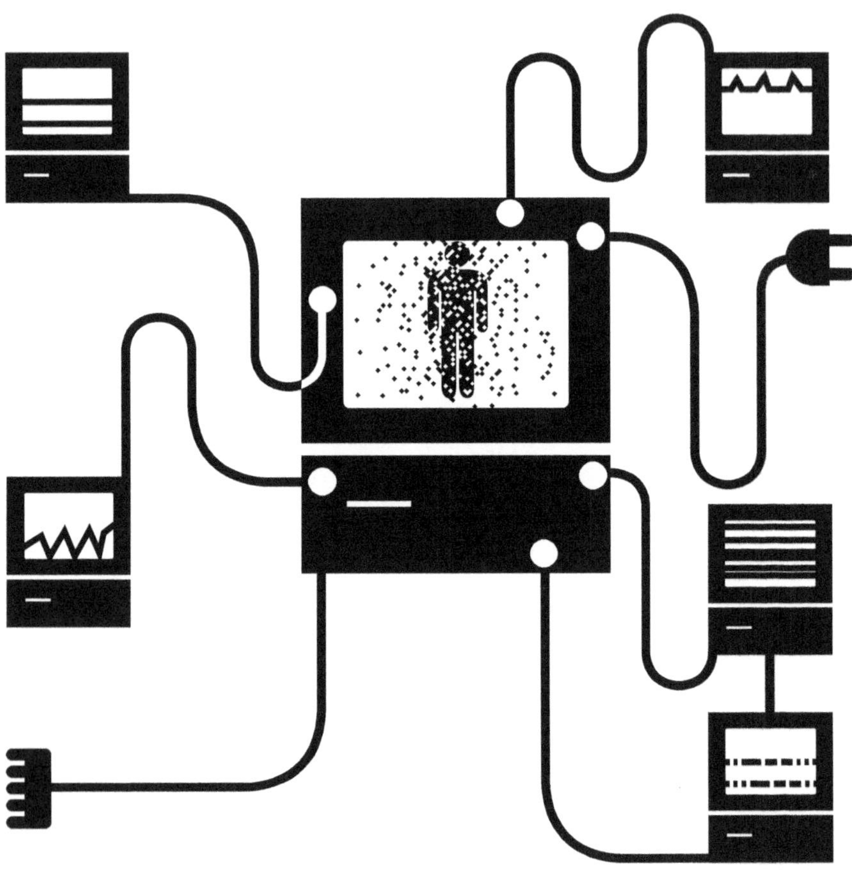

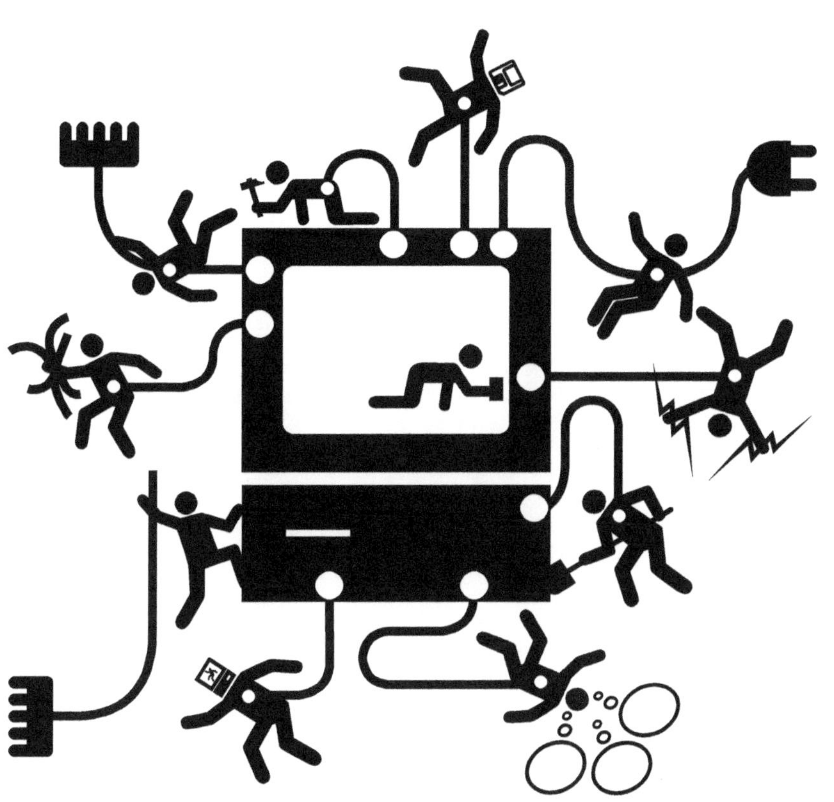

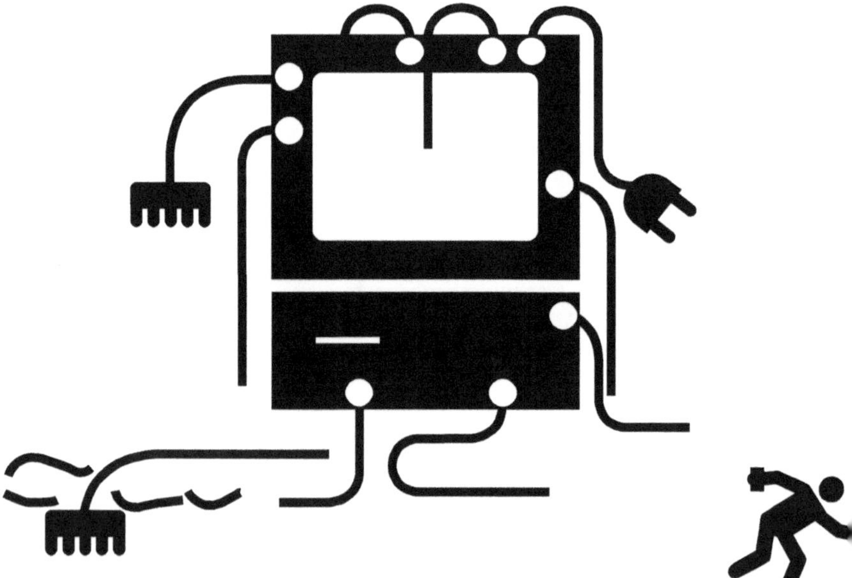

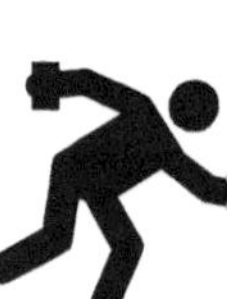

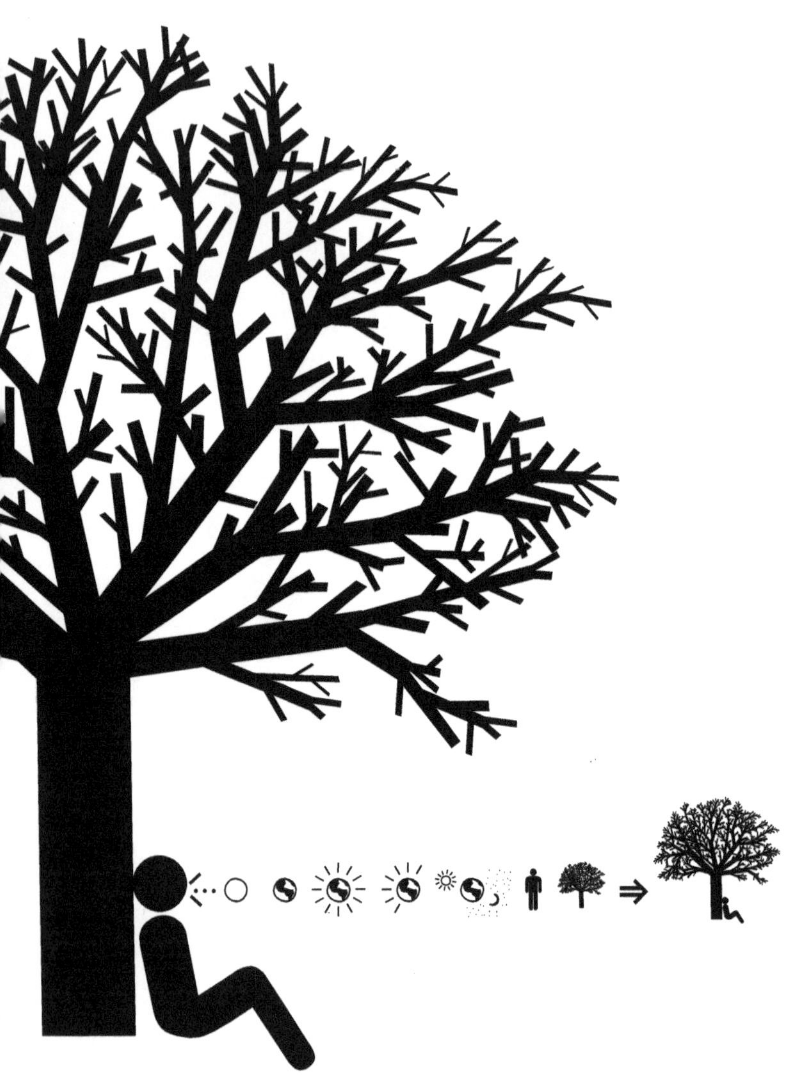

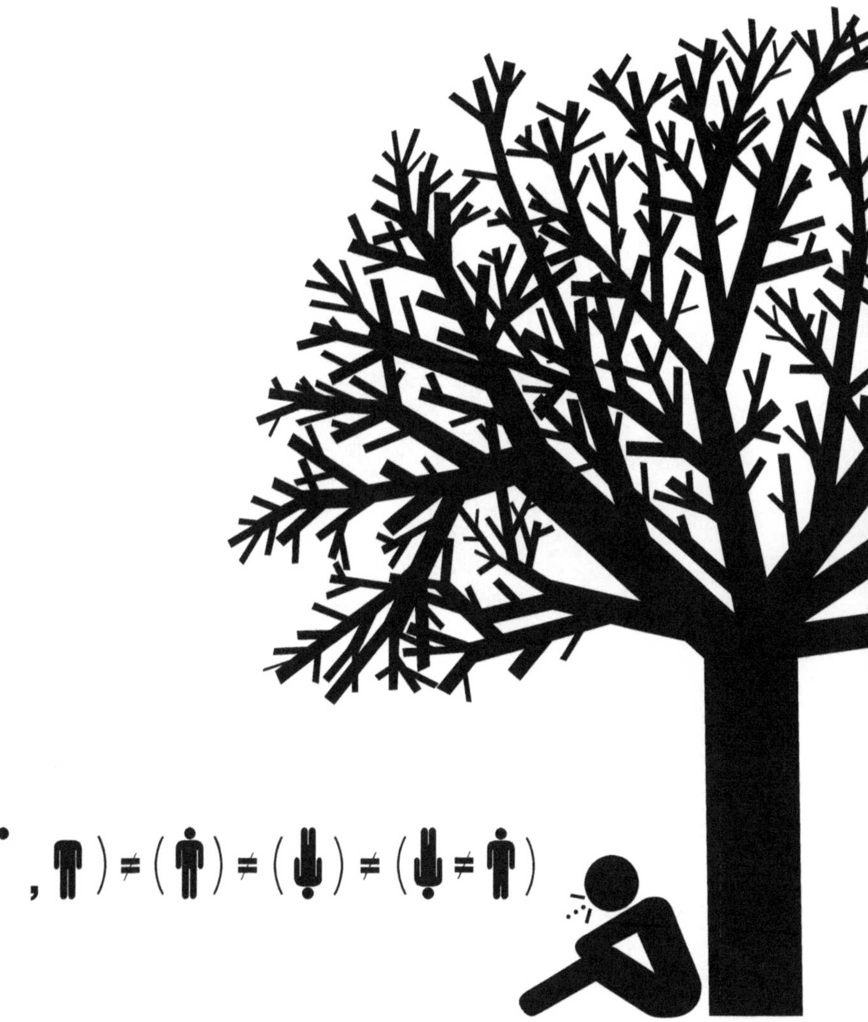

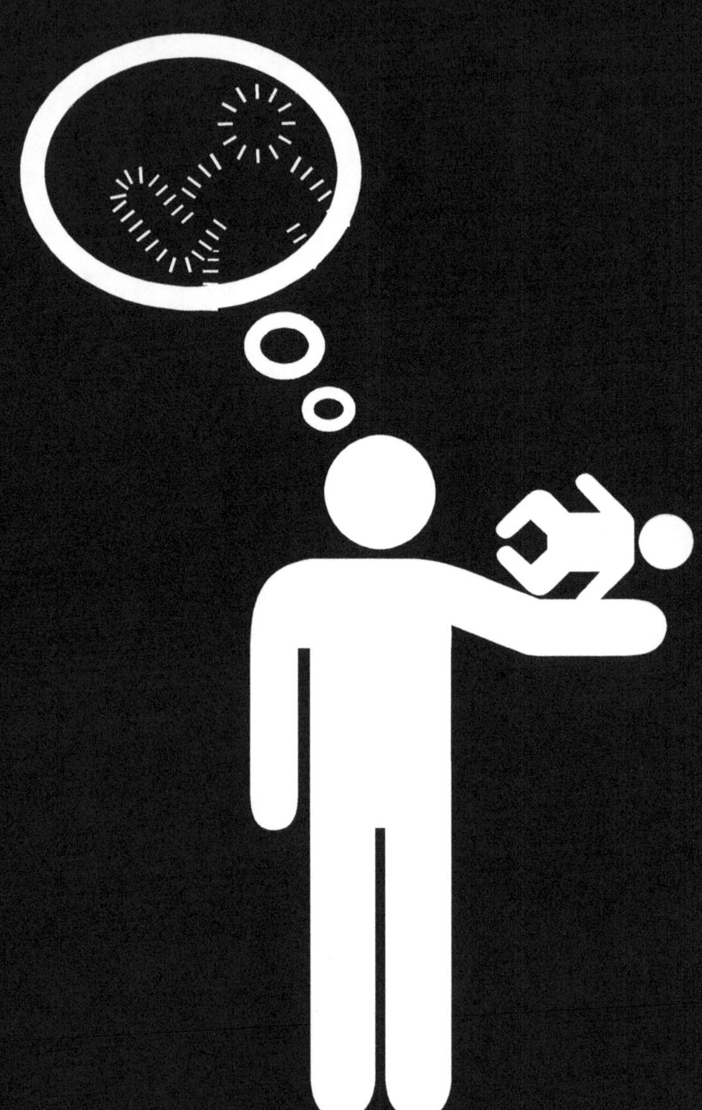

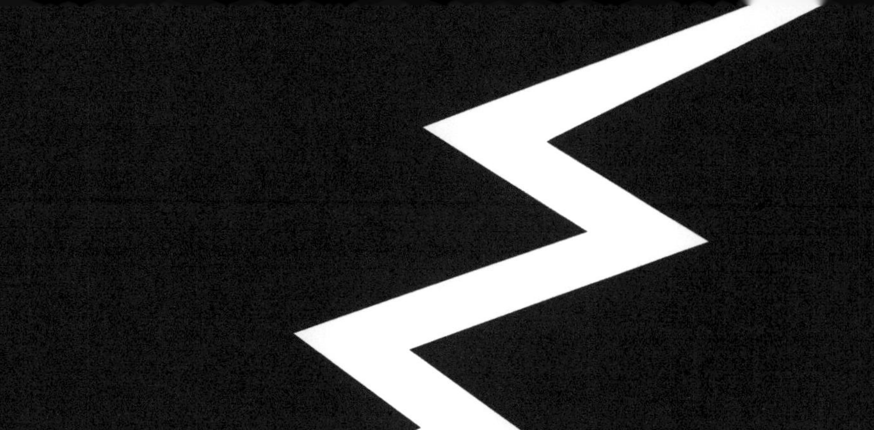

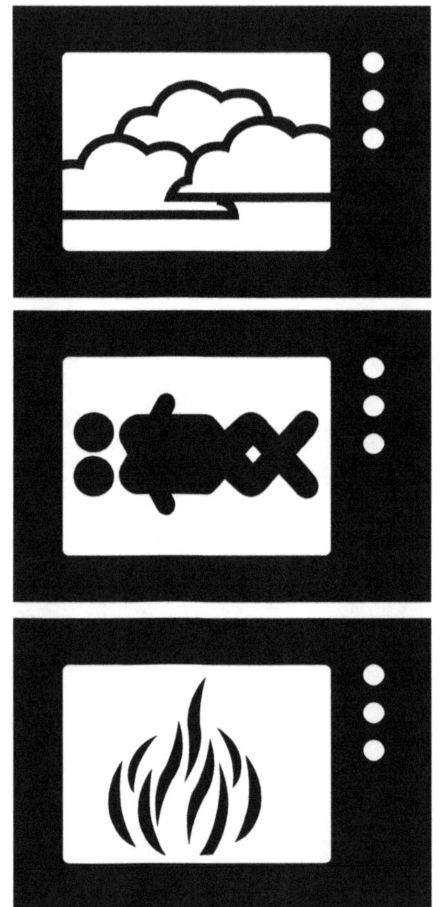

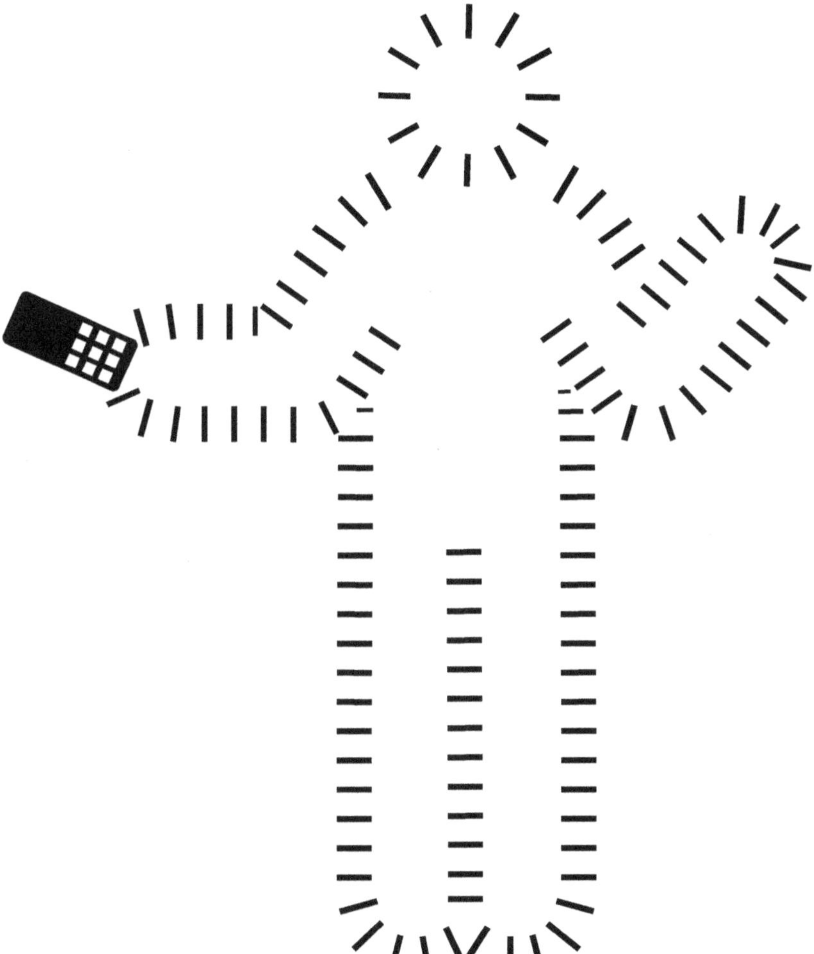

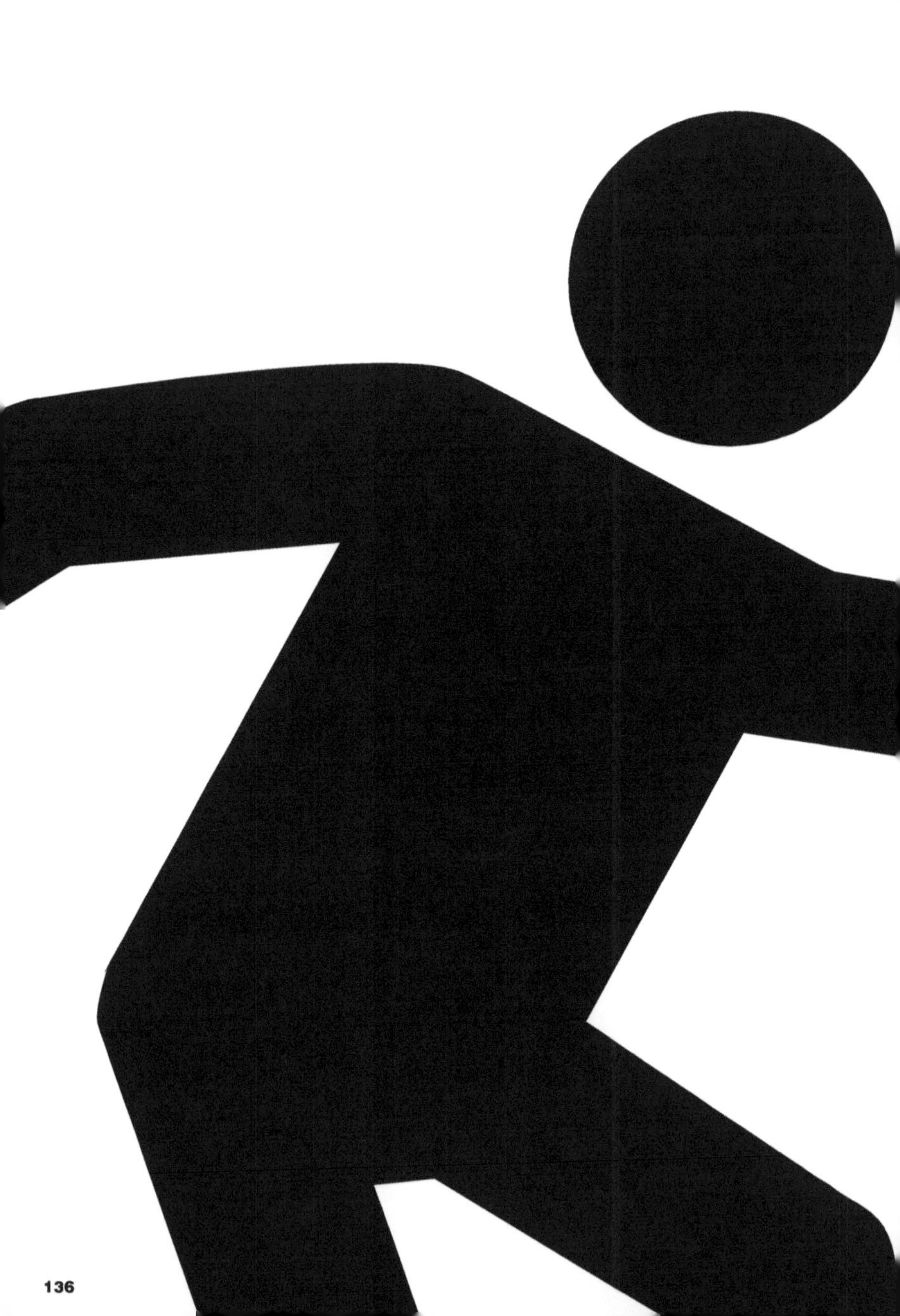

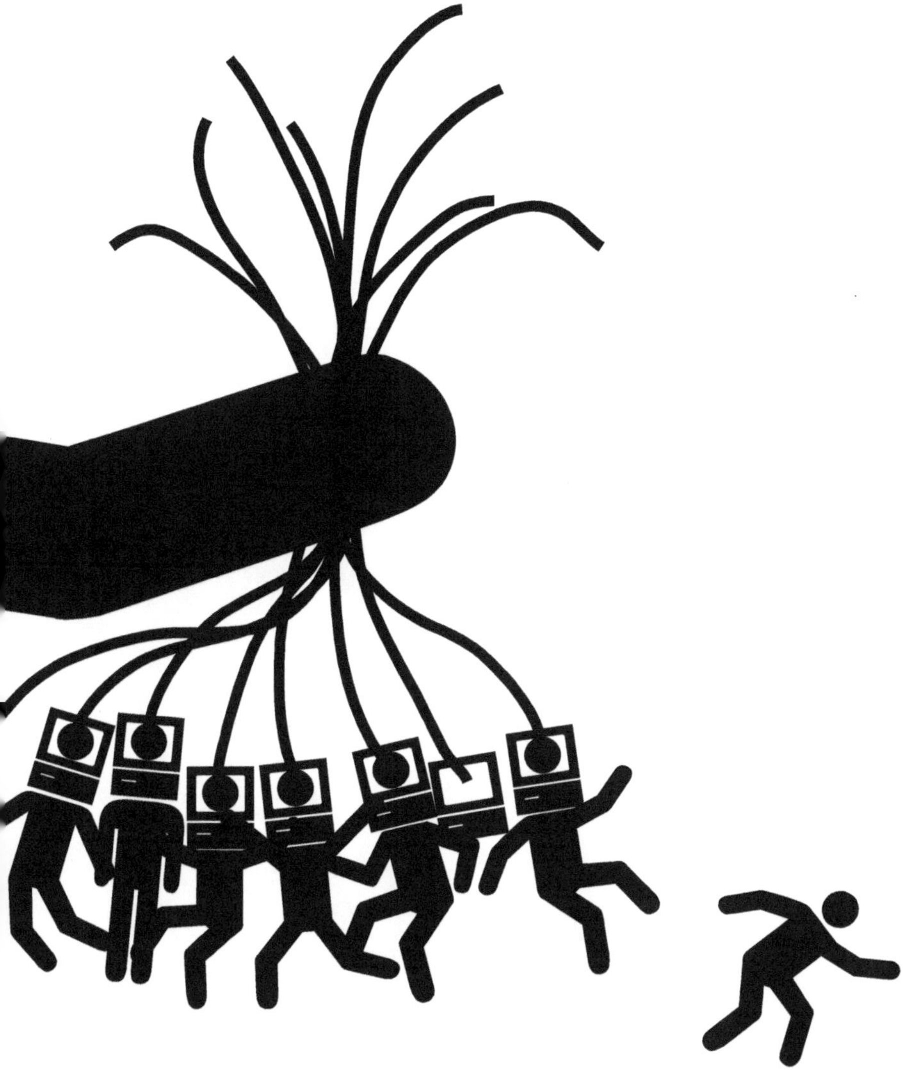

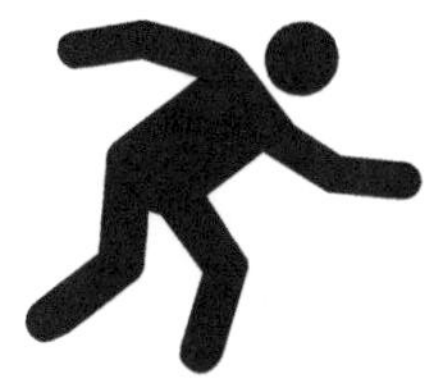

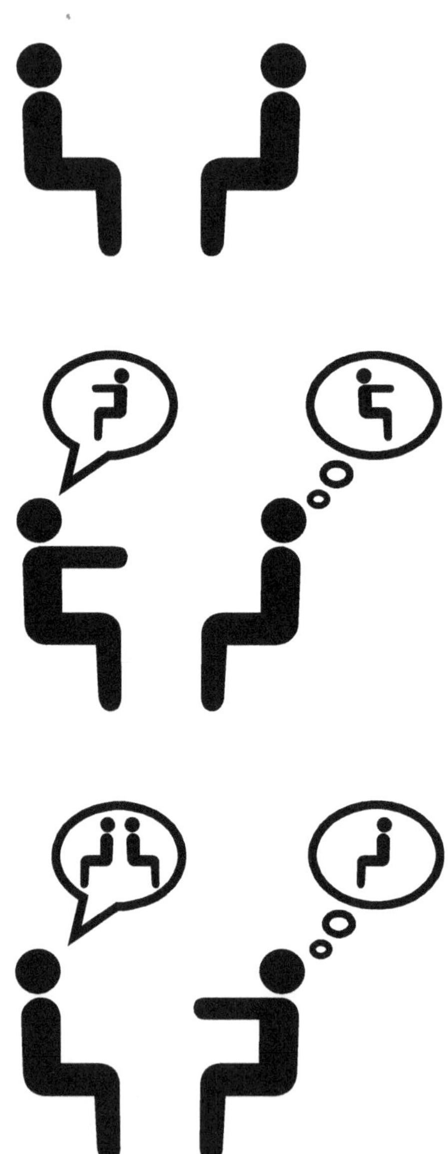

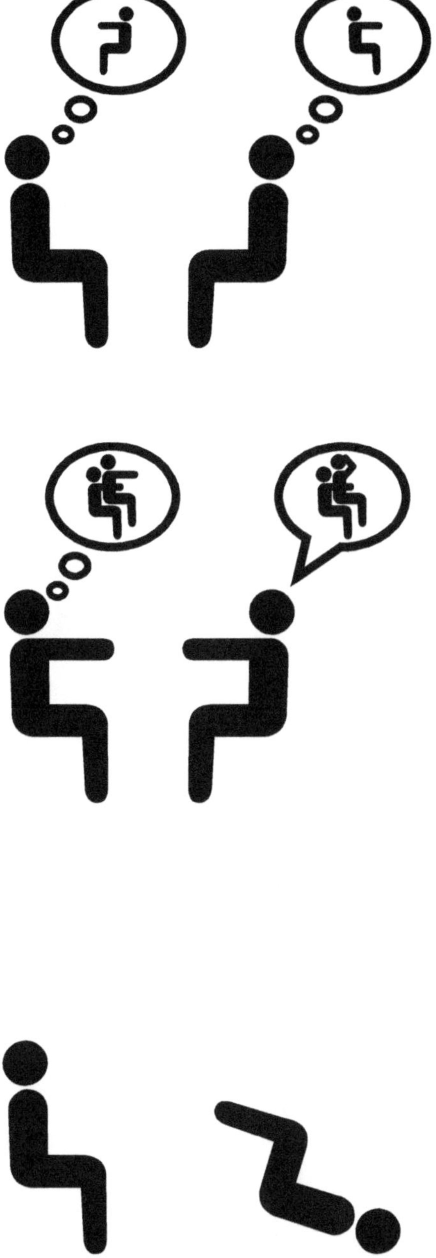

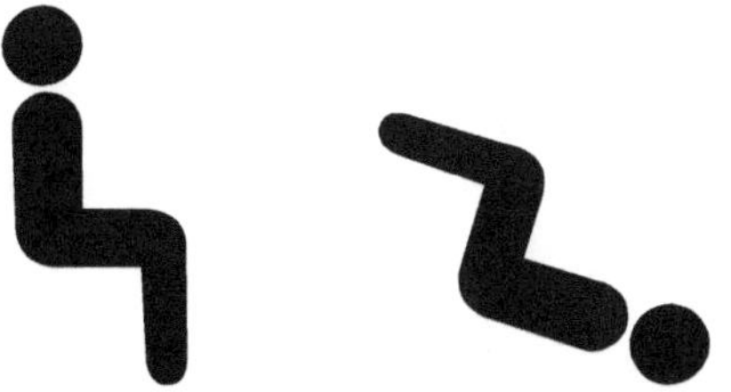

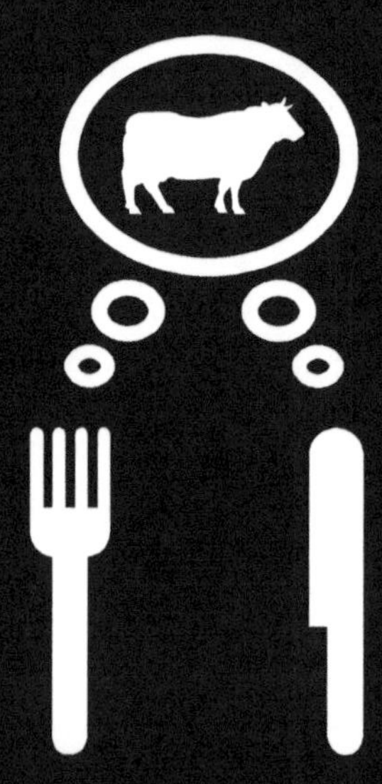

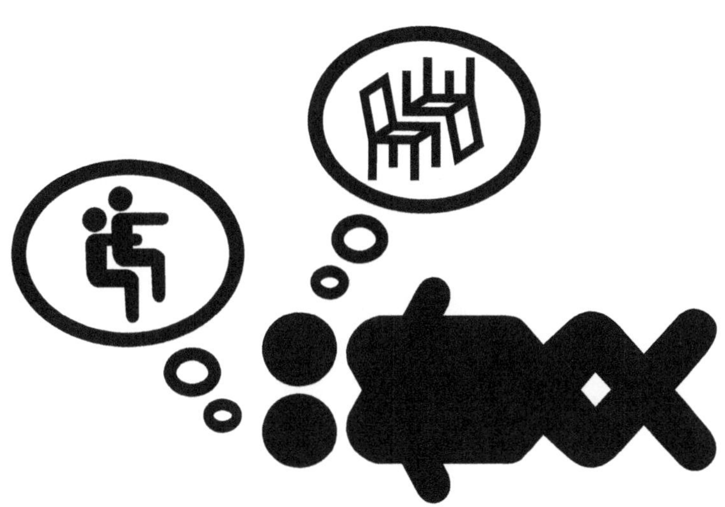

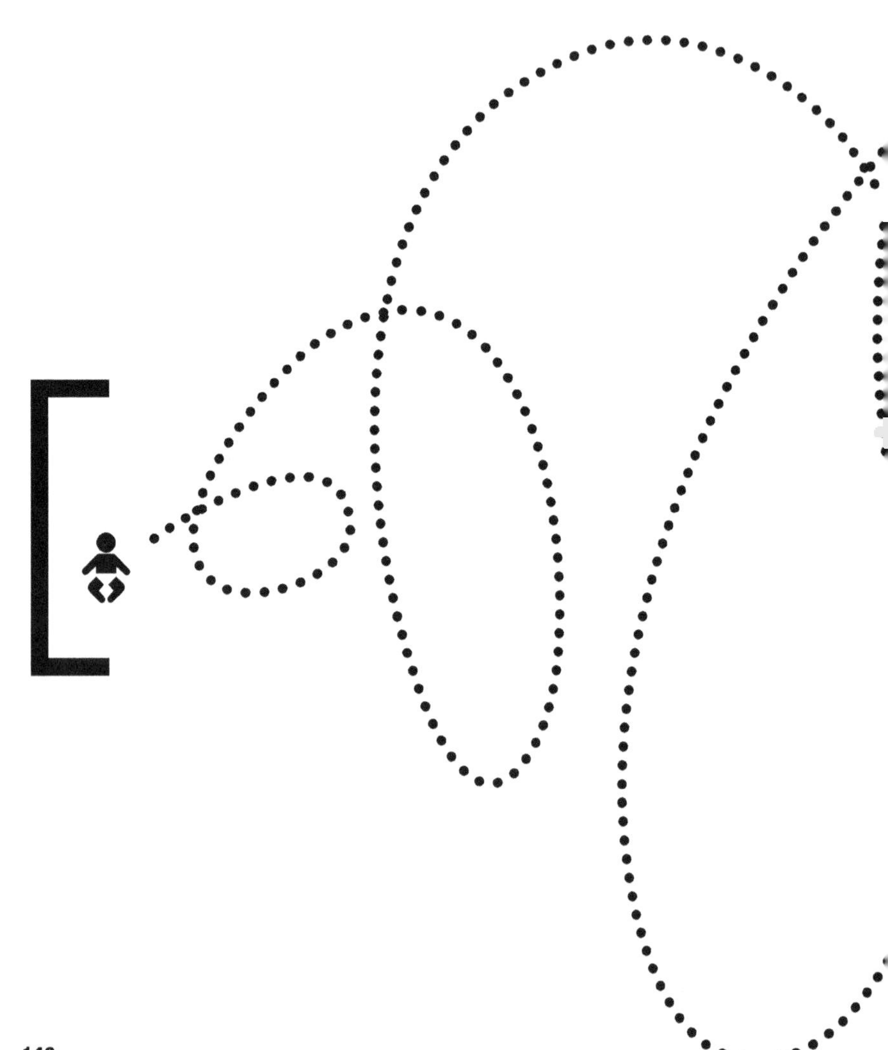

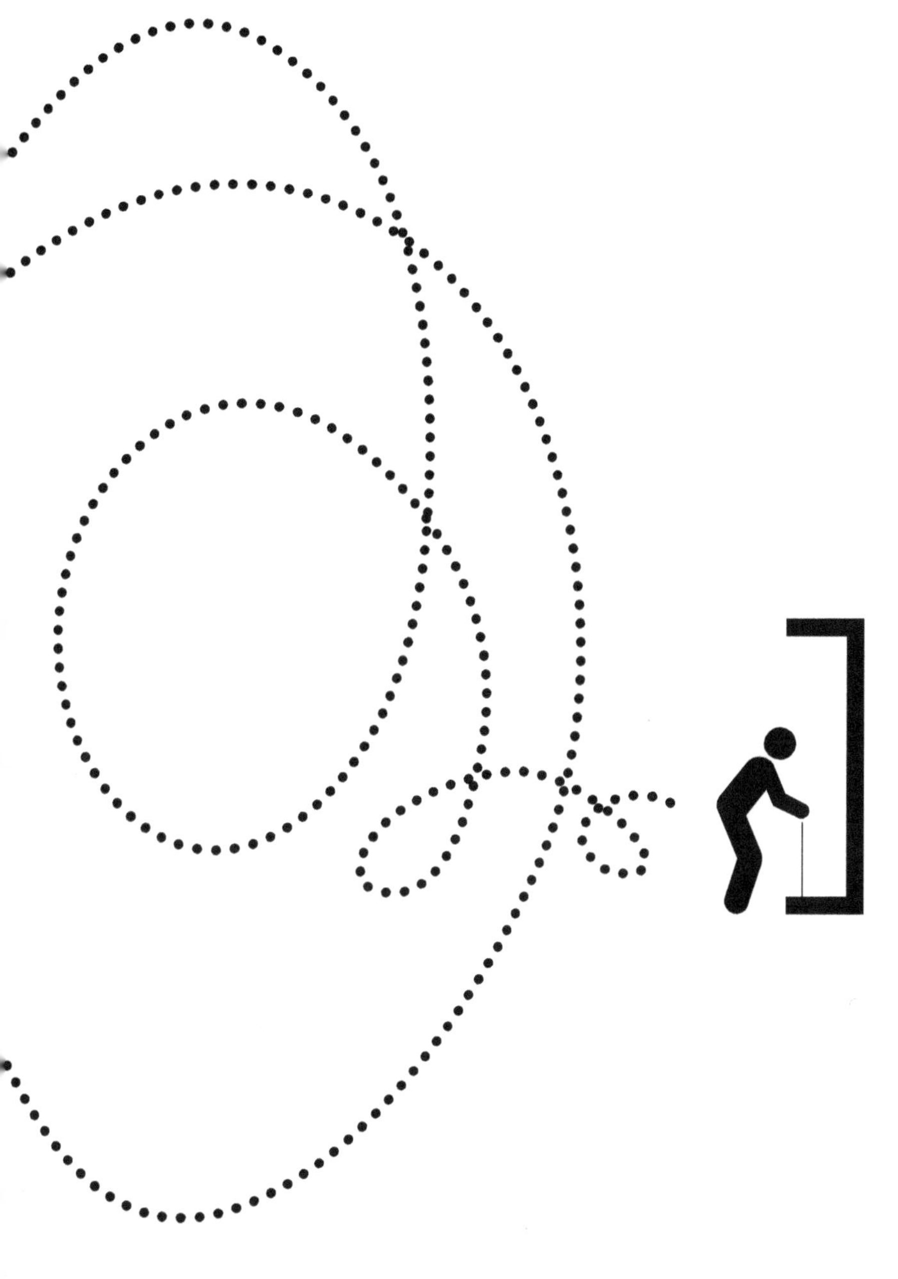

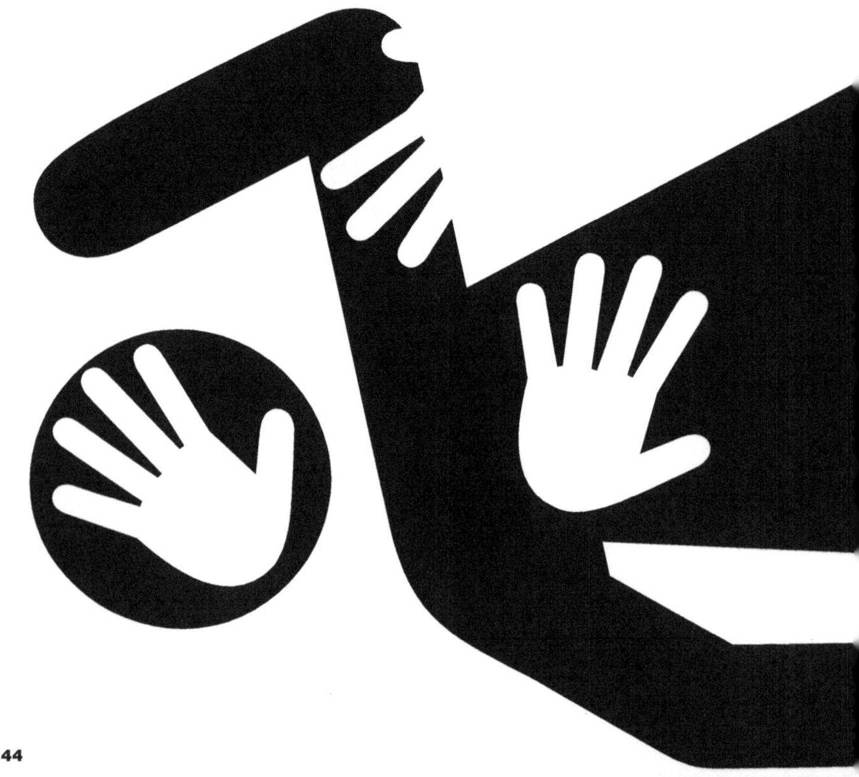

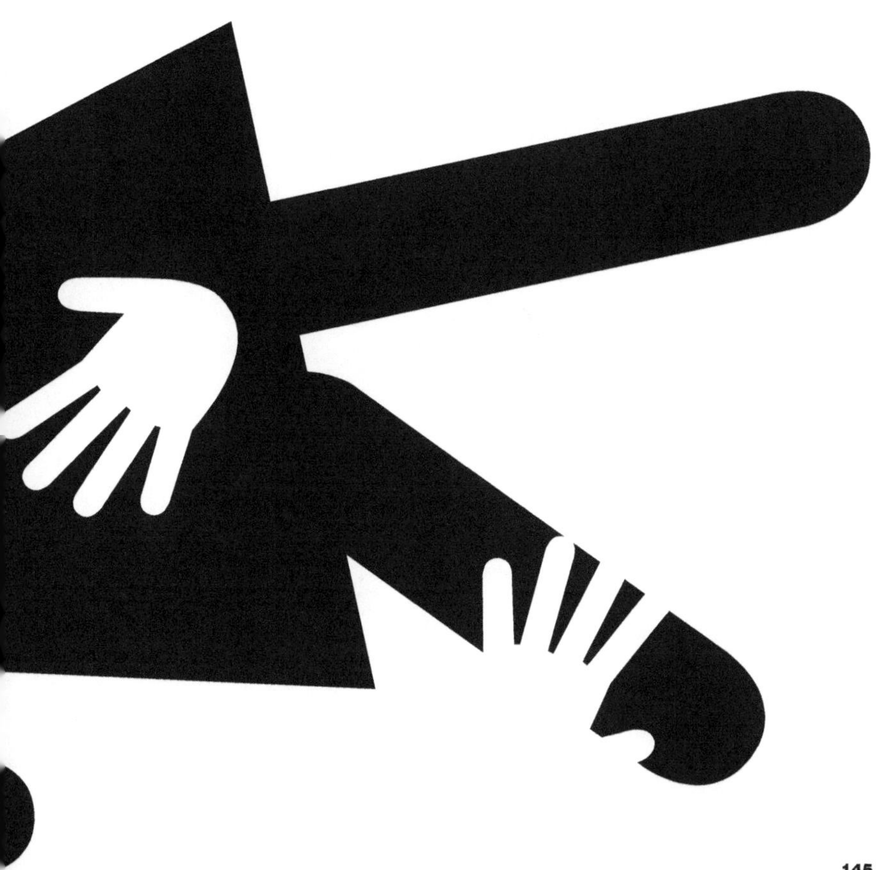

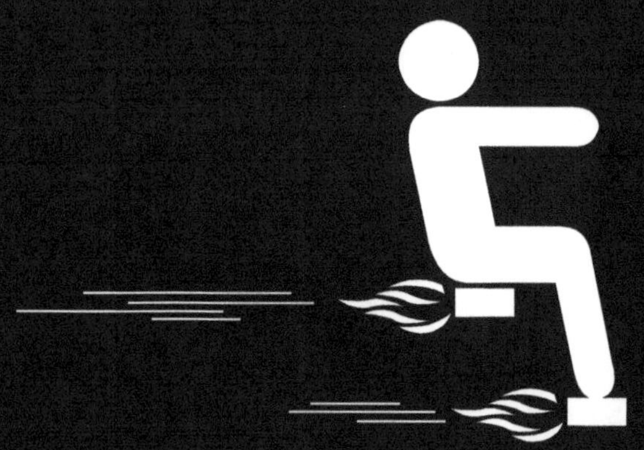

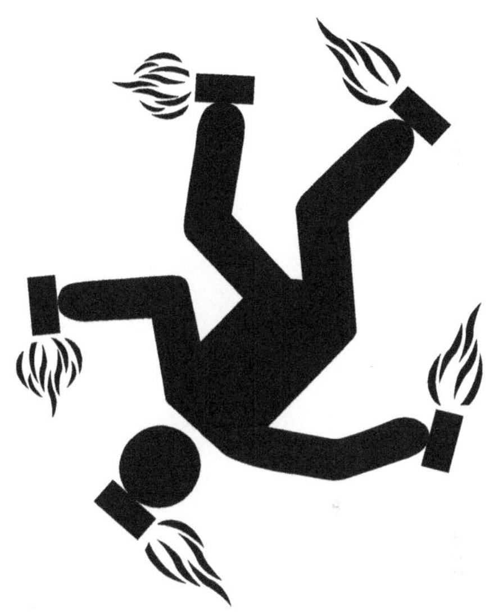

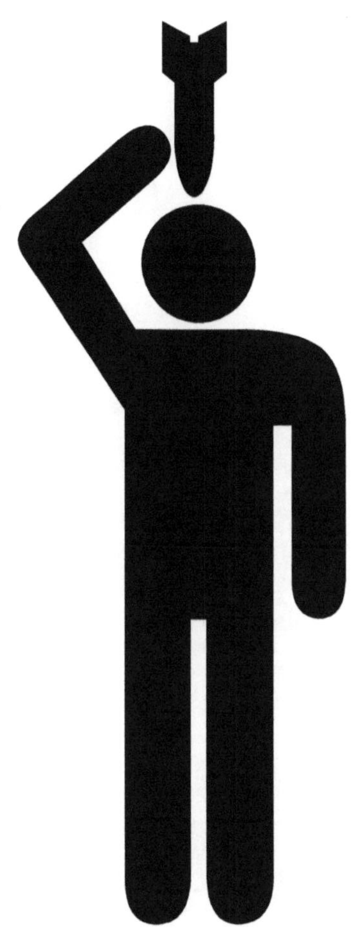

0001010101010101010100101011110101000101
11010001011111010001010100100011101
0101110111000101010101110100010111110
0111101010000101101110100001010001
01010100100111010001111011101000001
0111010001011110100000010101010100
1101000010100010101111010001011111110
0111101010000101110111010000101000101
0101010010011101000111101110100000001
0111010001011110100000010101010100
00111101110000001101010111011000101
000000101010101010010101111010100001
01111010001011111101000101010010011
0101011101110001010101011101000101111
0101111010100001011101110100001010000
00010101001001110100011110111010000000
0101110100010111101000000101010101010
0111010000101000101011110100010111111
0101111010100001011101110100001010000
0001010100100111010001111011101000000
0101110100010111101000000101010101010
100010100100010111010101000101000010
101000101011110100010111110100010100
00000011010101110111000101010101110
01010100101011110101000010111011101000
01111110100000010101010101001010111
101000101011110100010111111010001010
10000001101010111011100010101010110
010101001010111000010000010111000101
00001000010101010001001110100101000001
00101010010011101000111101110100000000
10111010001011110100000010101010101010
111010000101000101011110100010111111
101111010100001011101110100000101000001
0010101001001110100011110111010000000
001010101011101000101111010000001010
001011101110100000101000101011110100
010100101011110101000010111011101000
1111100000101010010010011101000111101110111
0010101010111010001011110100000010101
00010111000101001000101110101010001001
1110100101000101011110100010111111101
0100011111011101000000011010101011101110

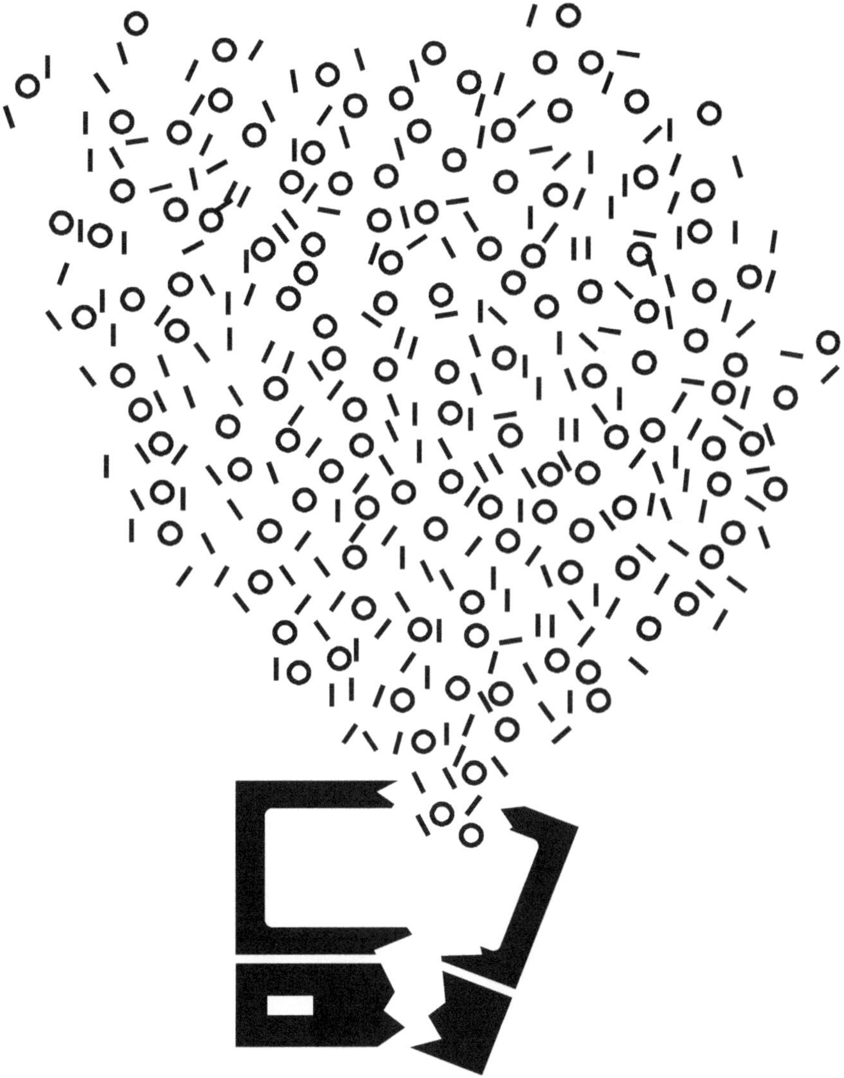

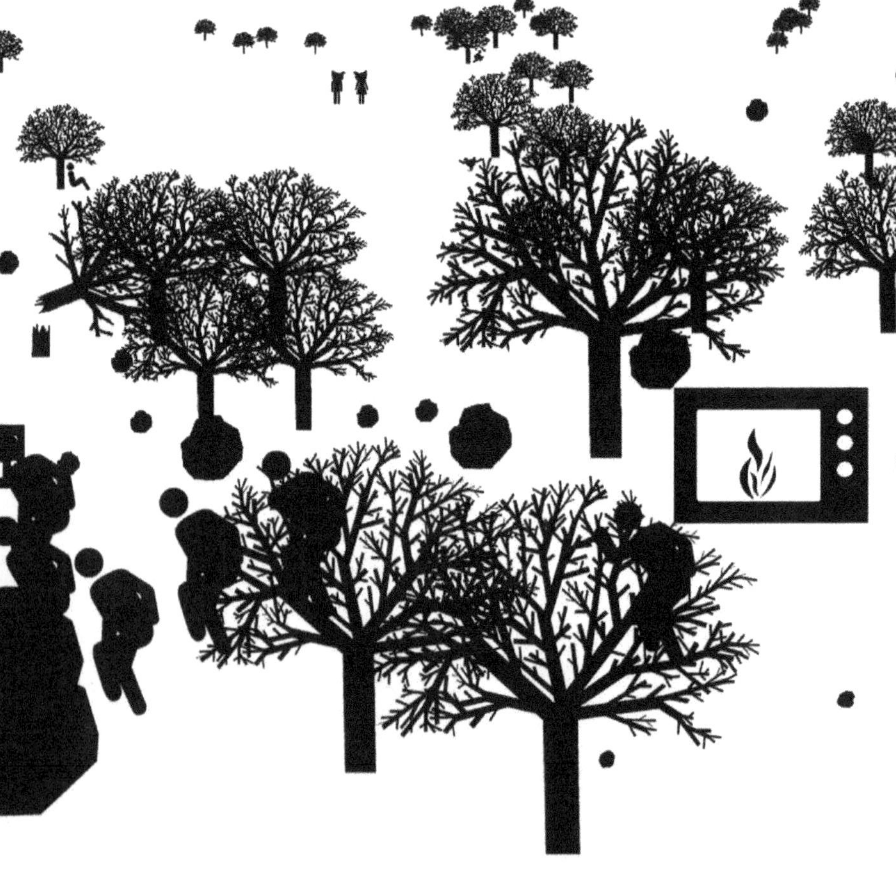

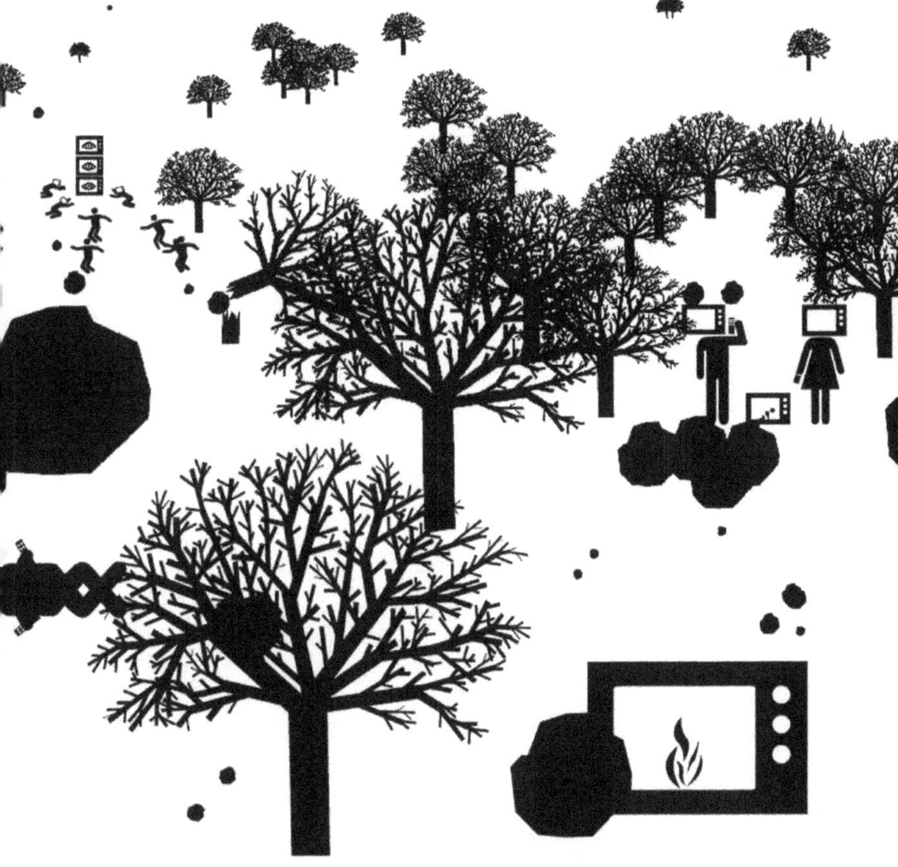

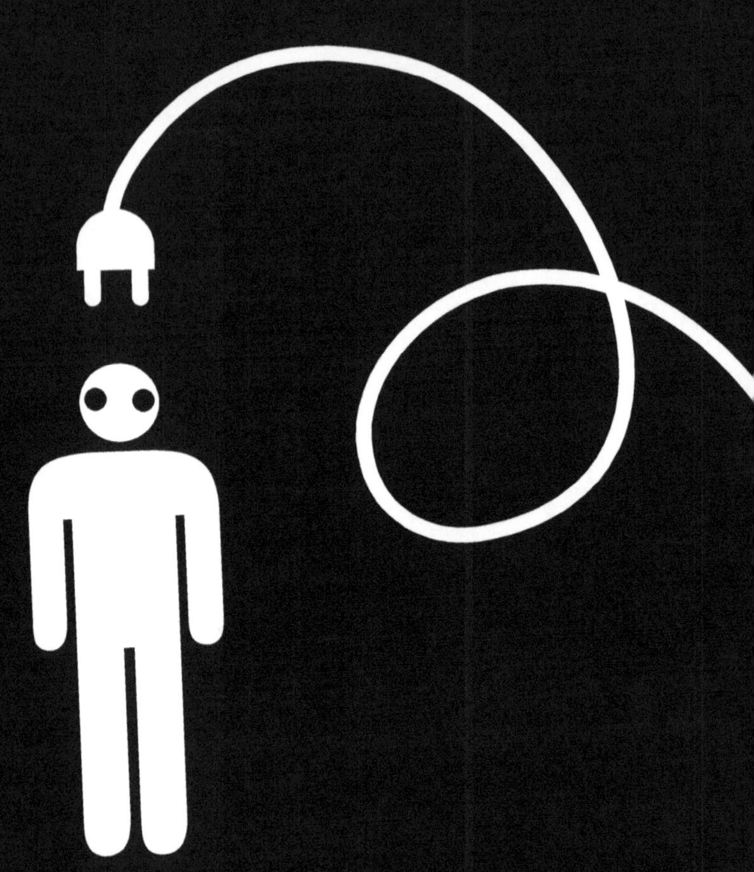

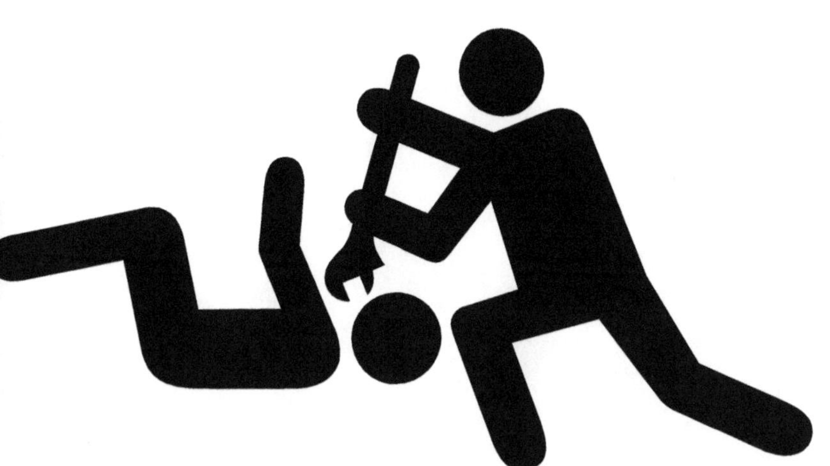

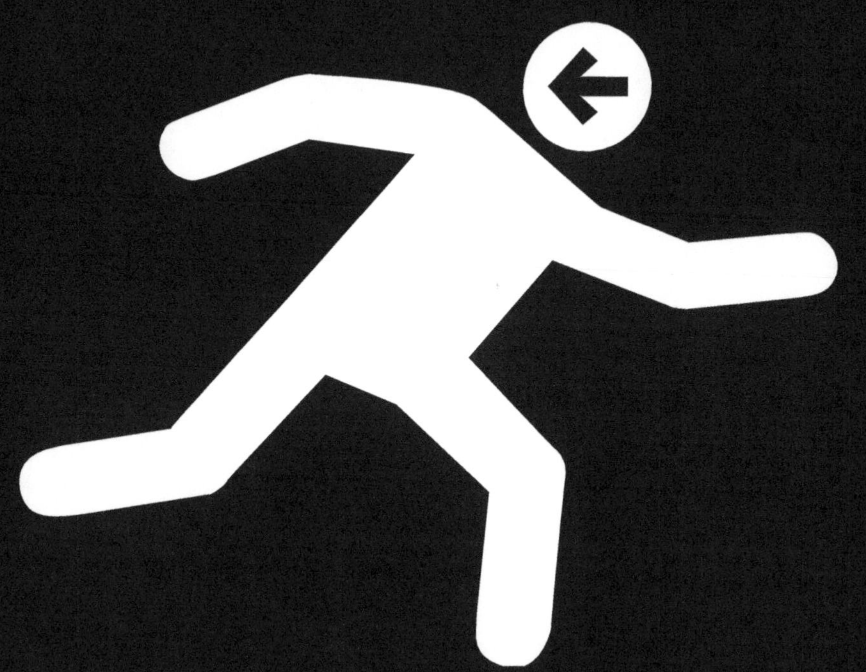

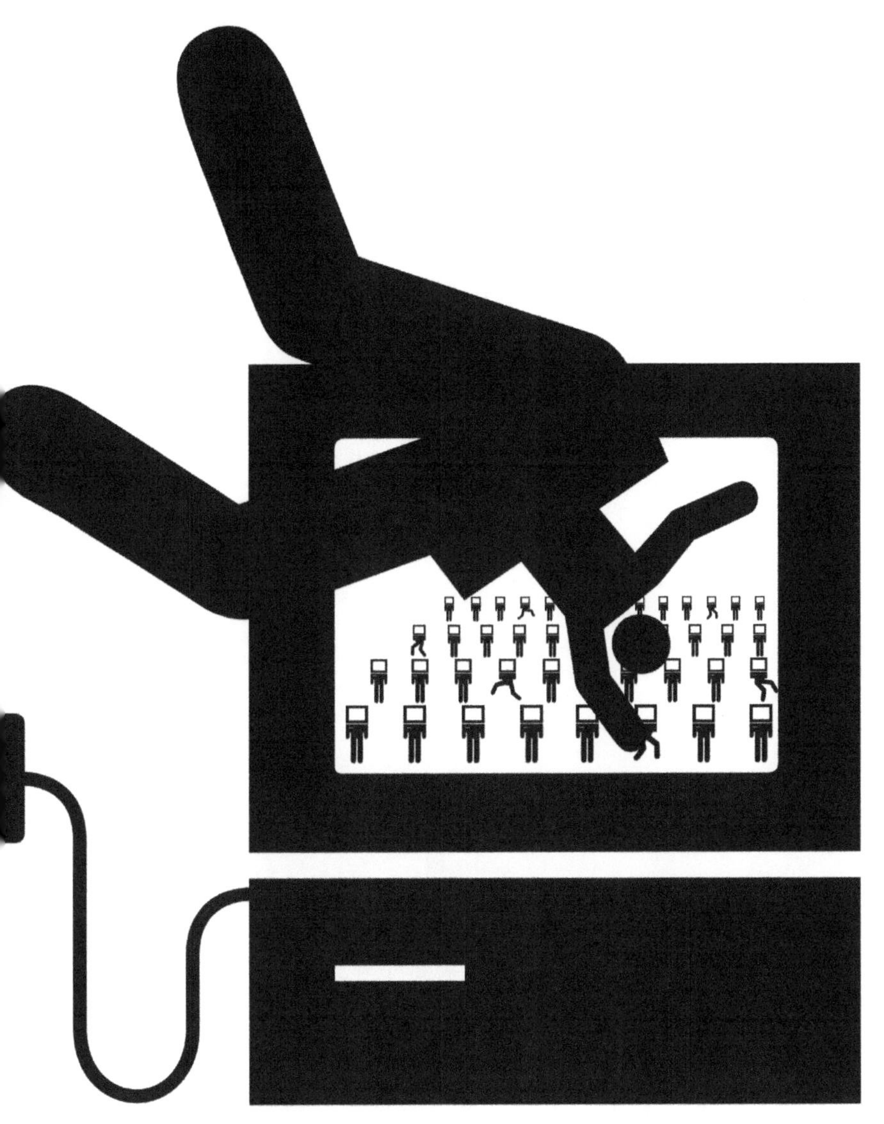

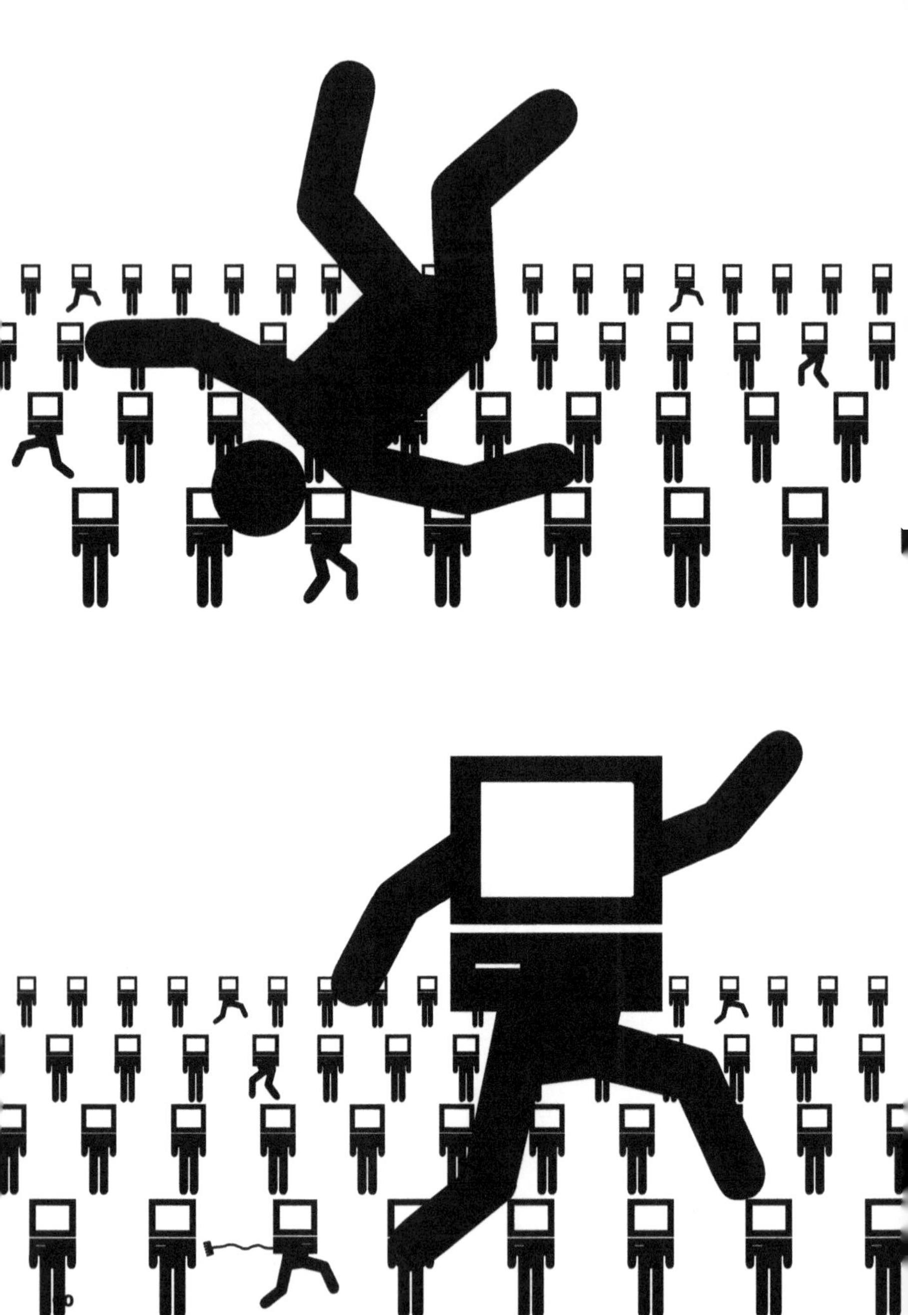

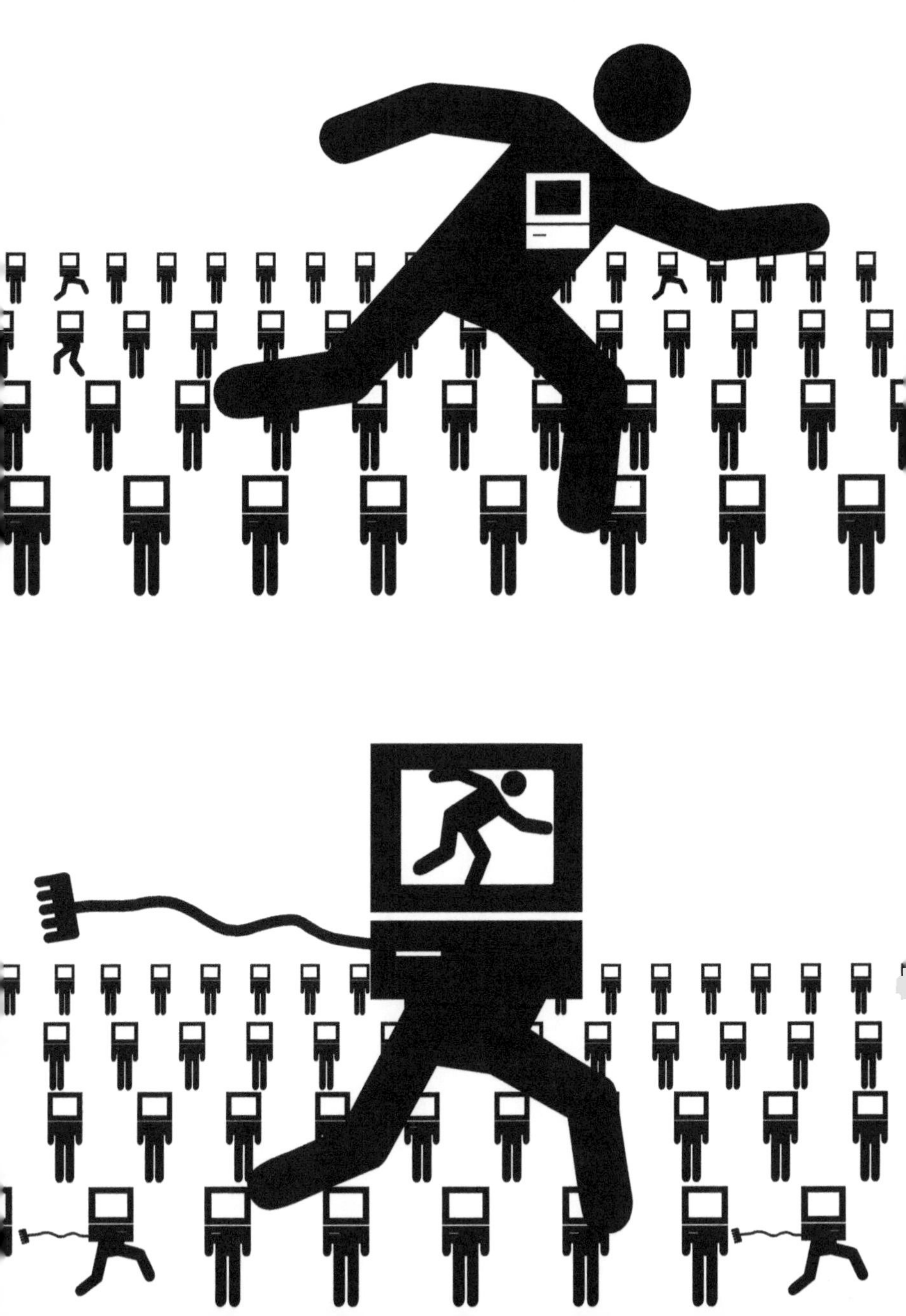

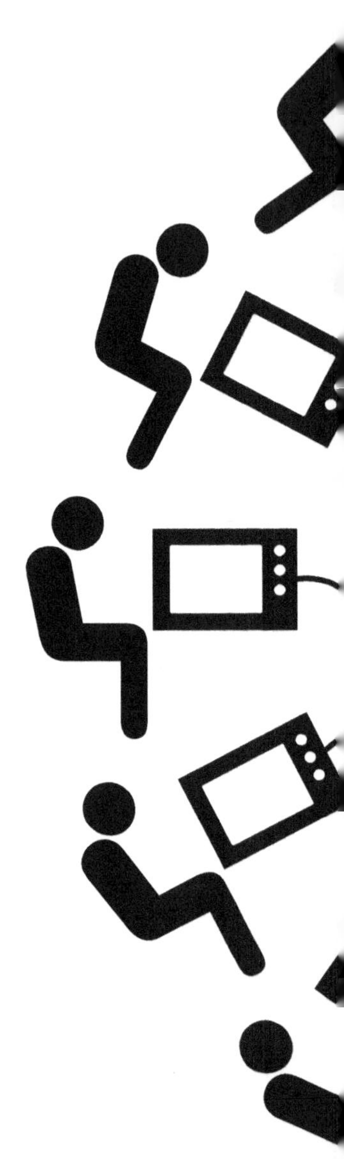

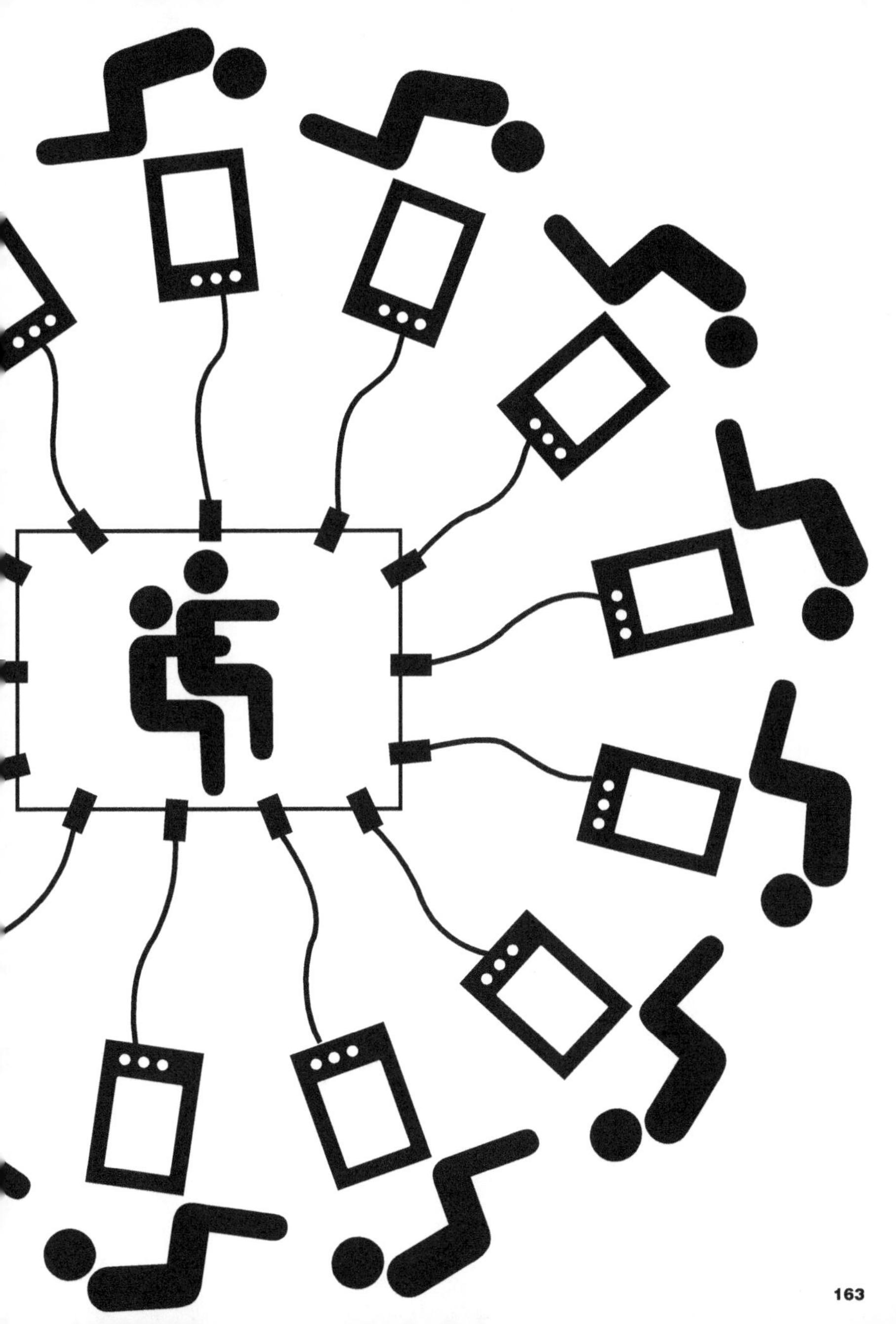

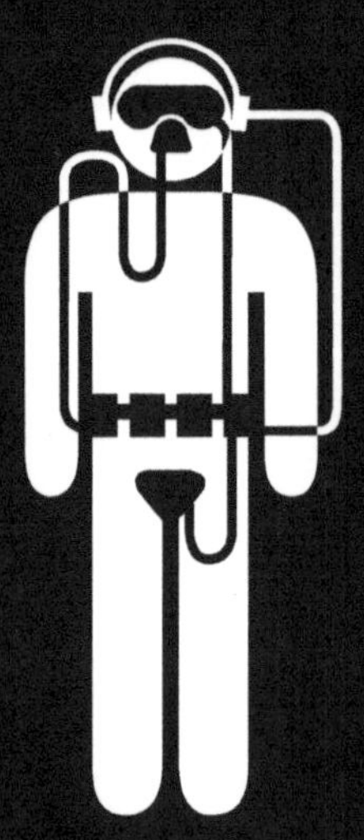

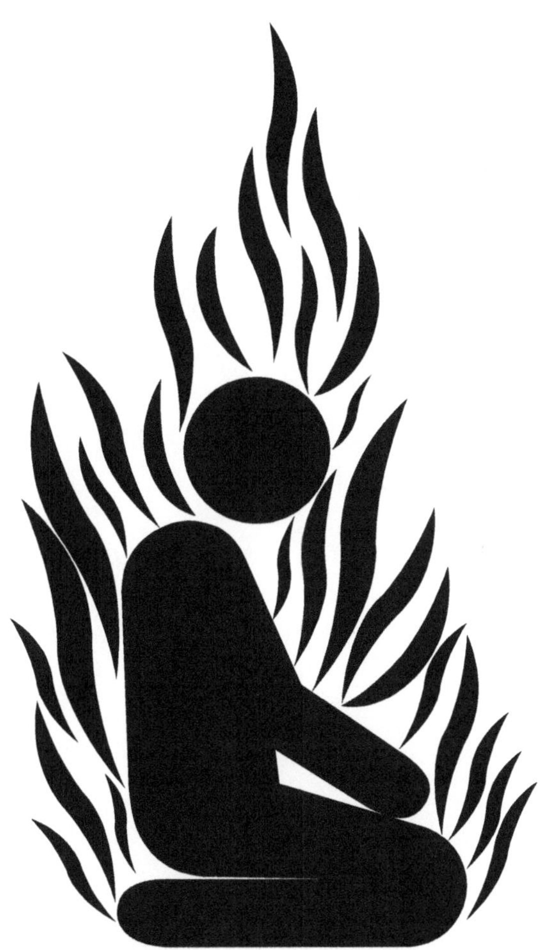

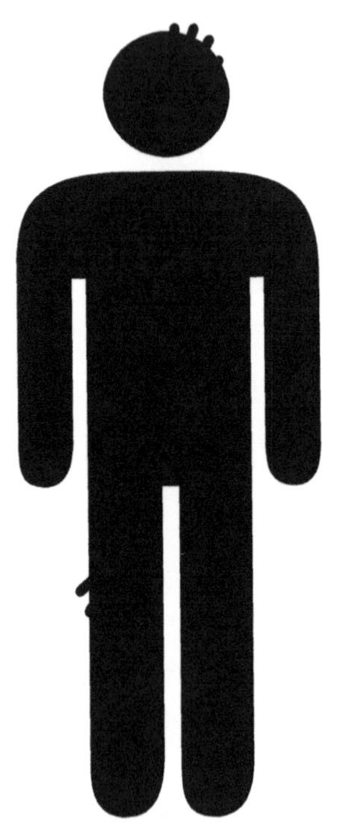 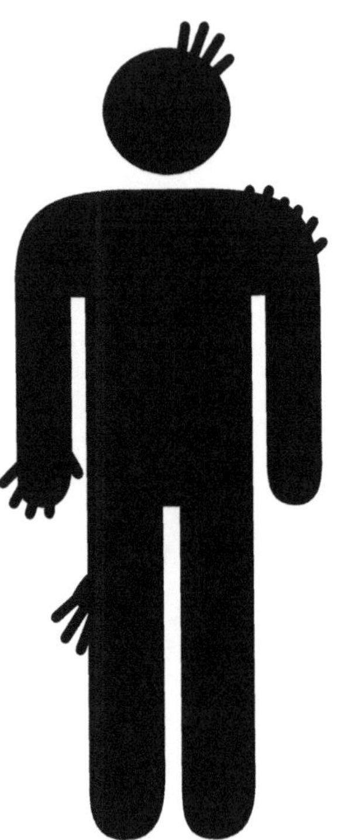

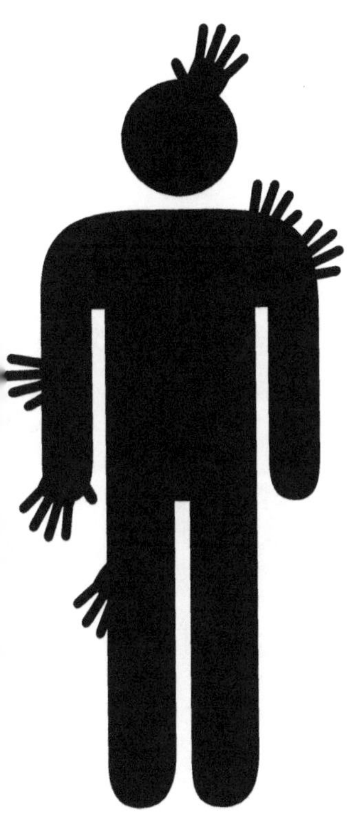
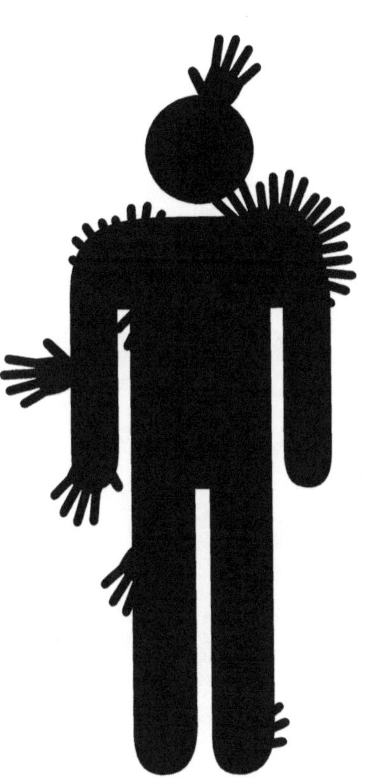

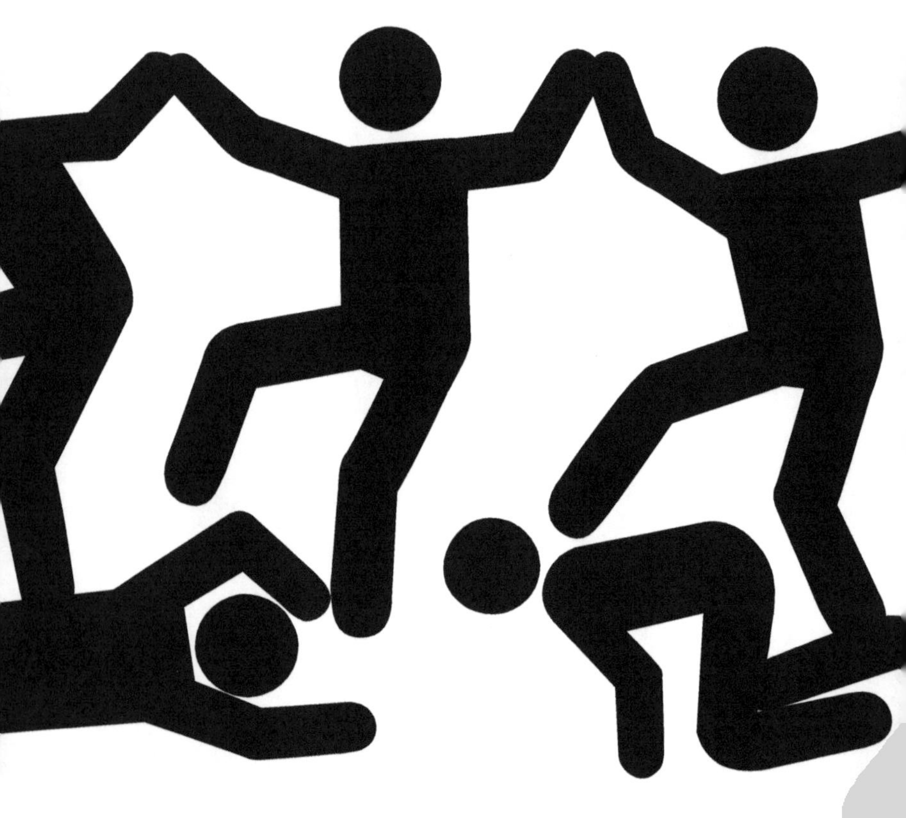

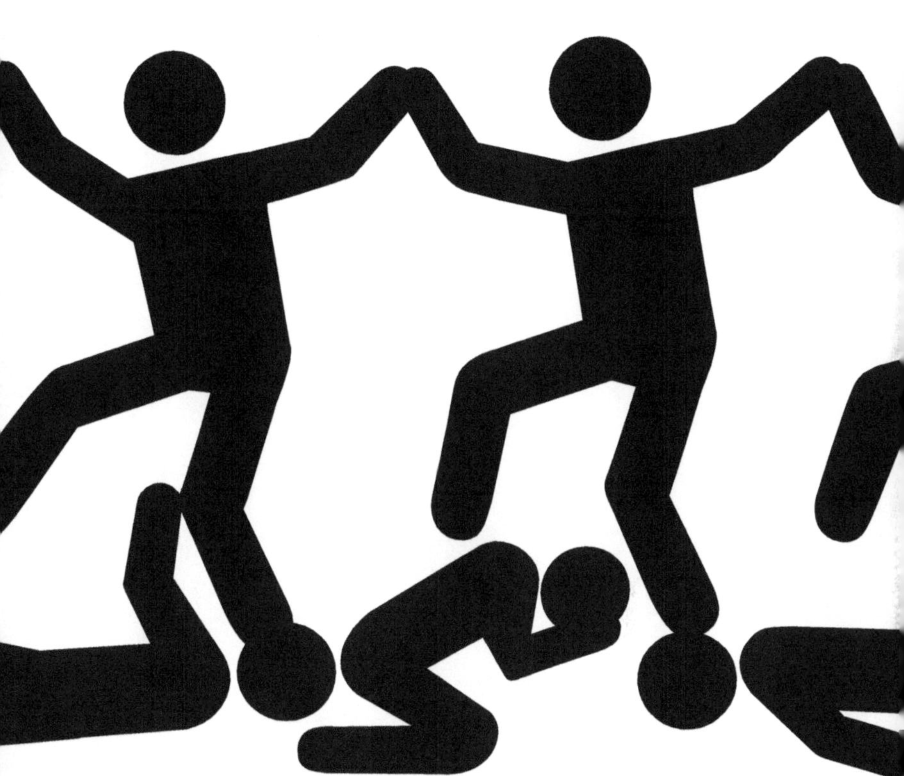

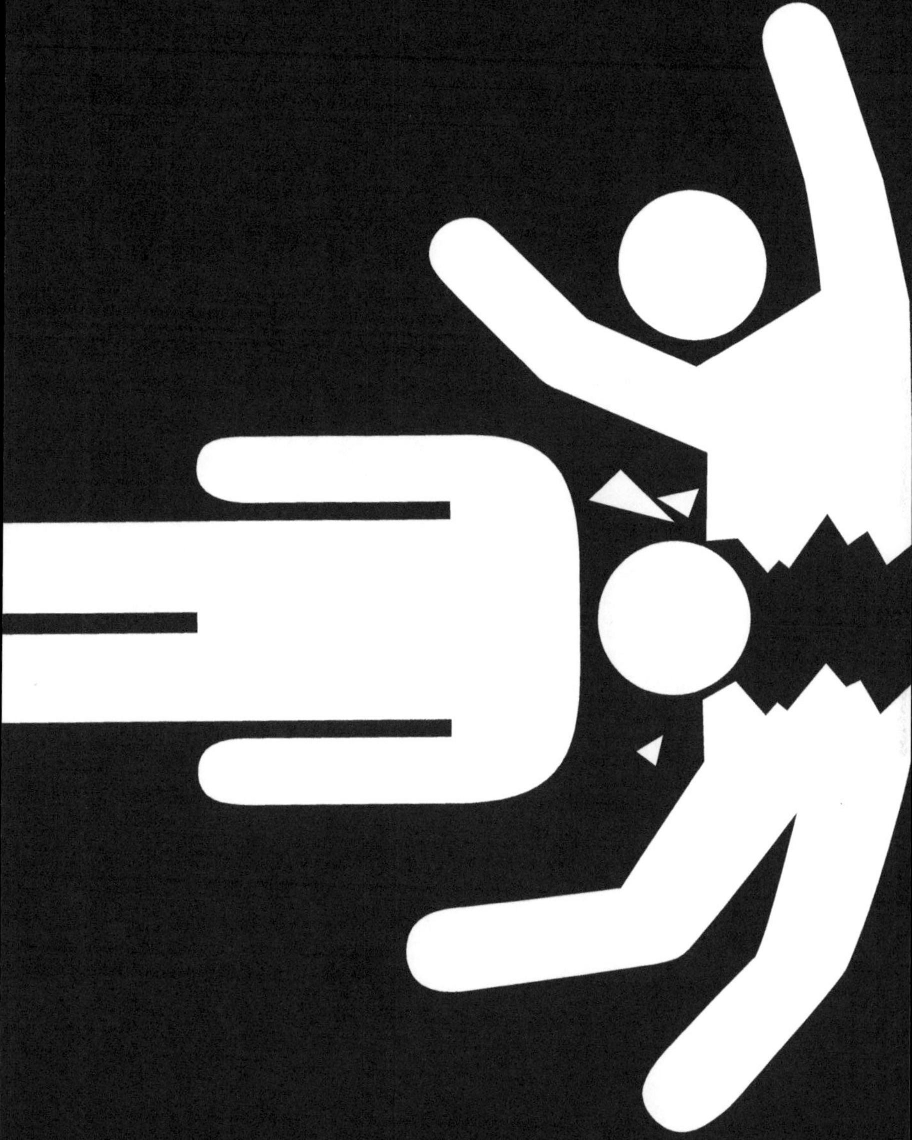

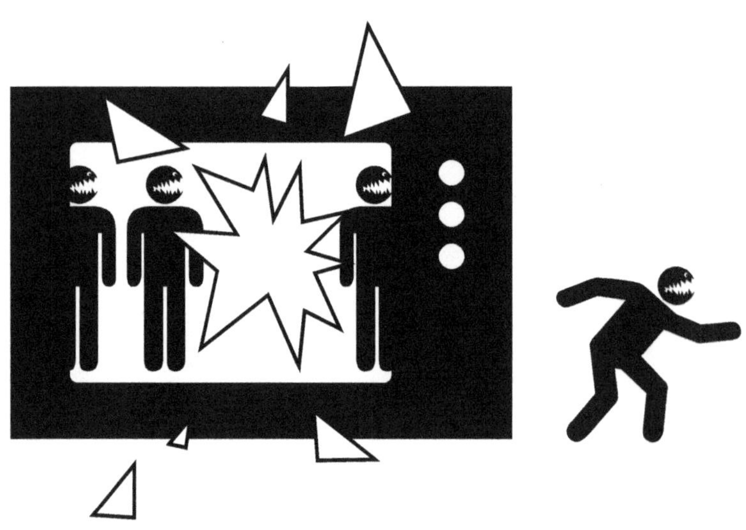

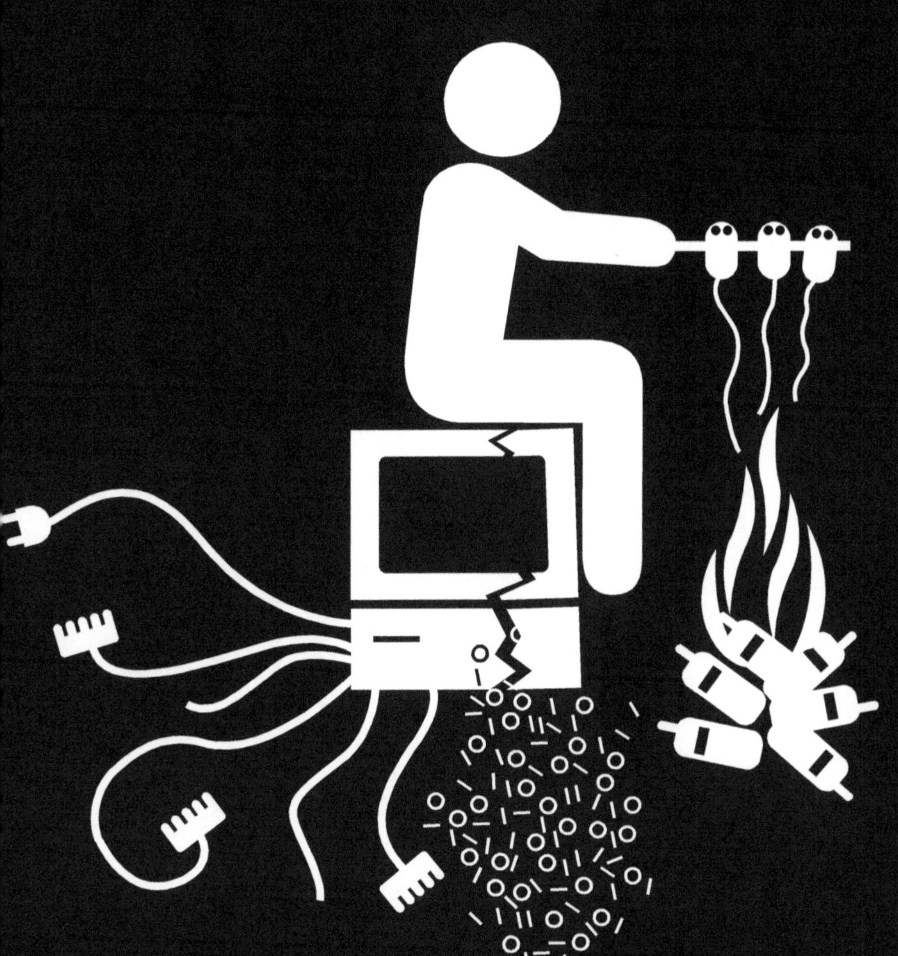

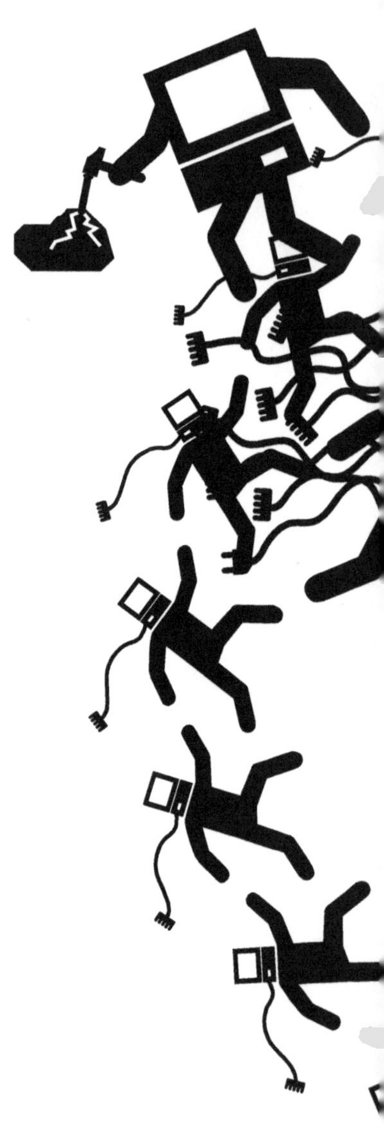

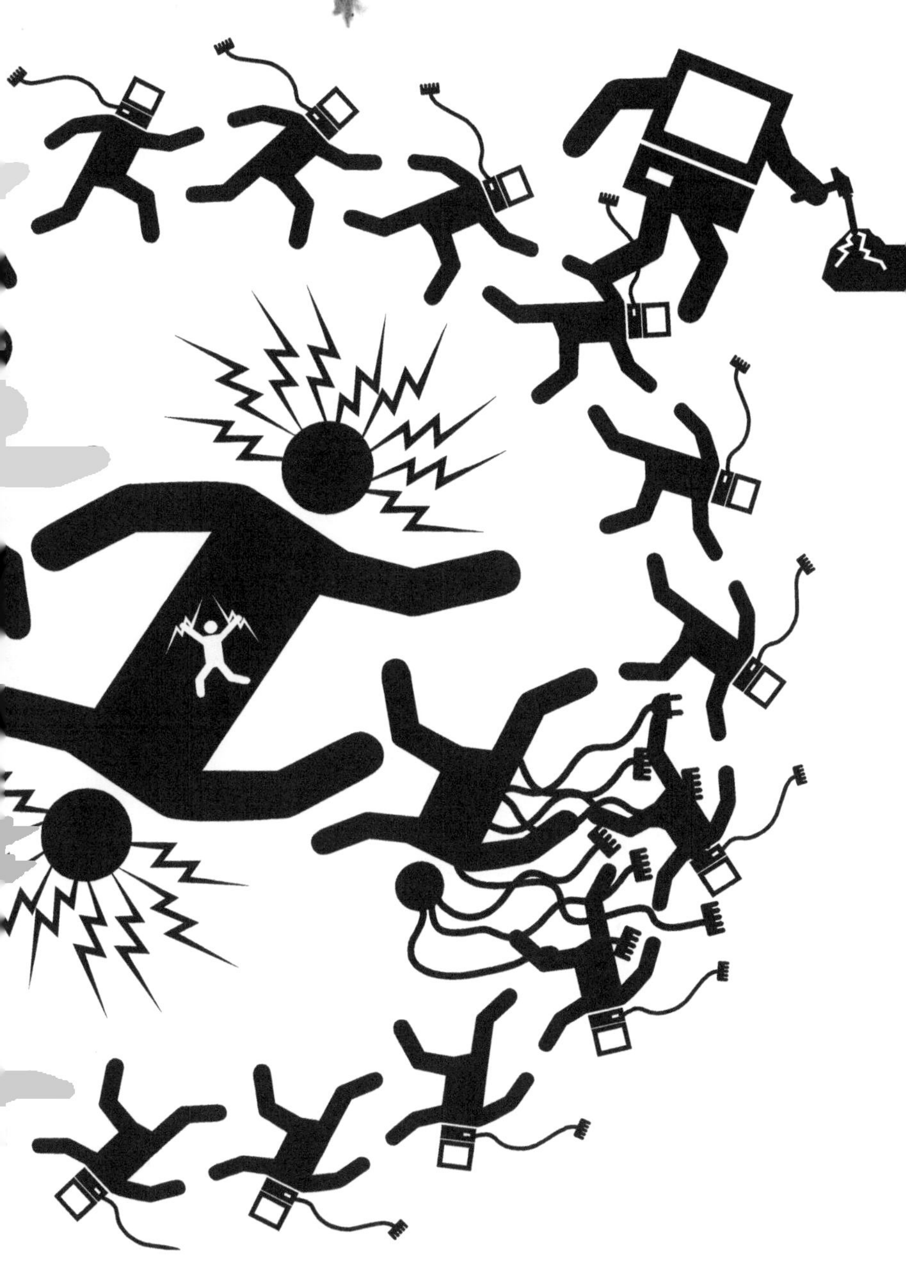

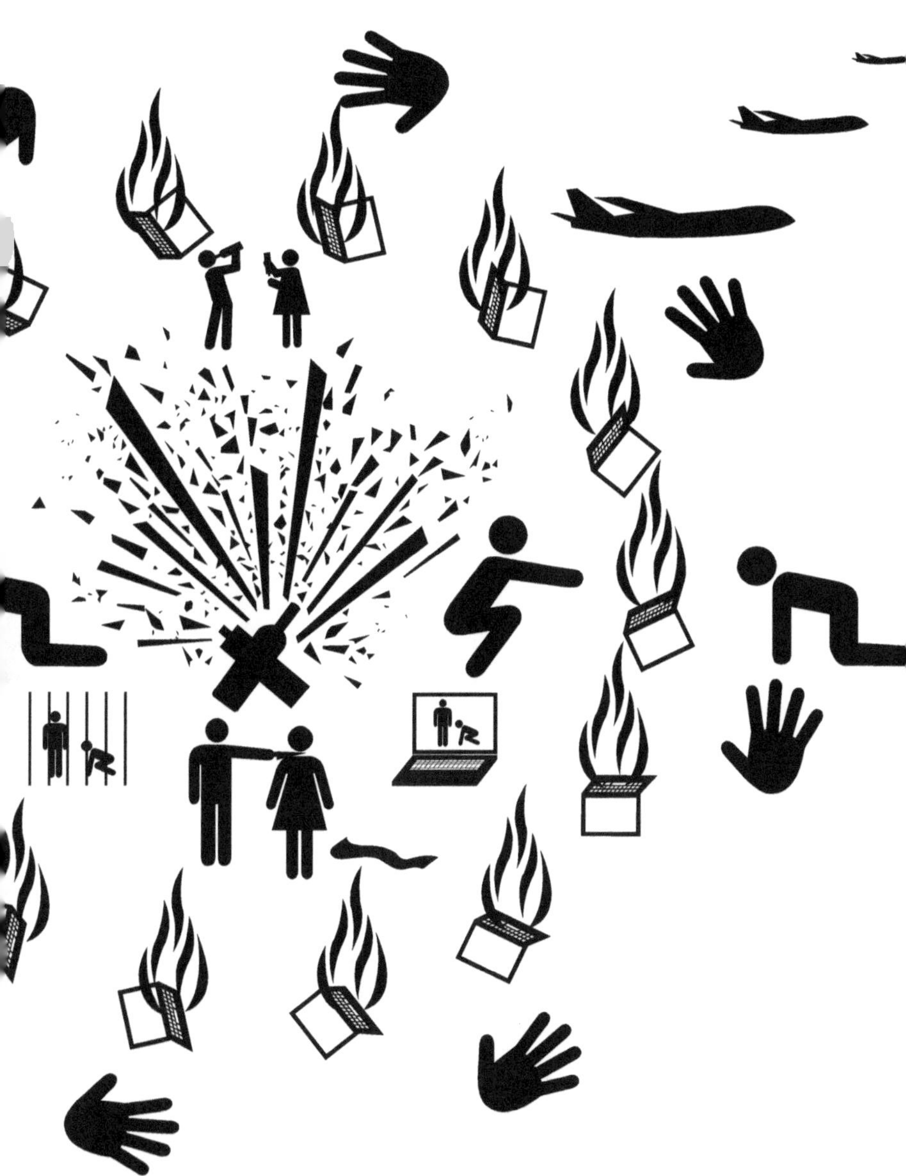

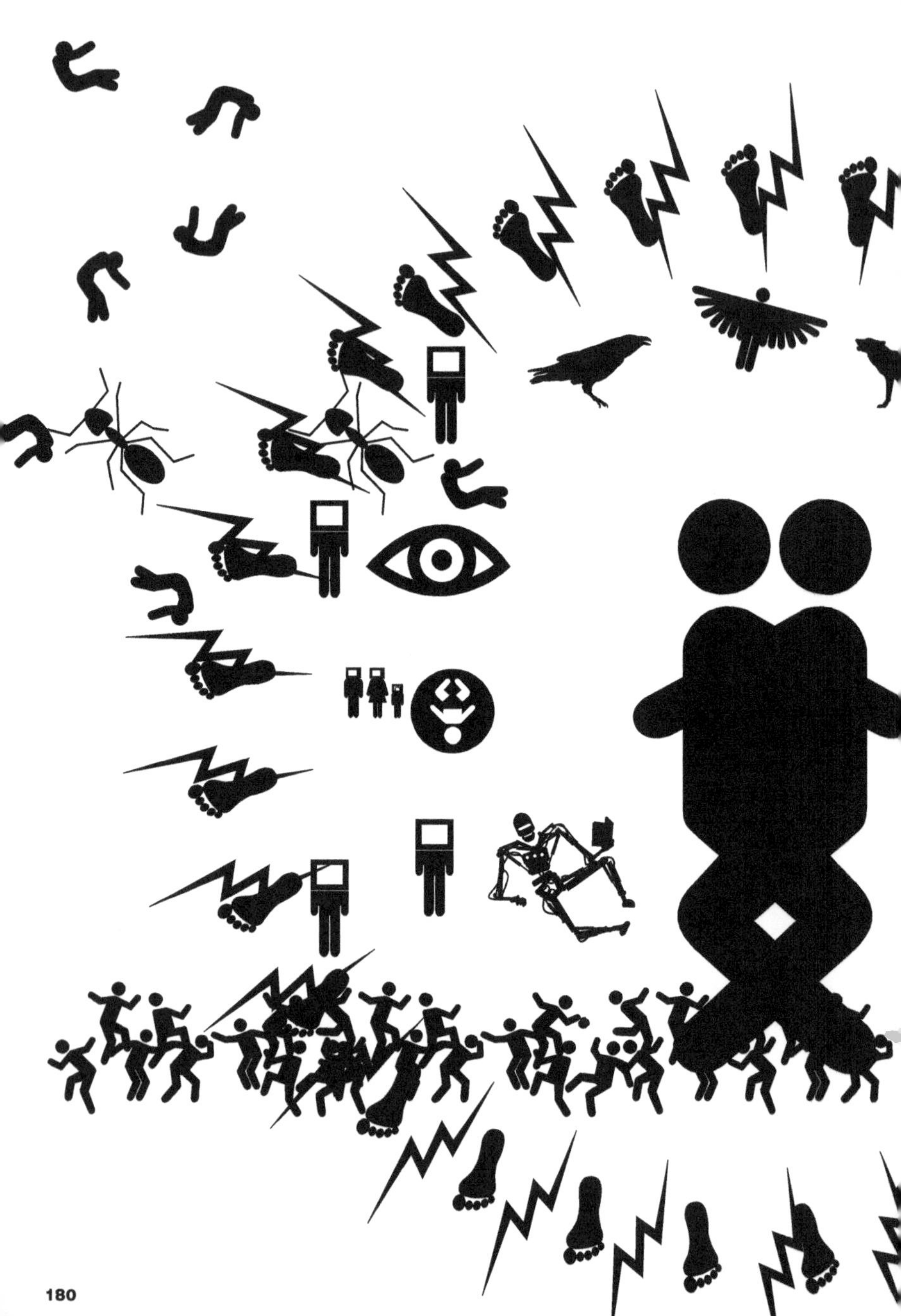

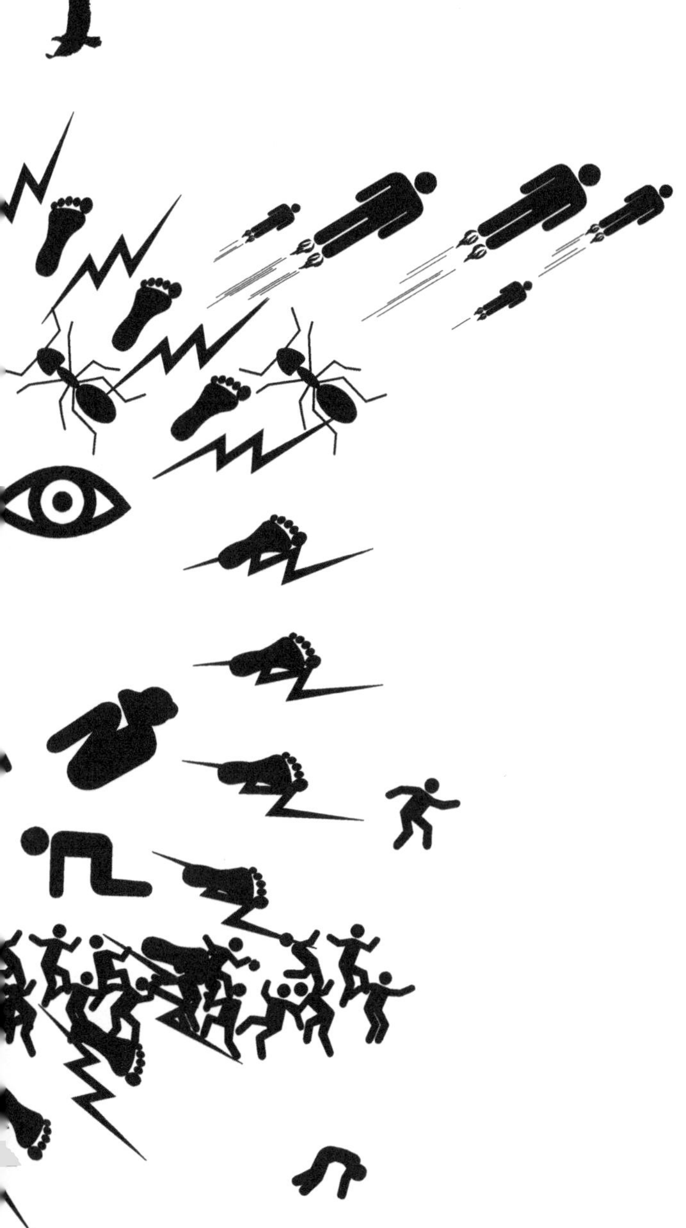

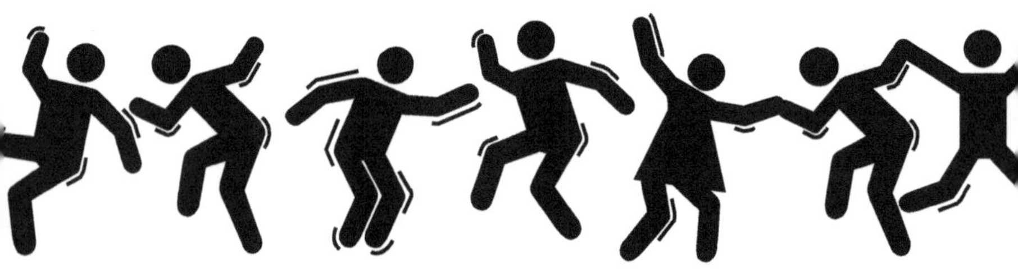

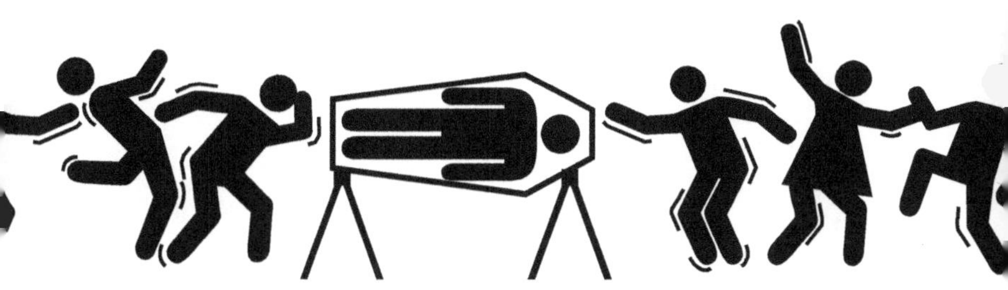

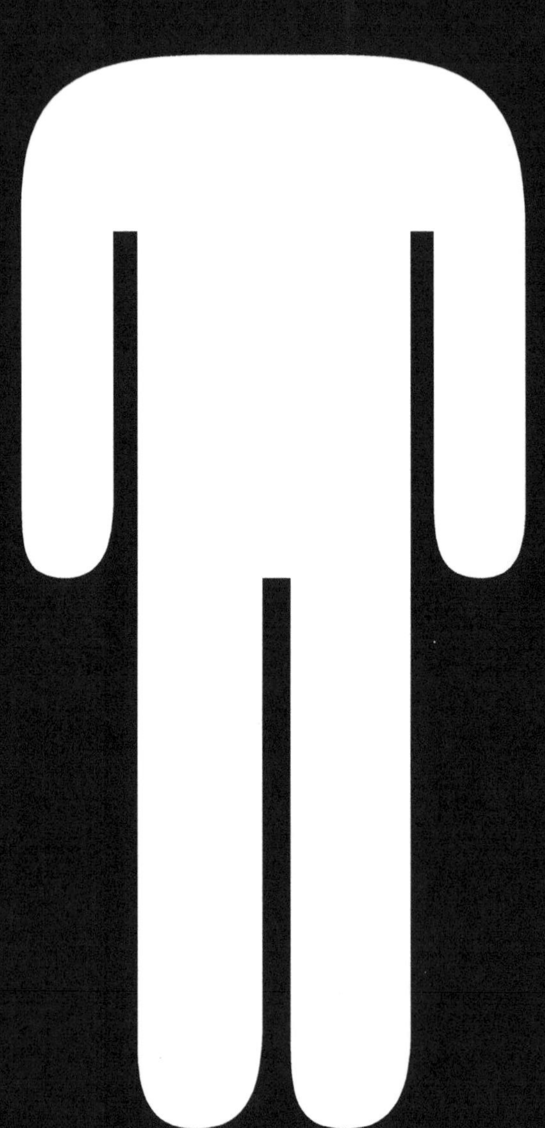

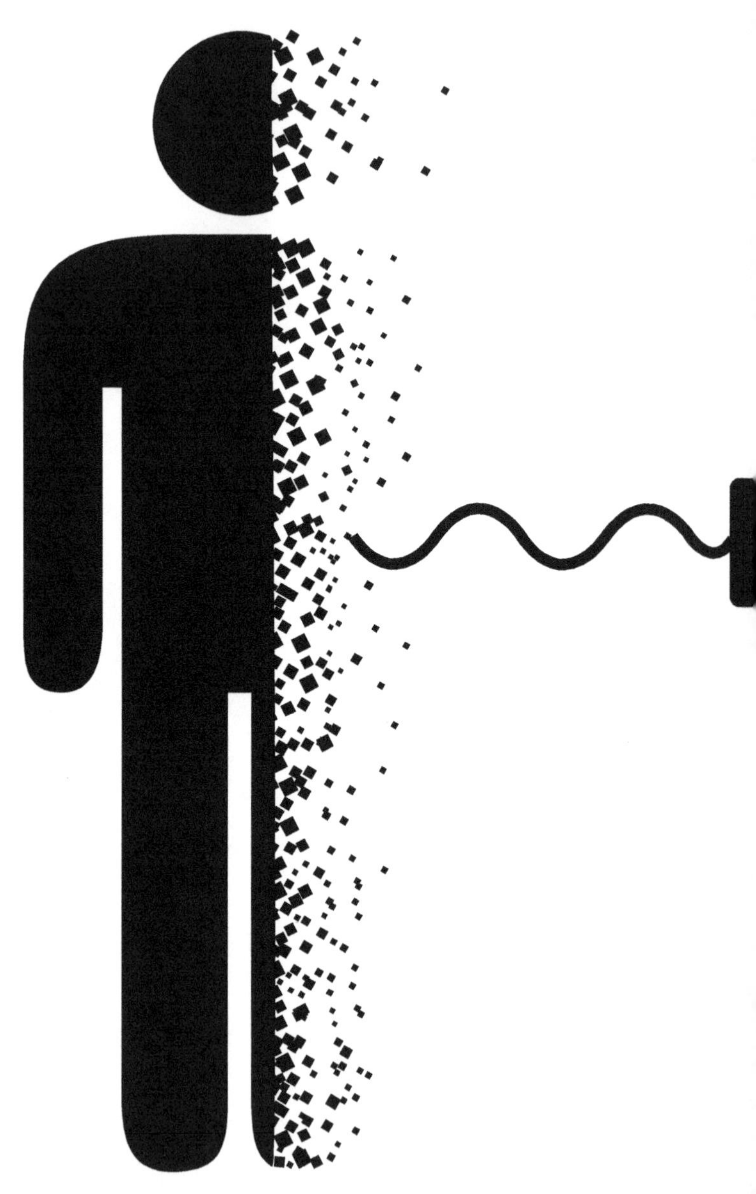

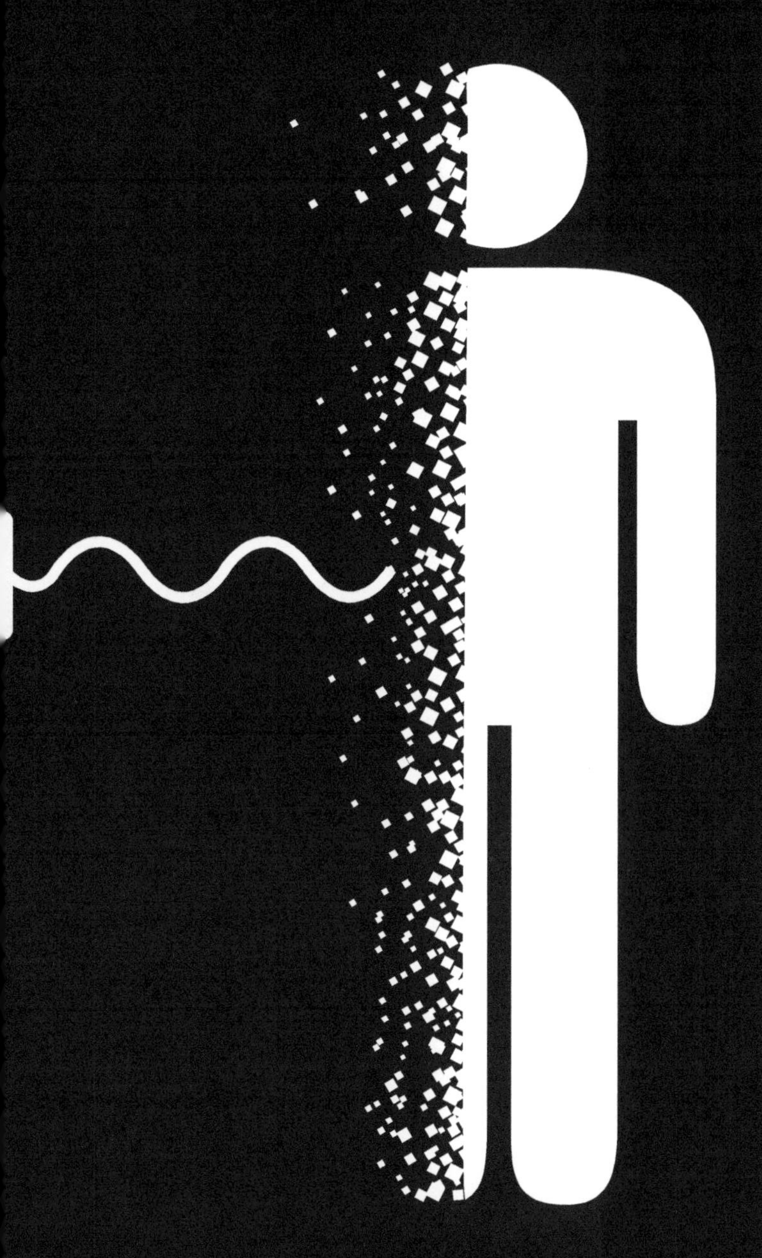

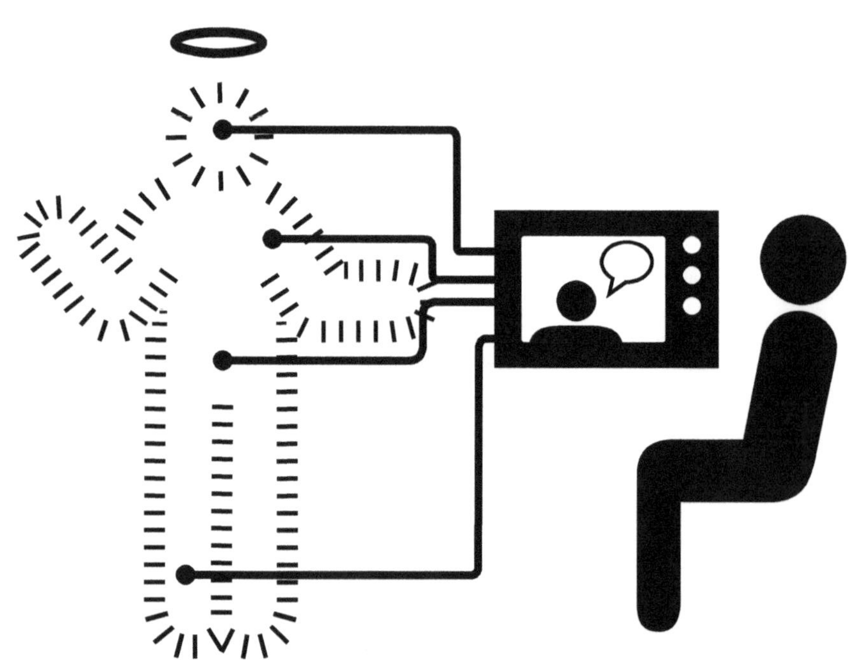

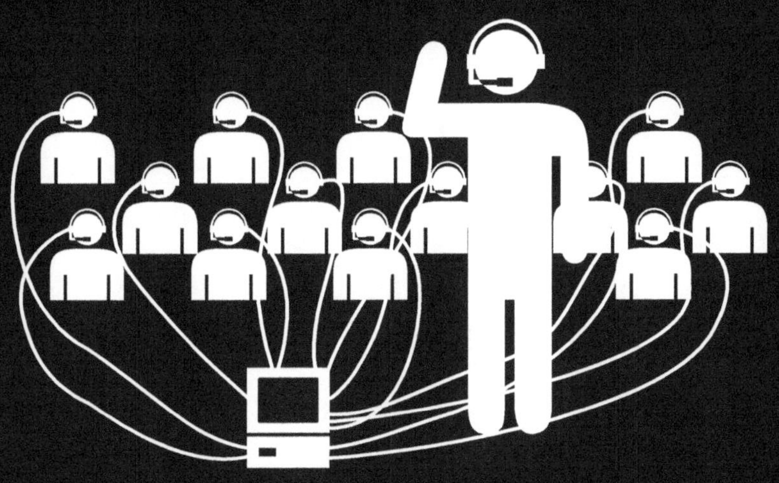

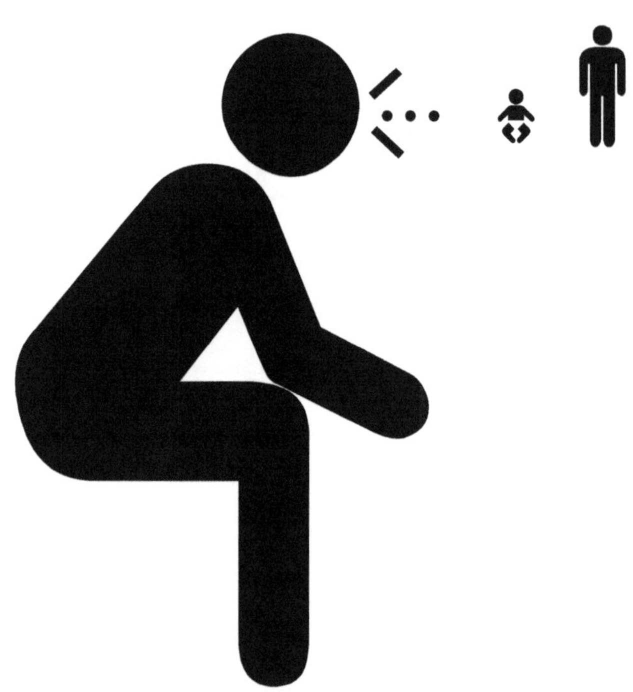

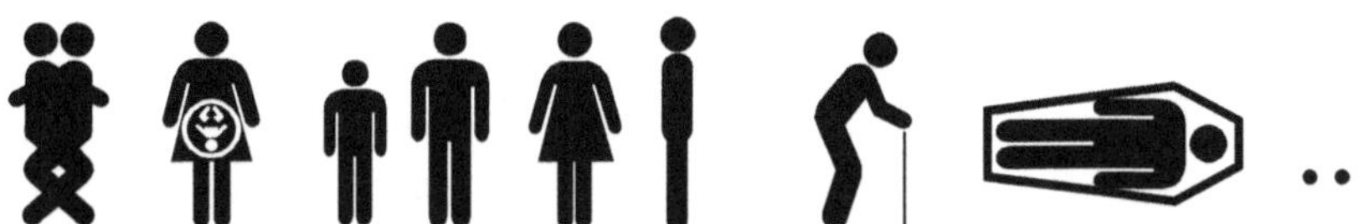

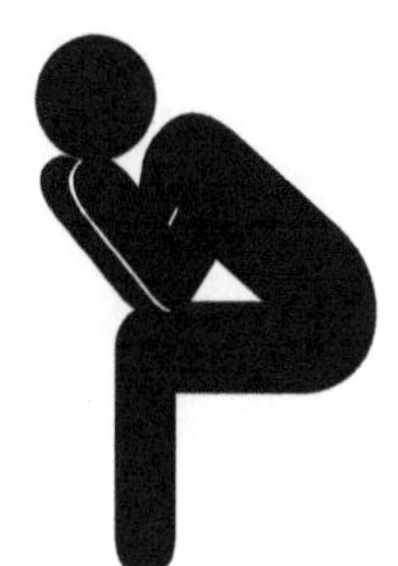

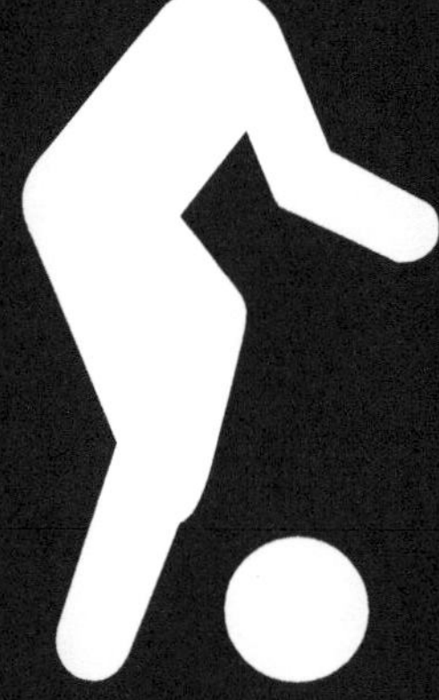

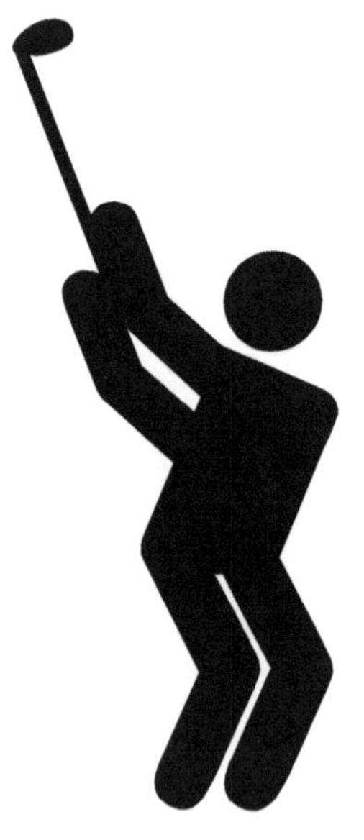

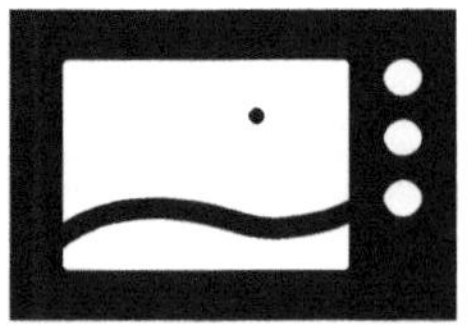

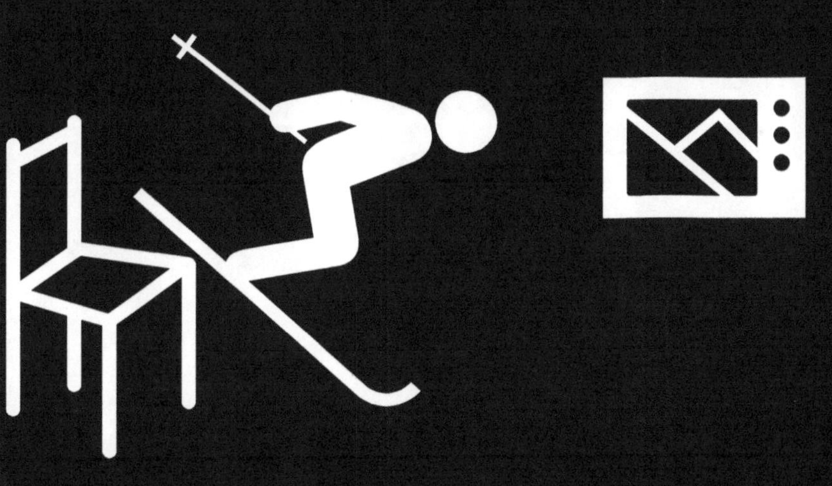

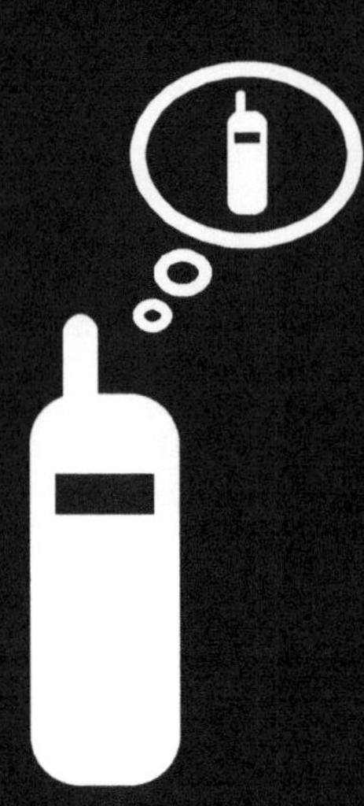
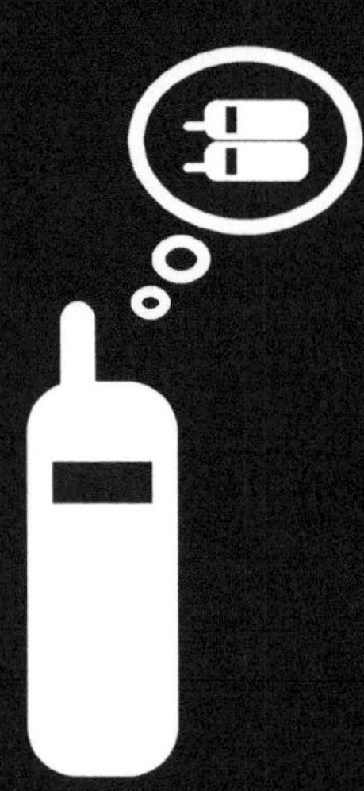

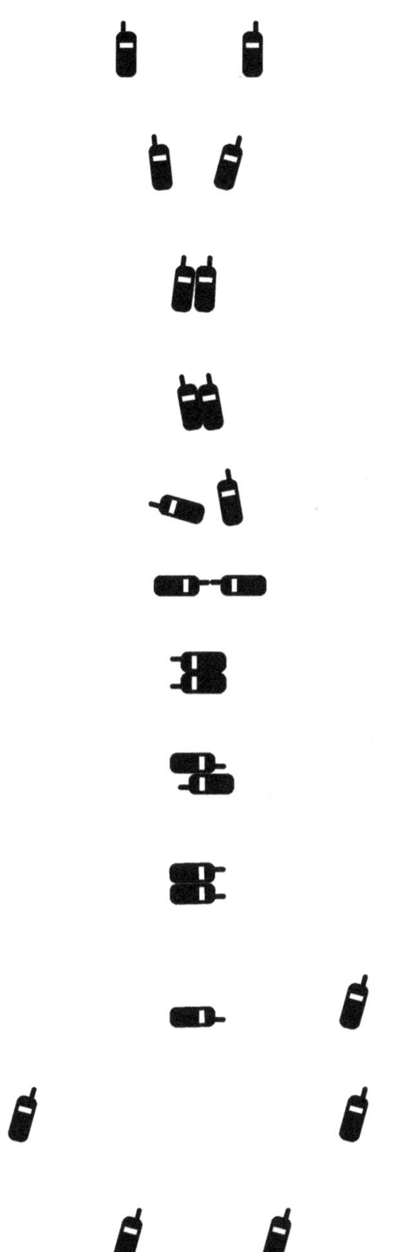

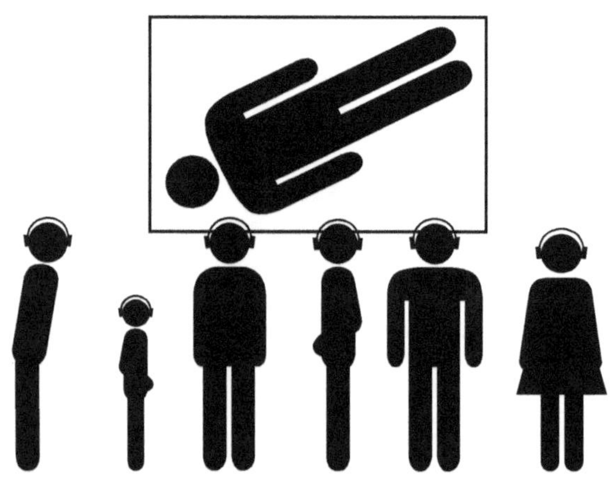

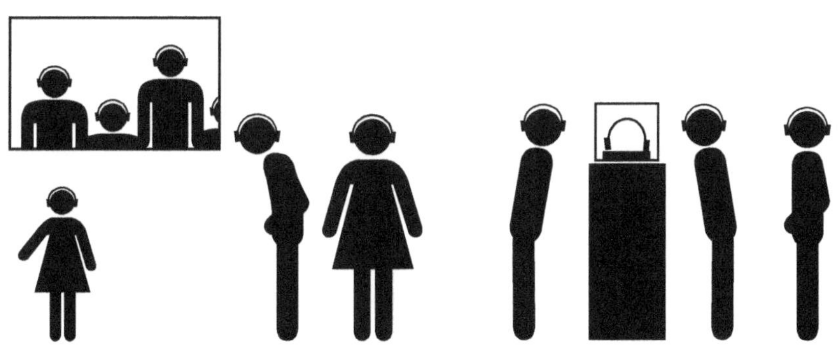

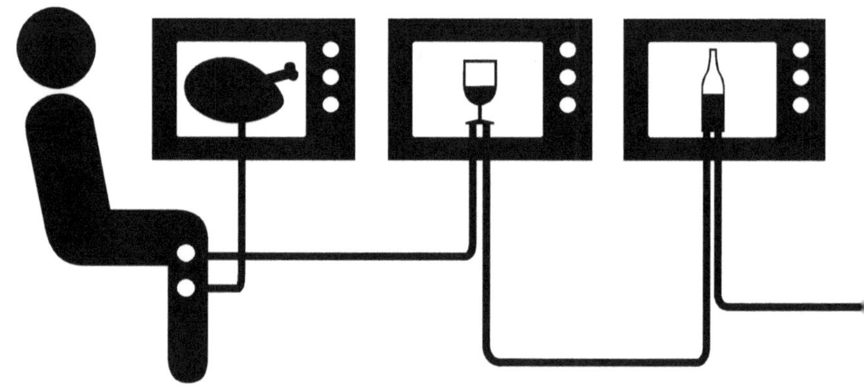

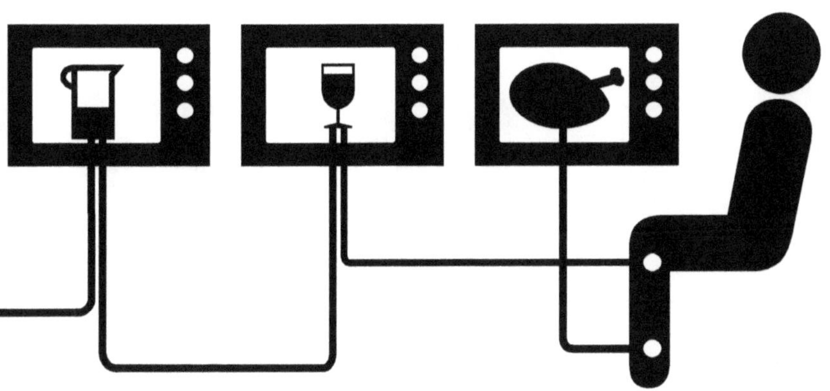

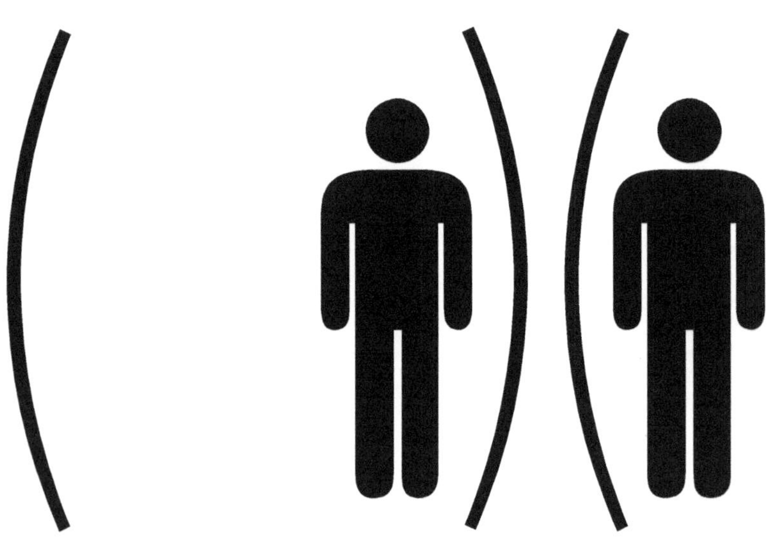

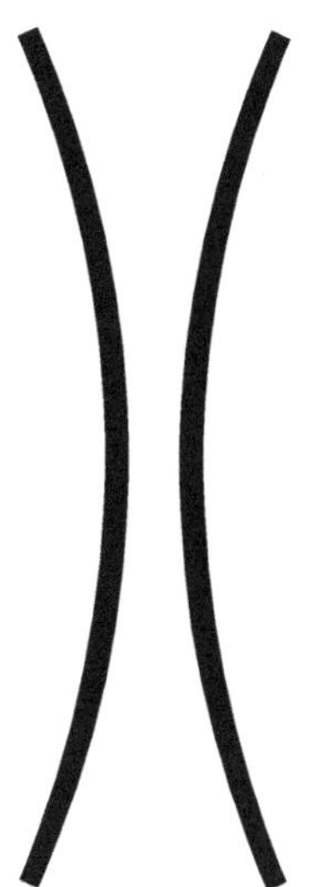

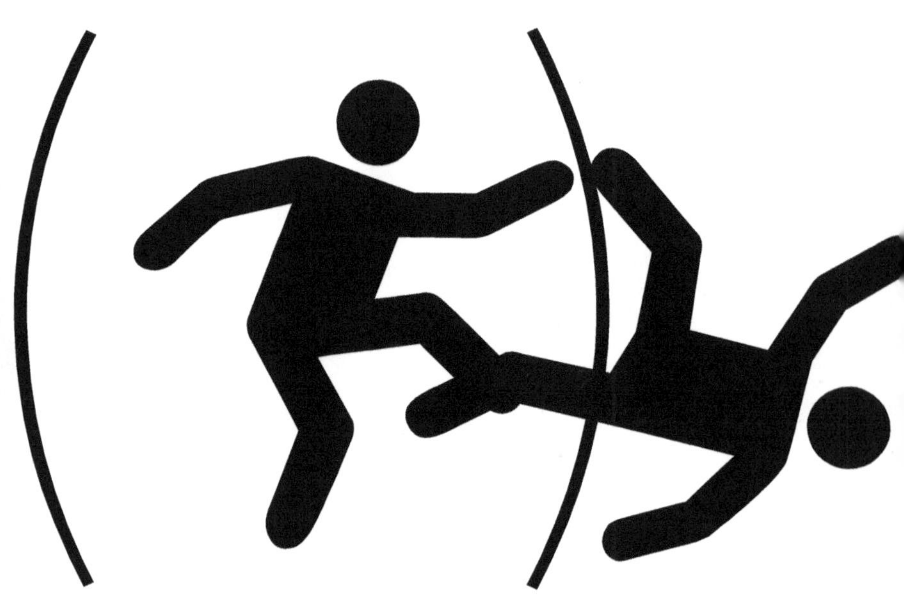

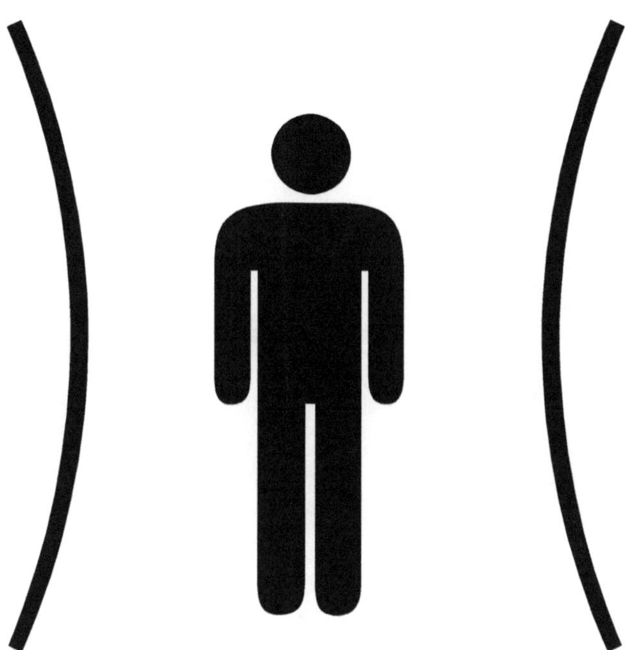

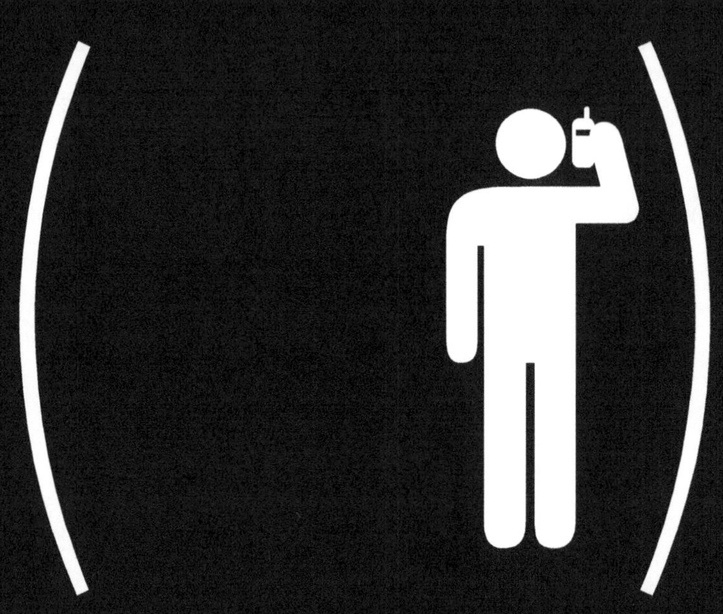

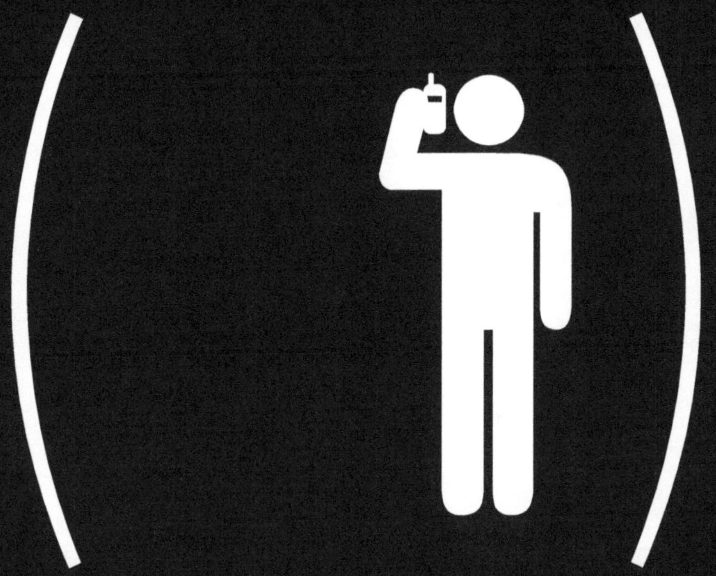

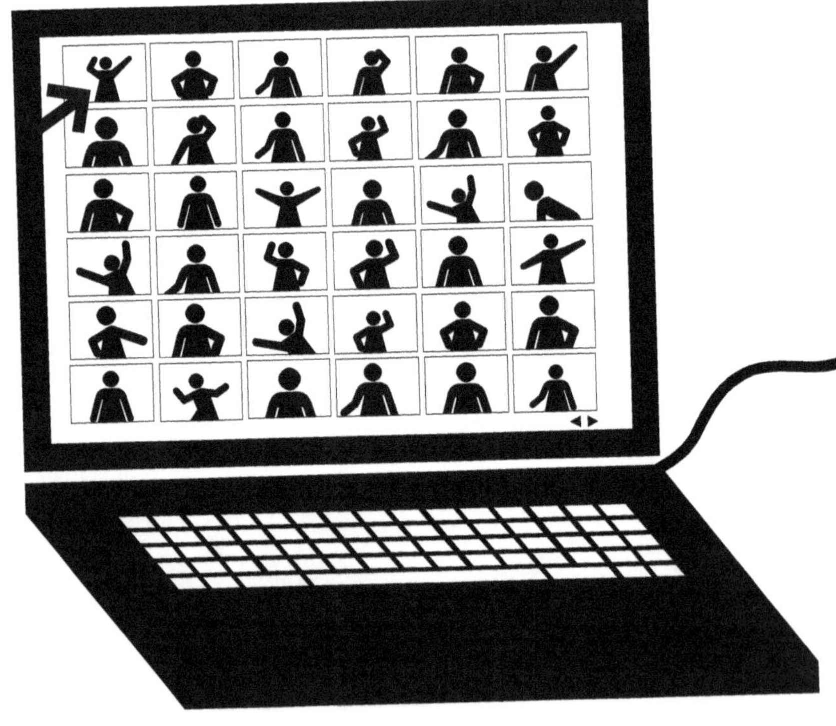

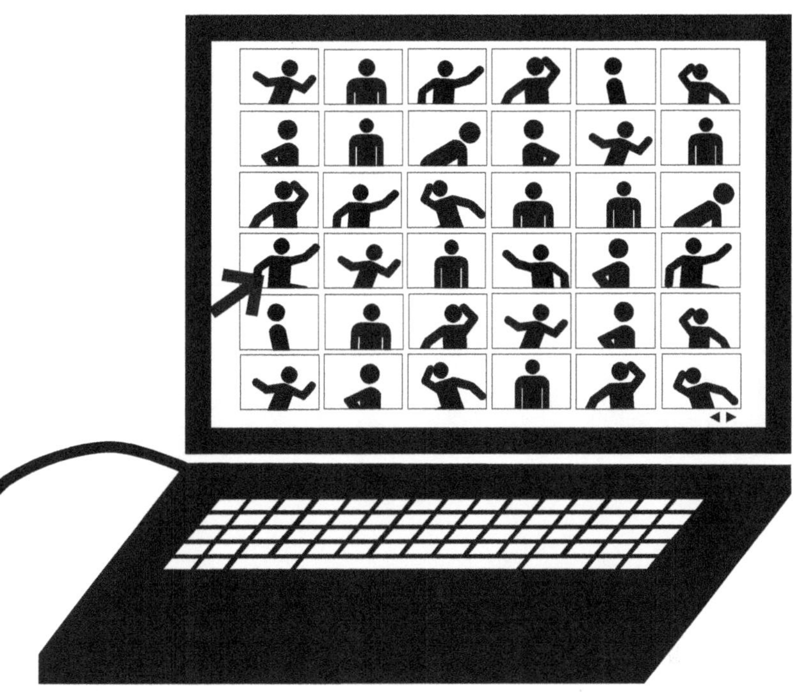

213

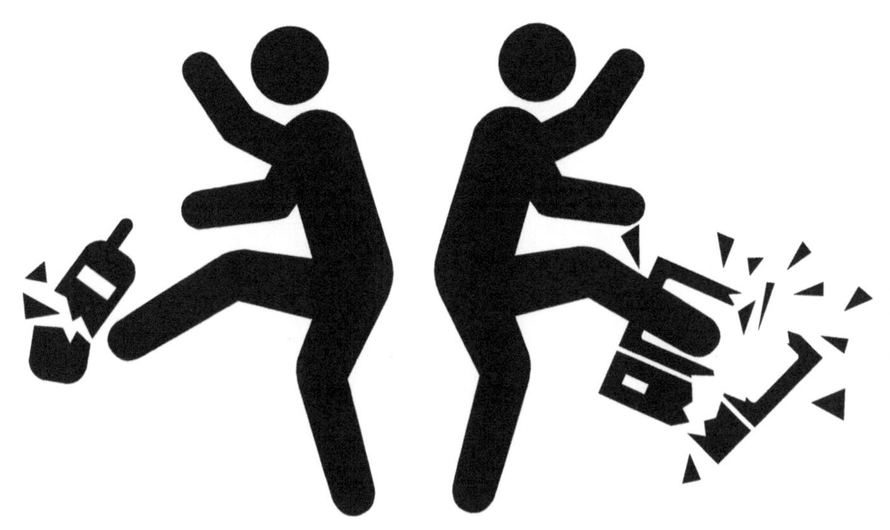

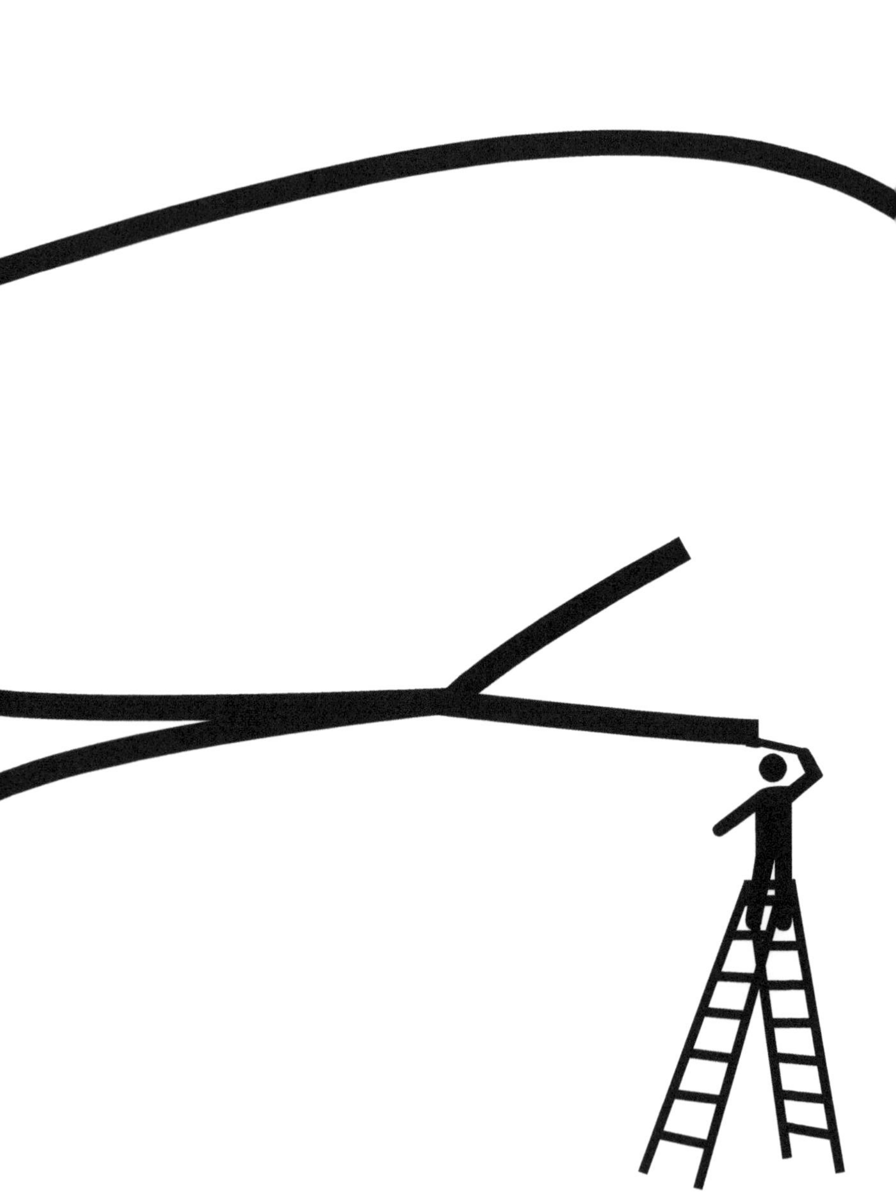

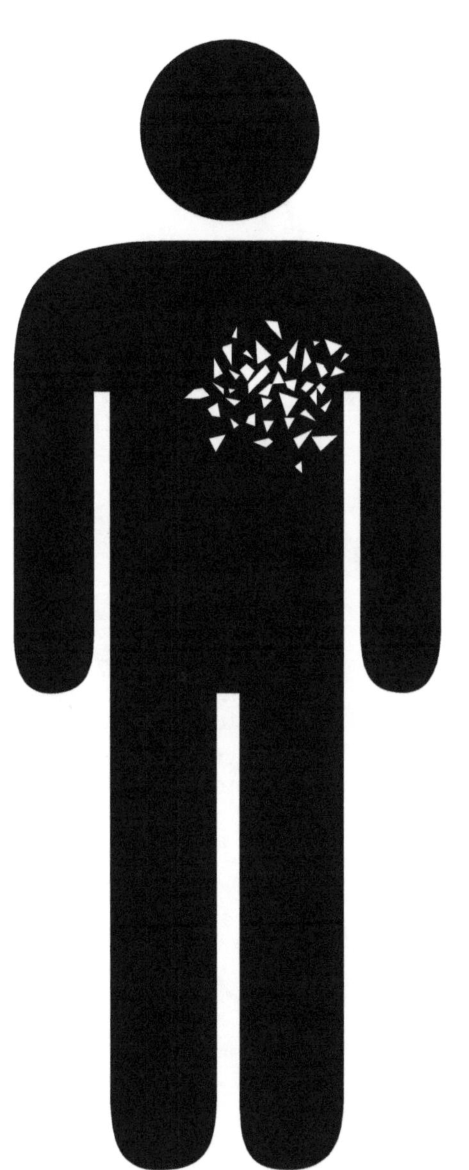

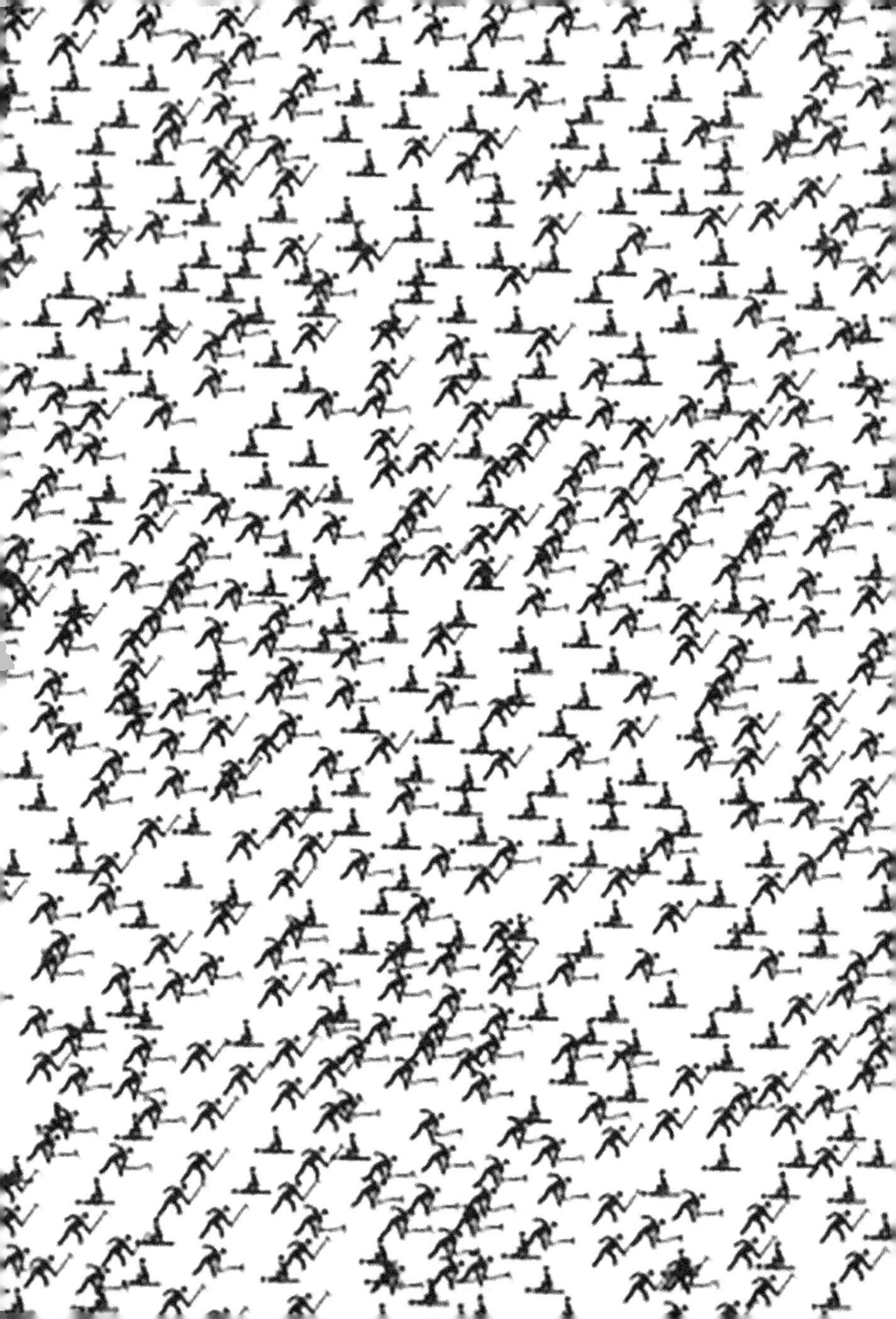

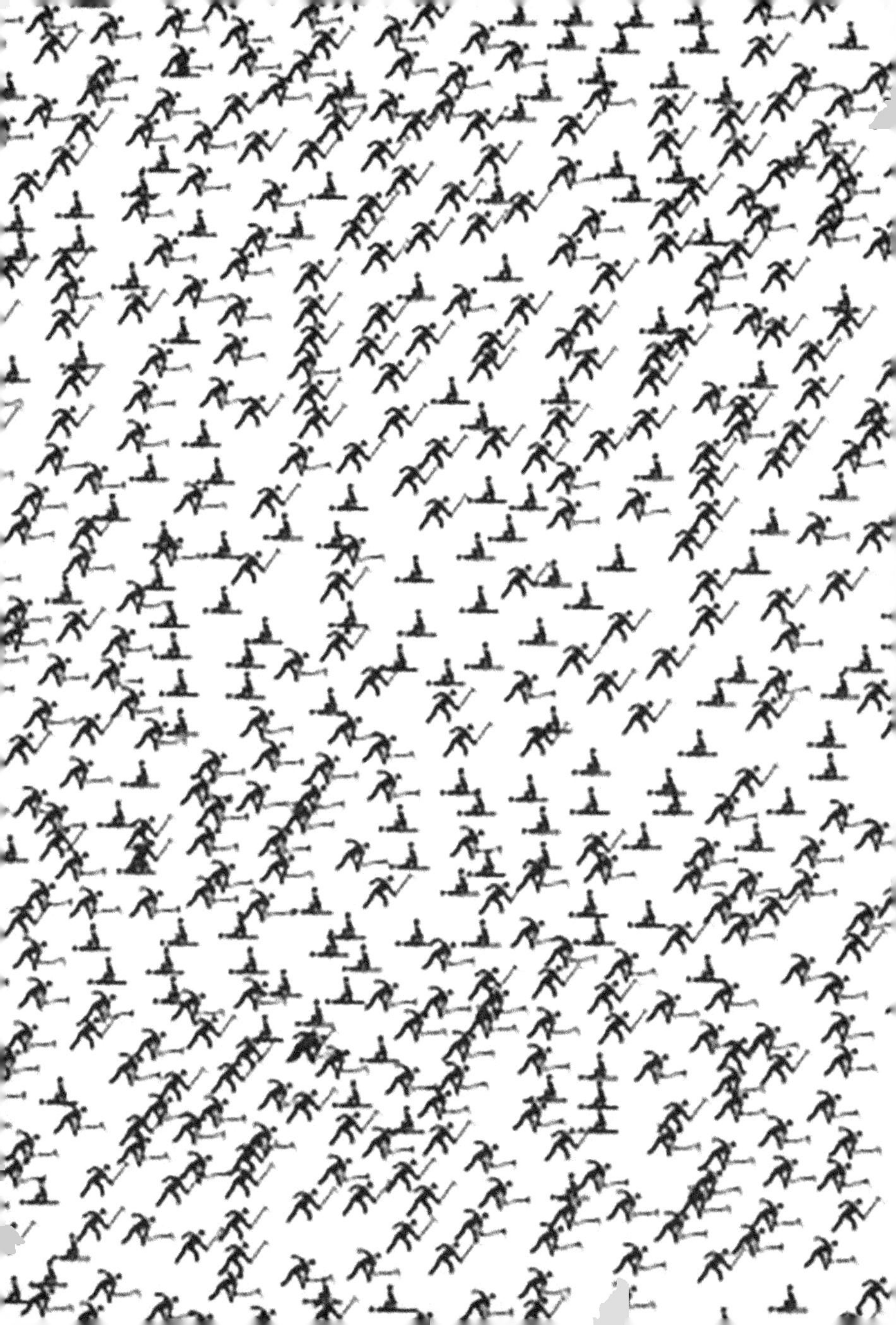

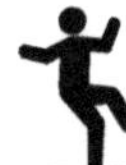

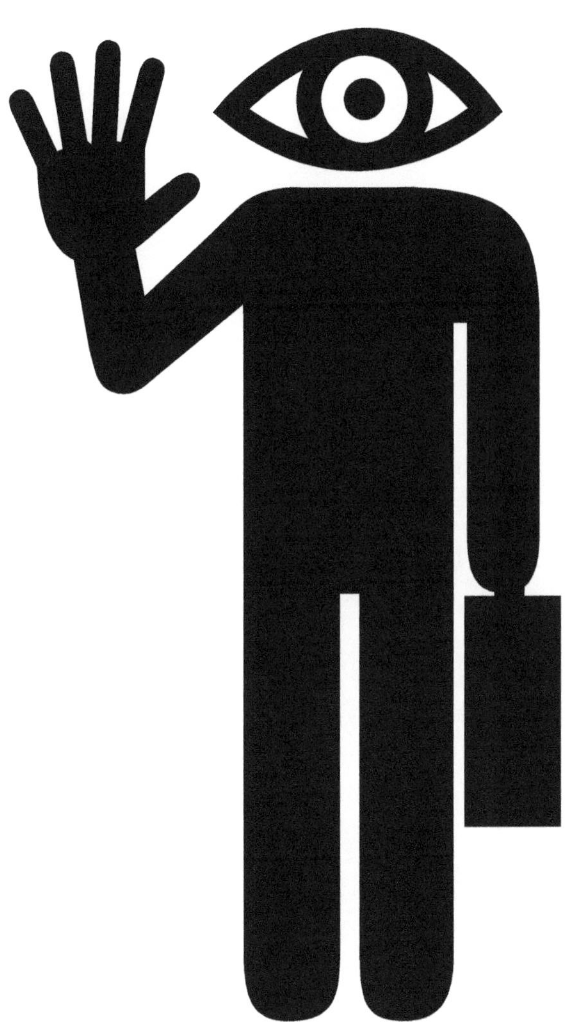

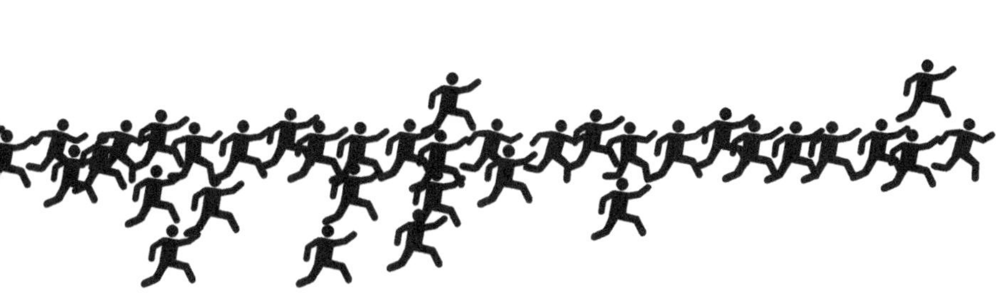

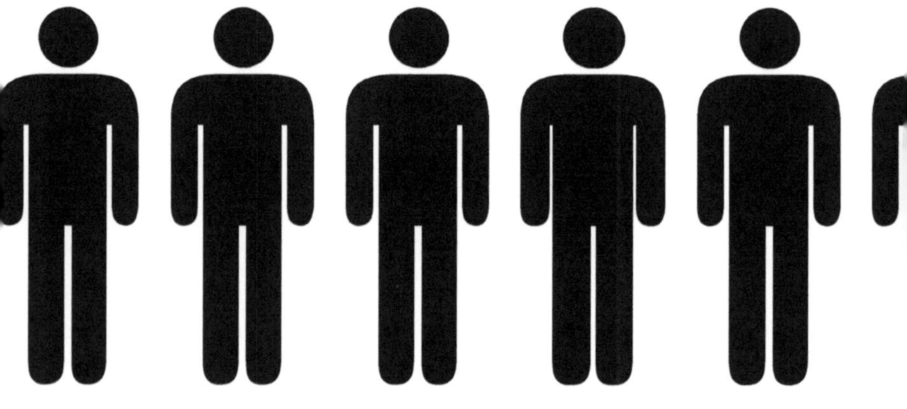

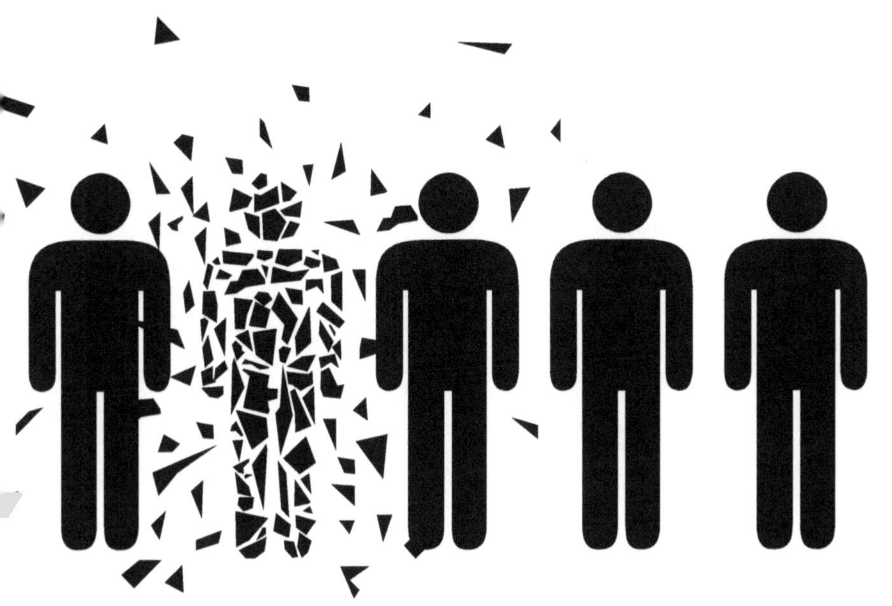

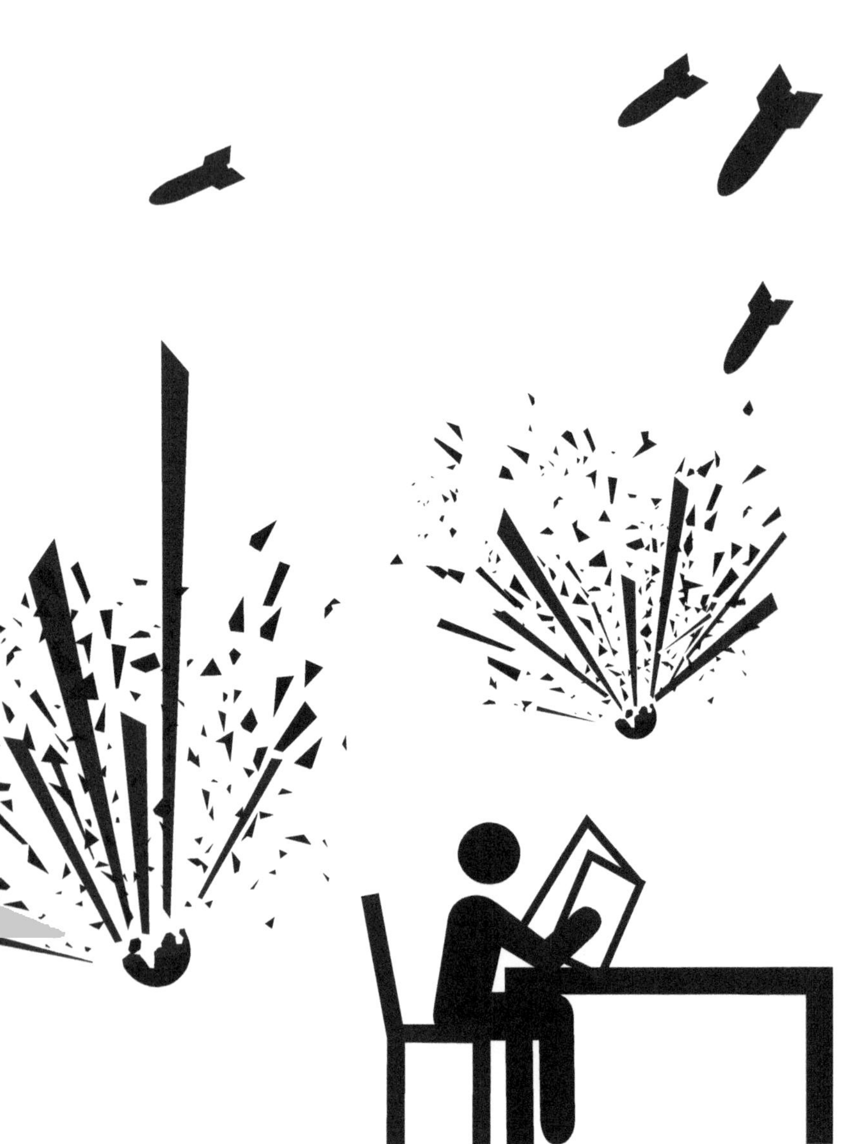

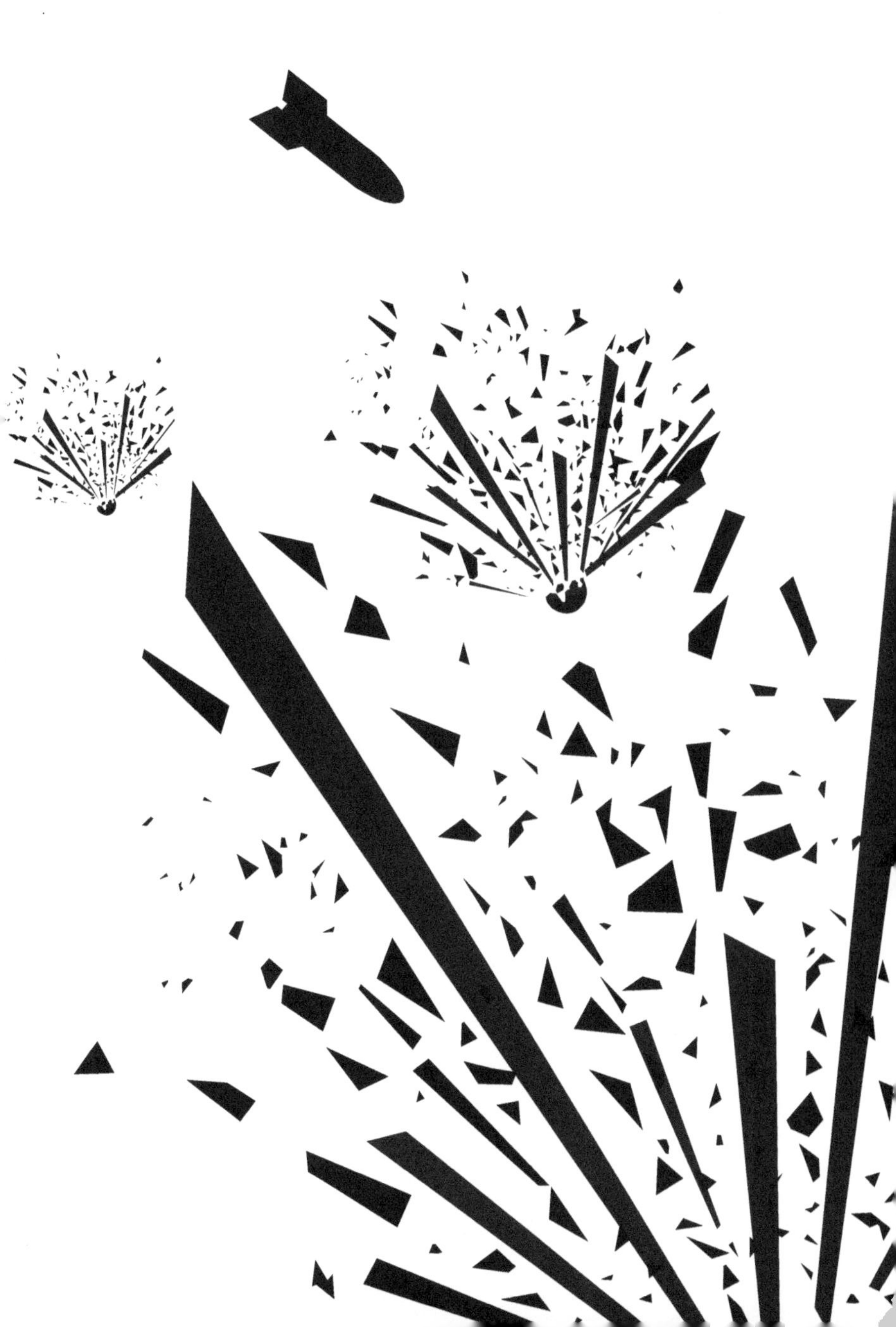

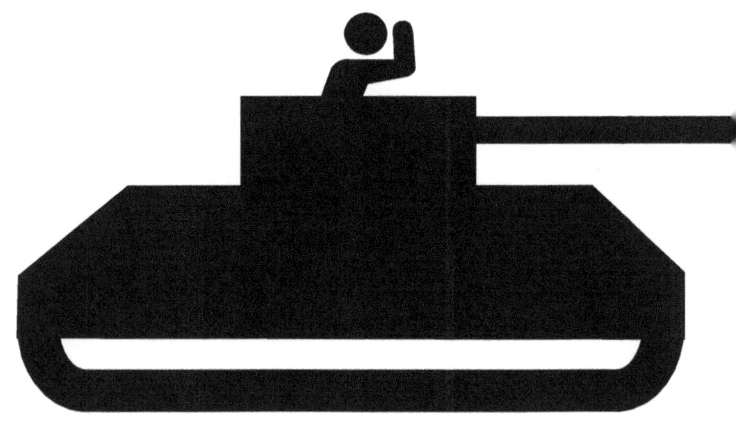

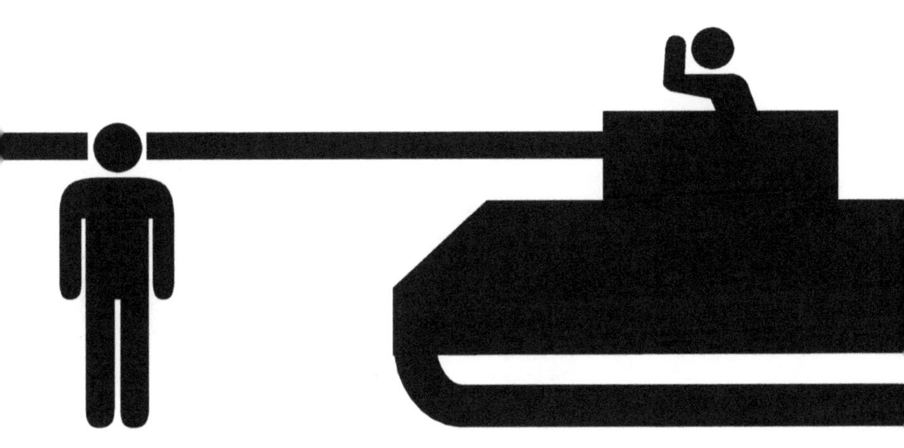

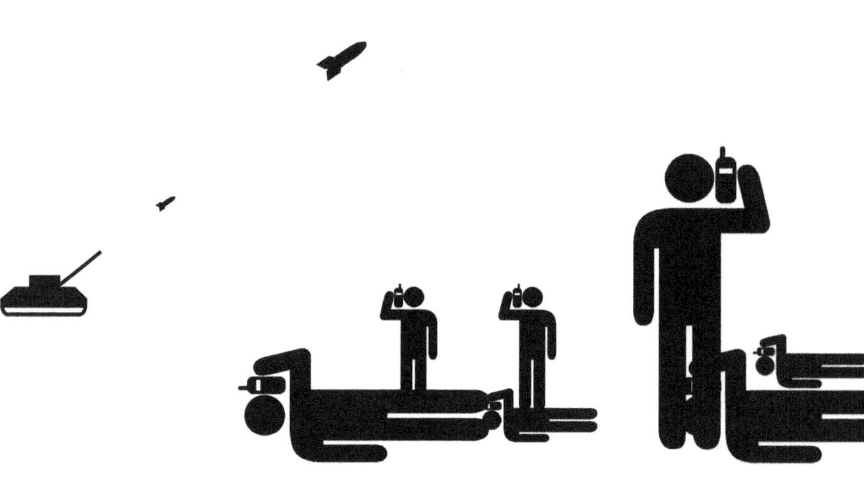

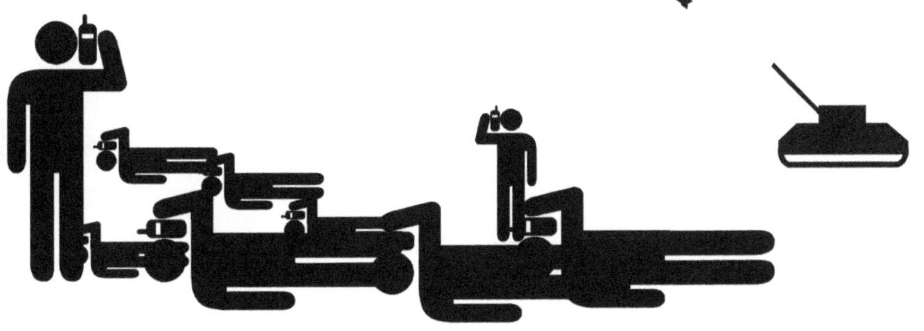

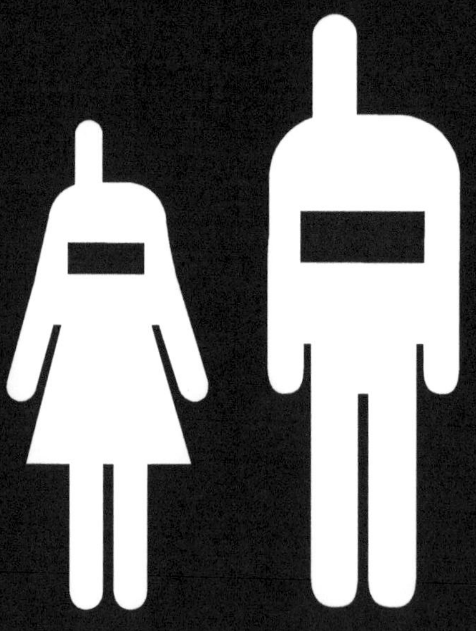

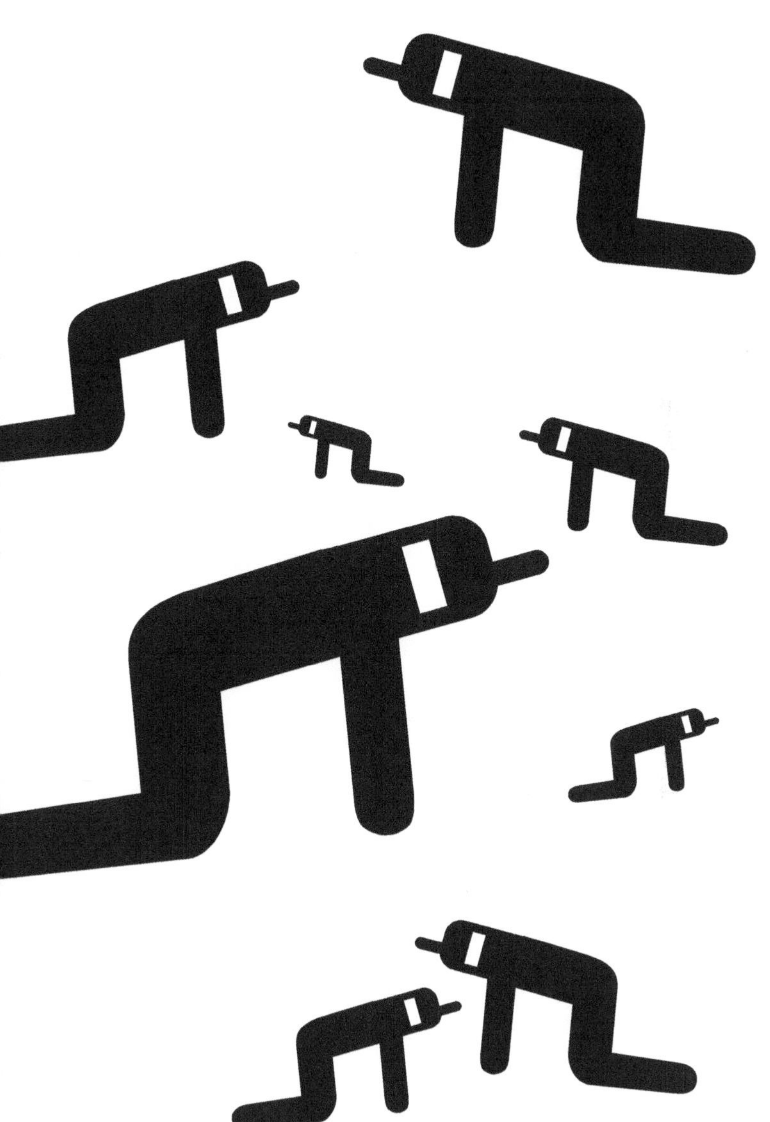

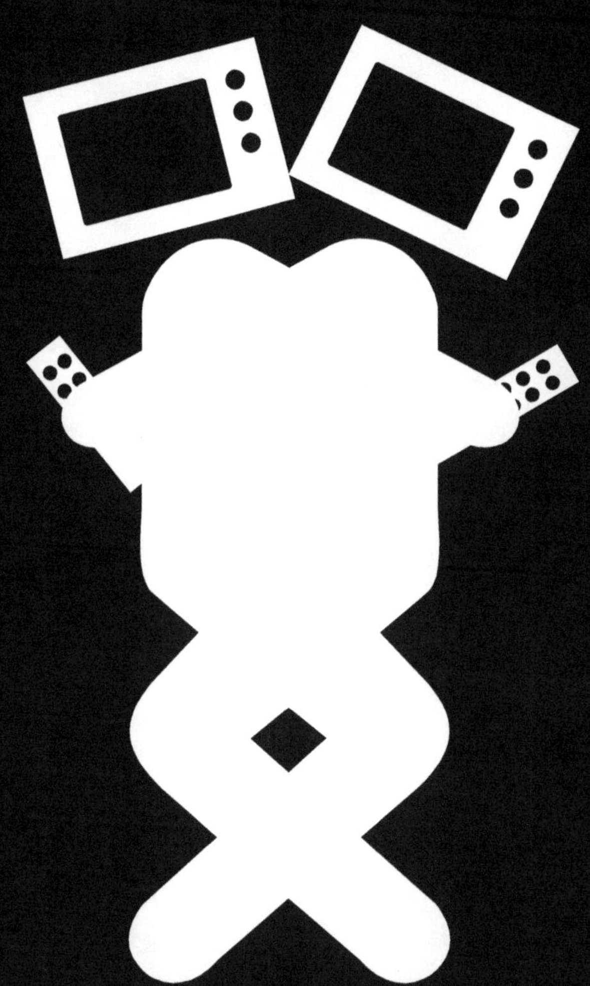

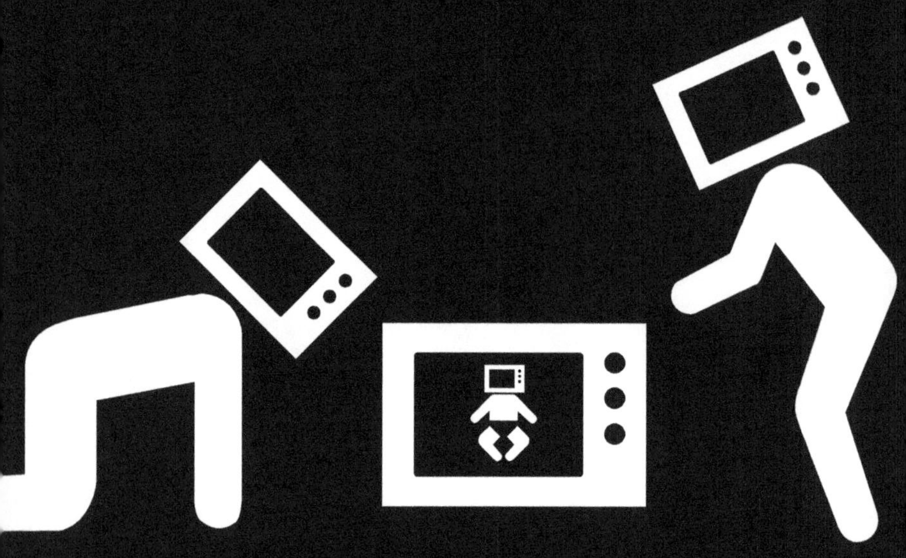

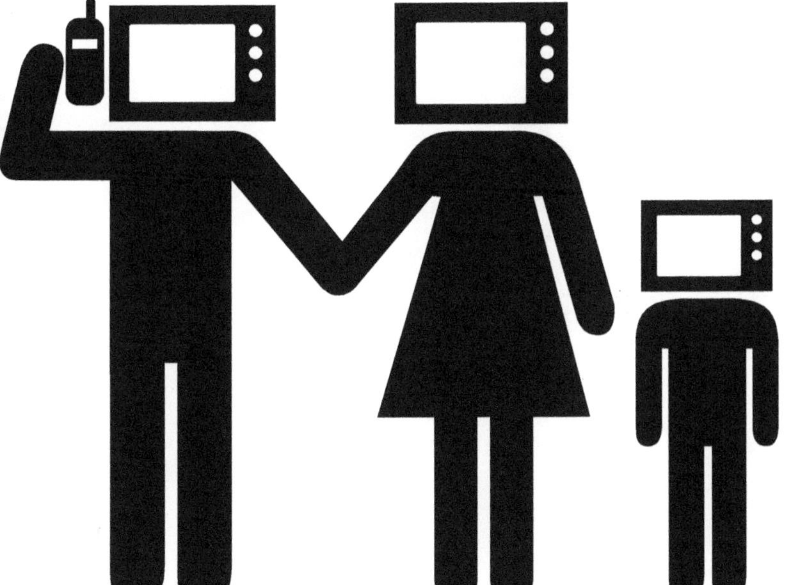

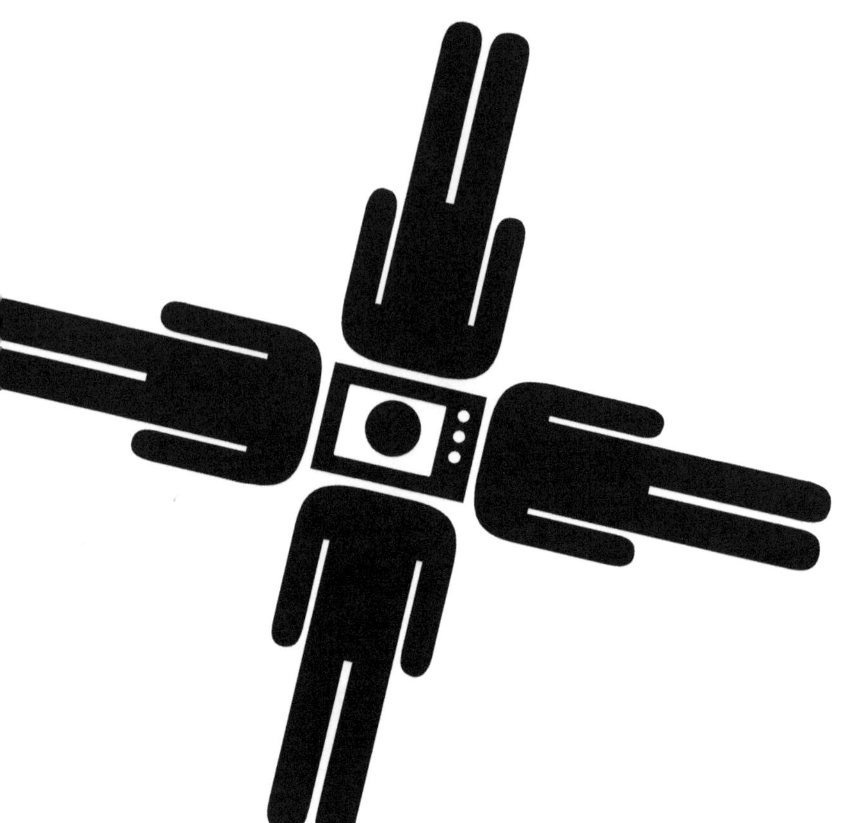

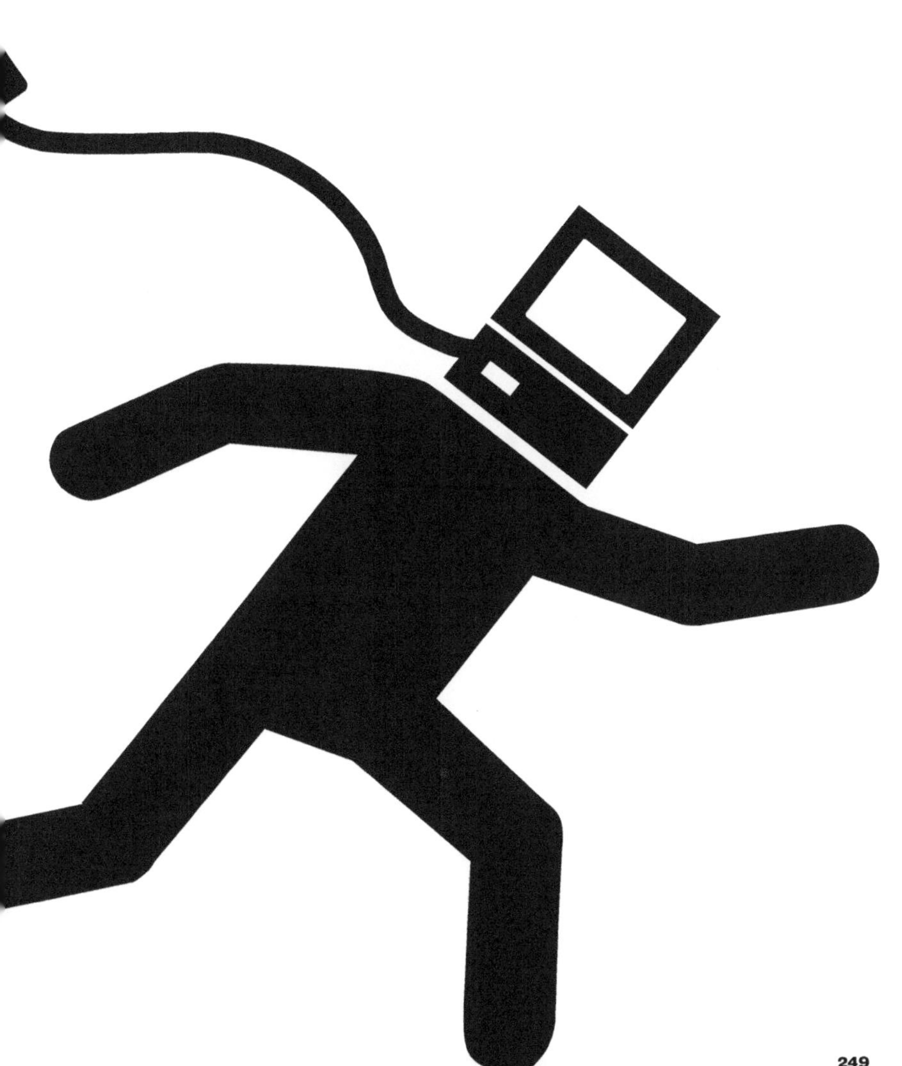

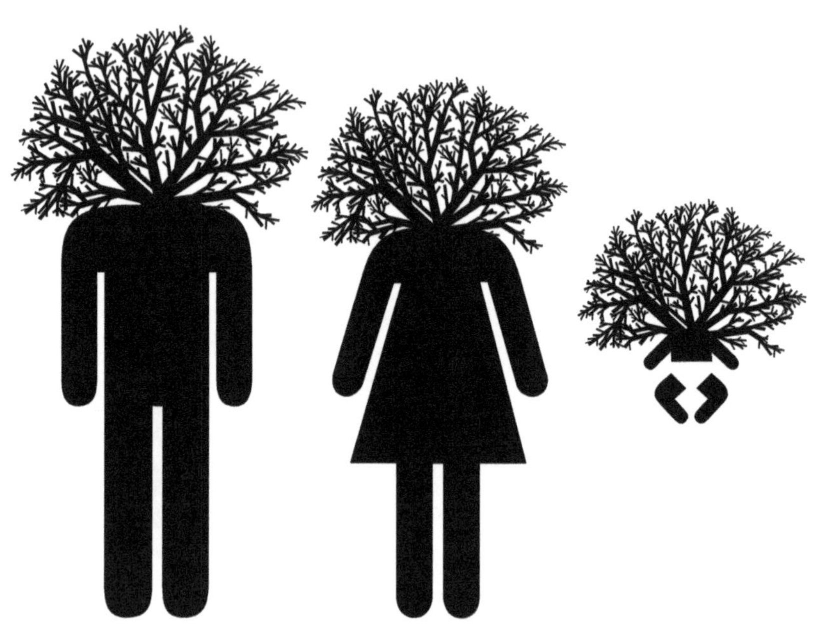

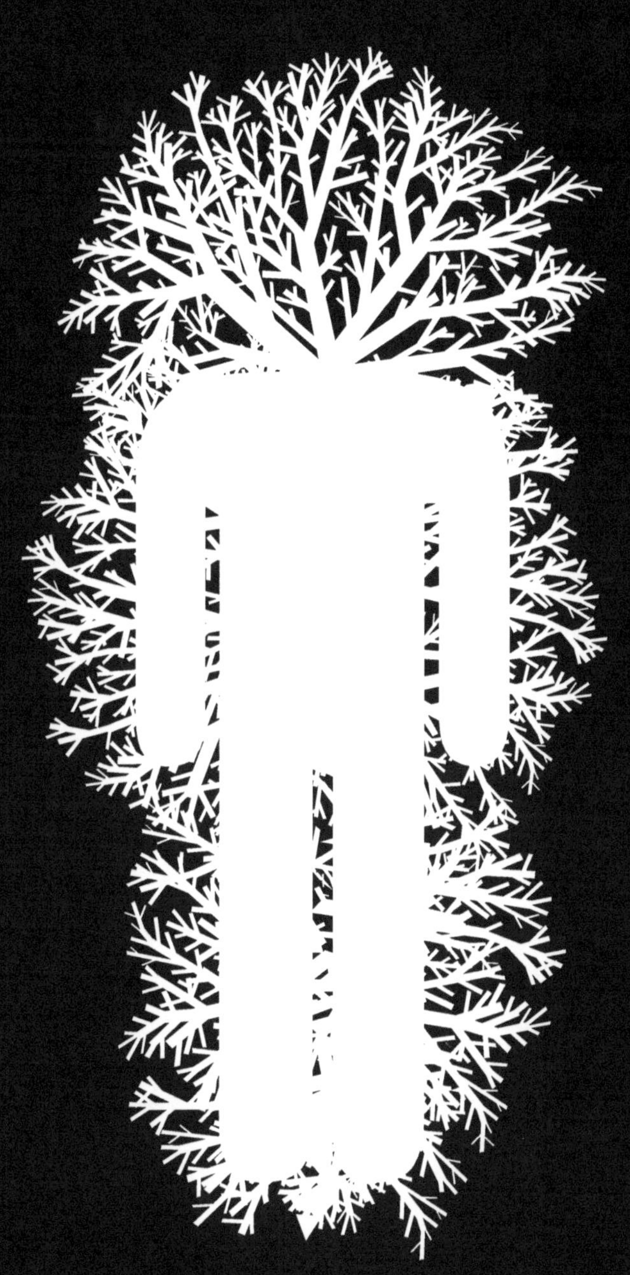

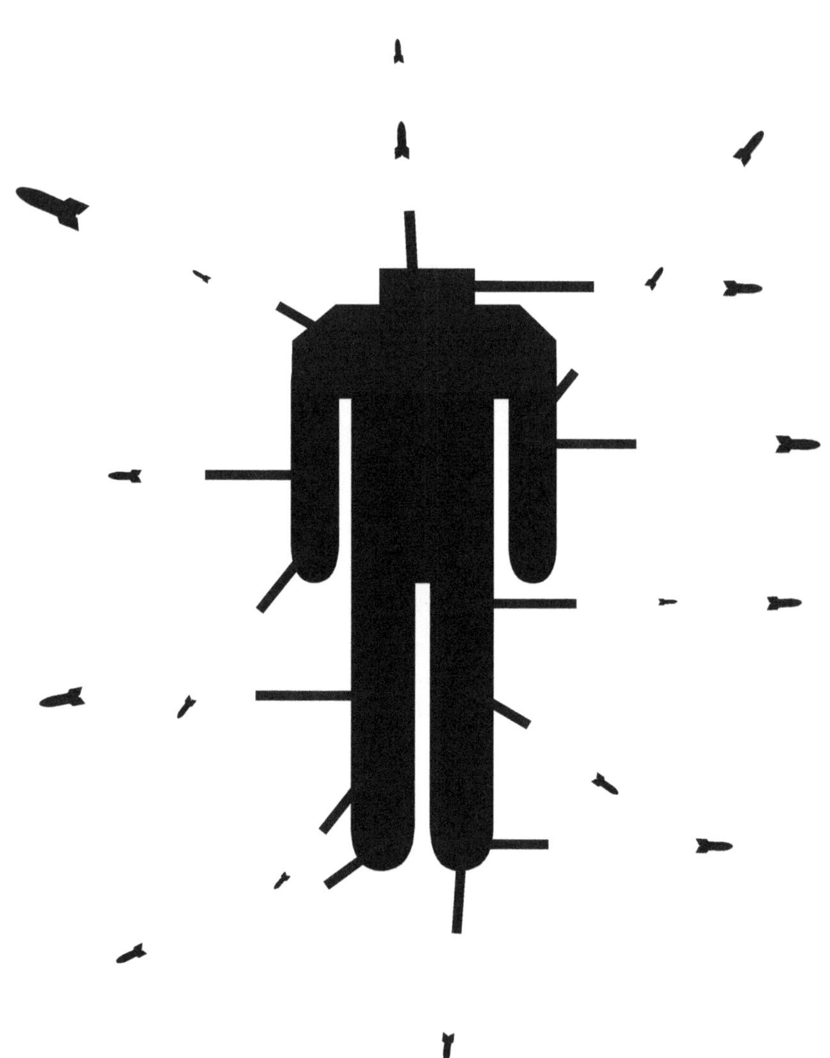

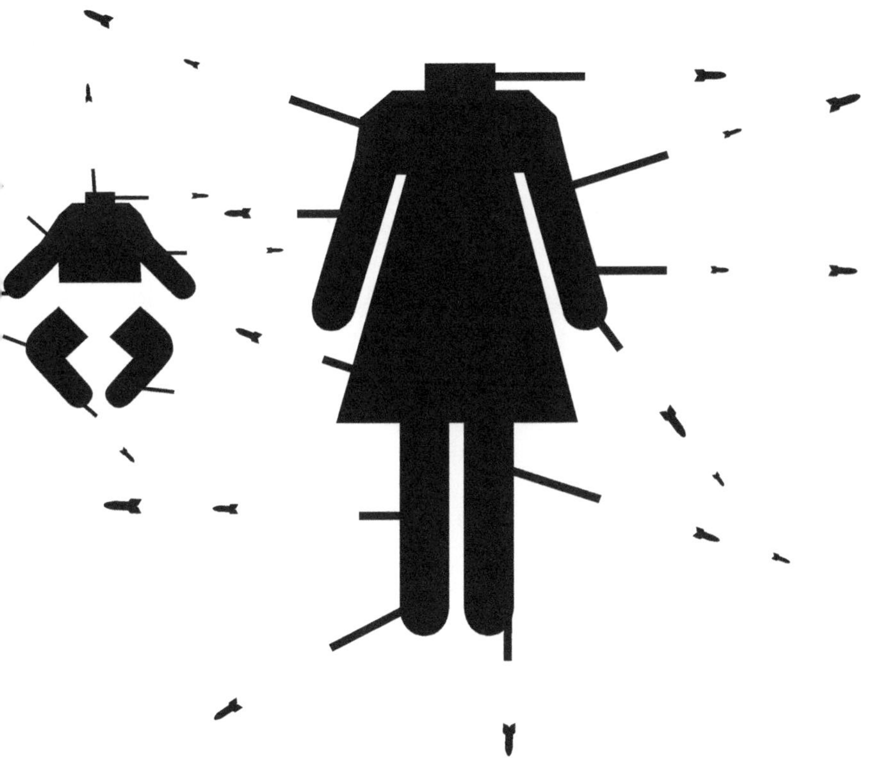

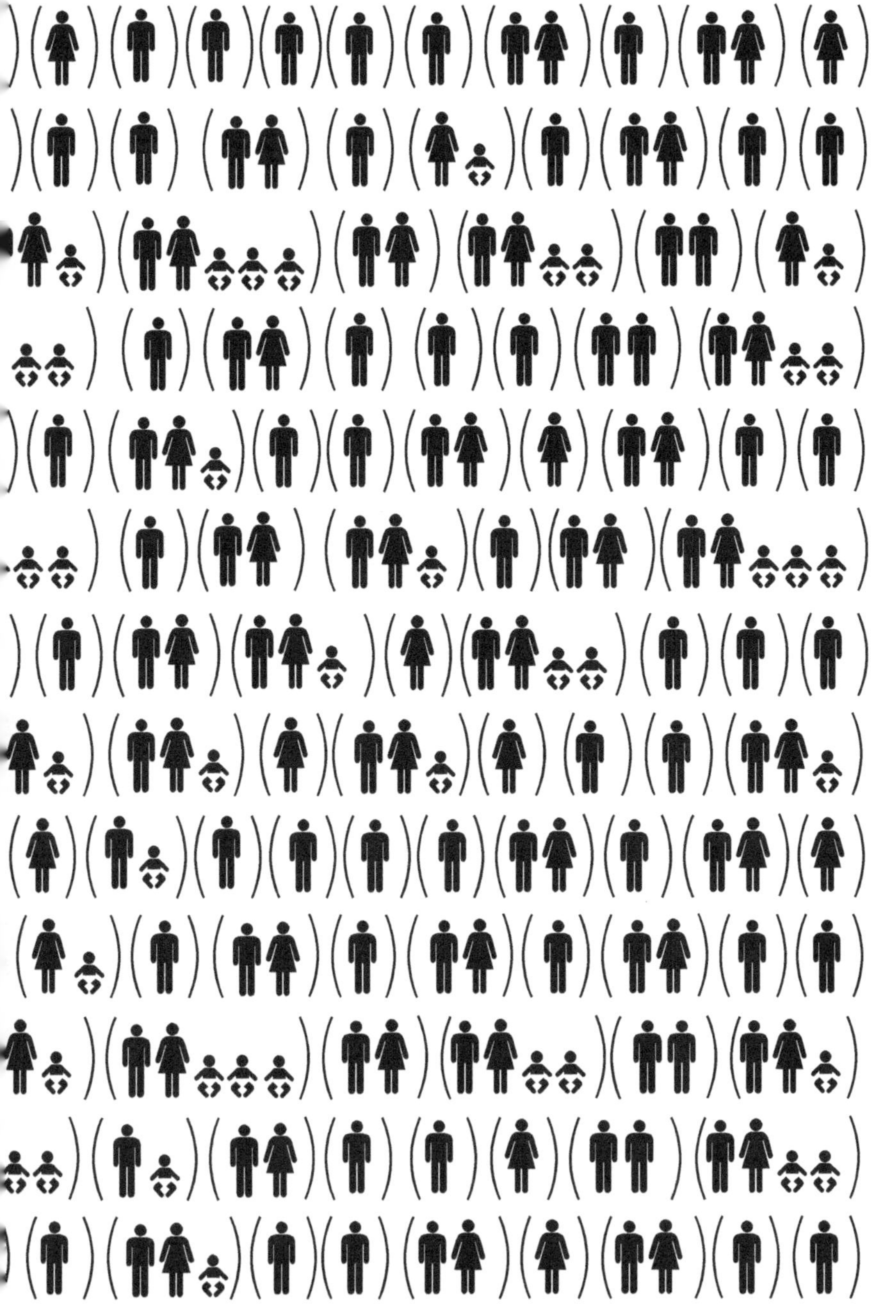

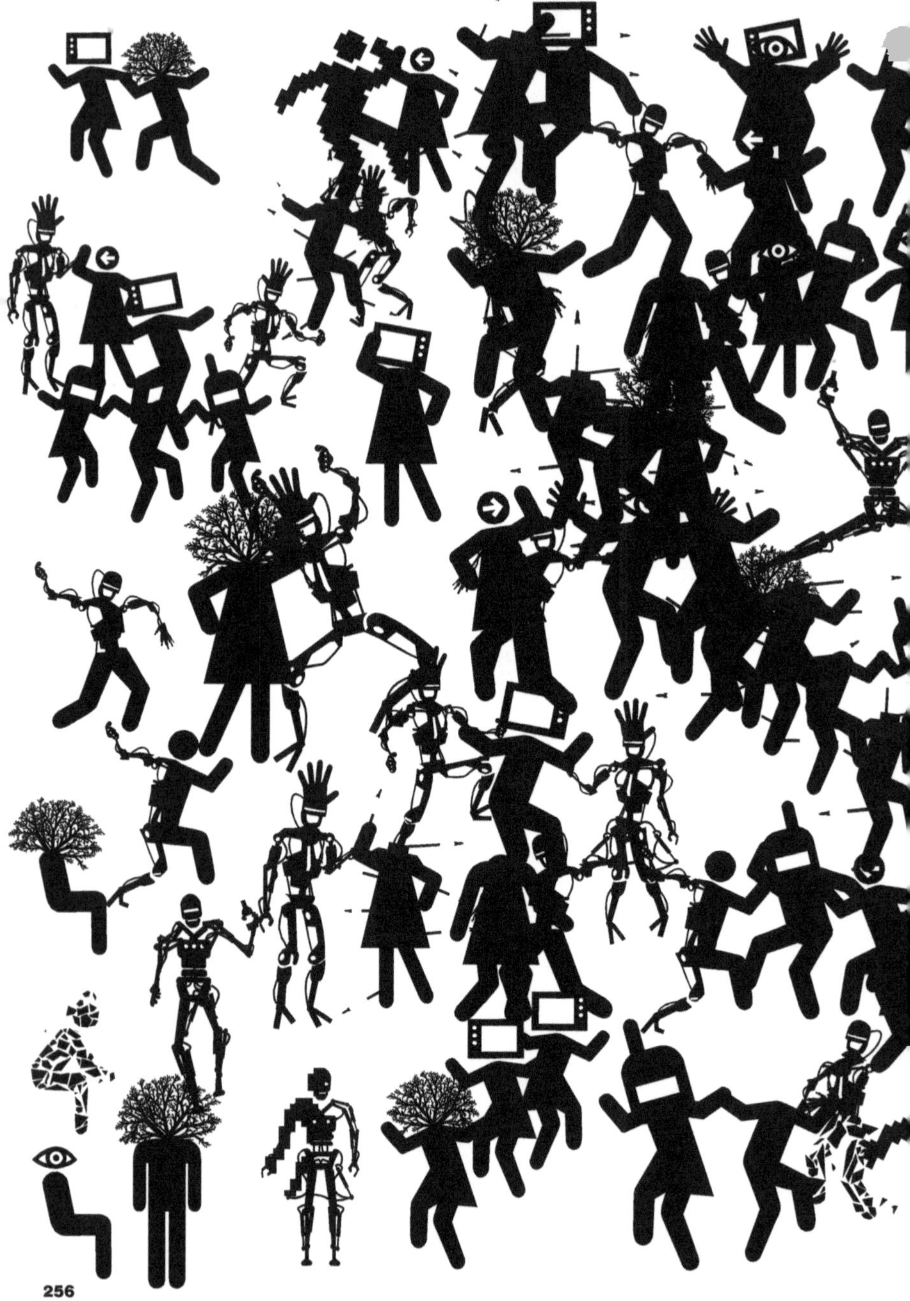

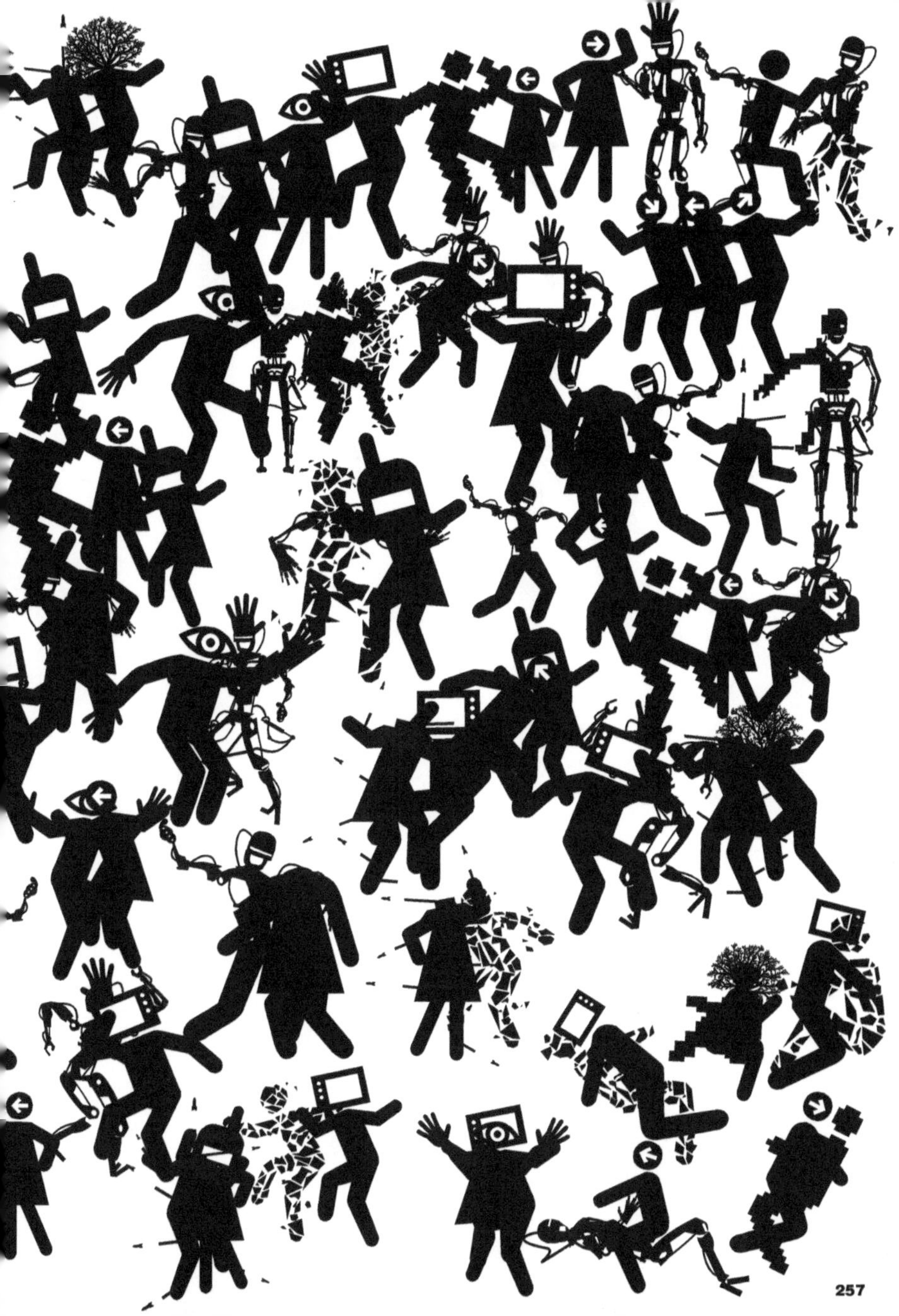

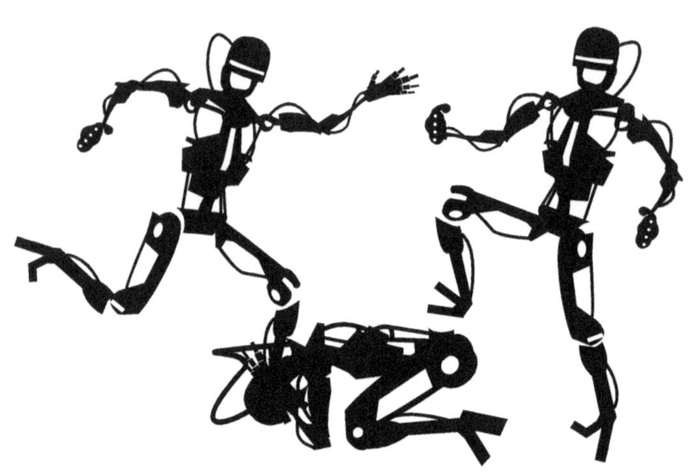

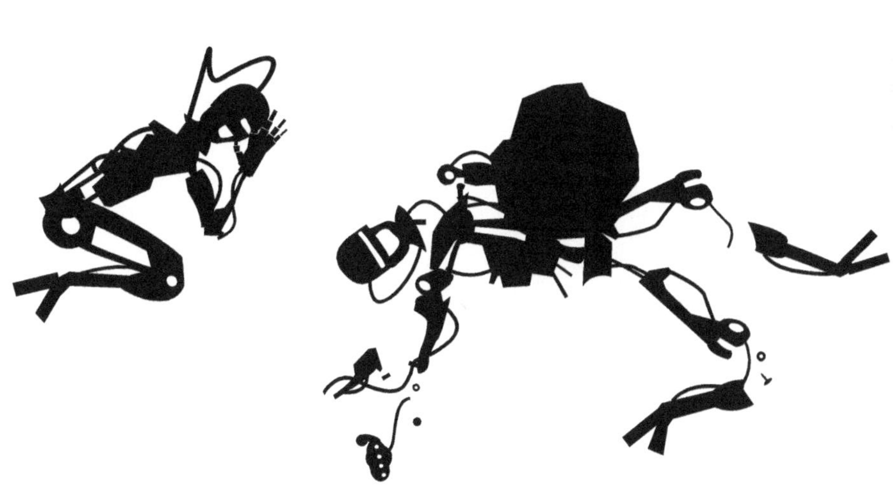

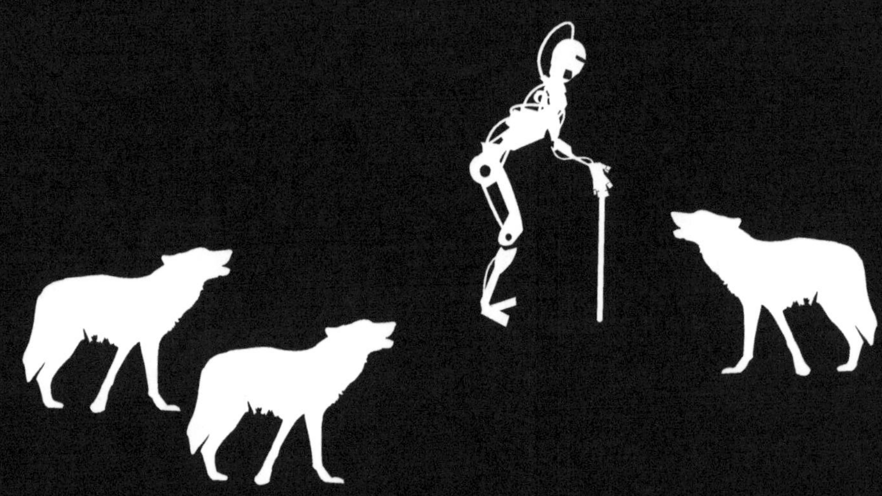

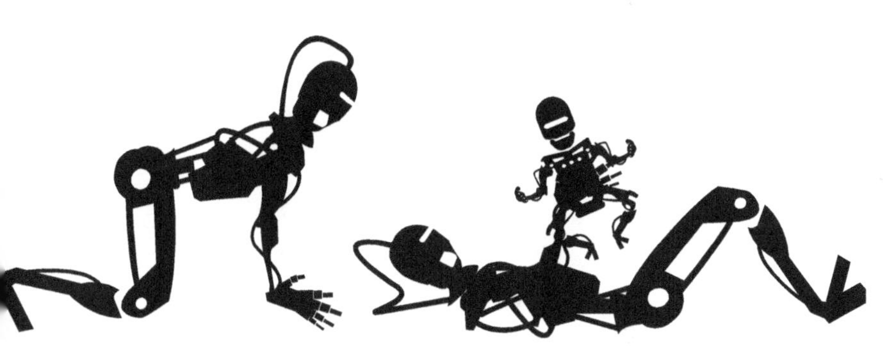

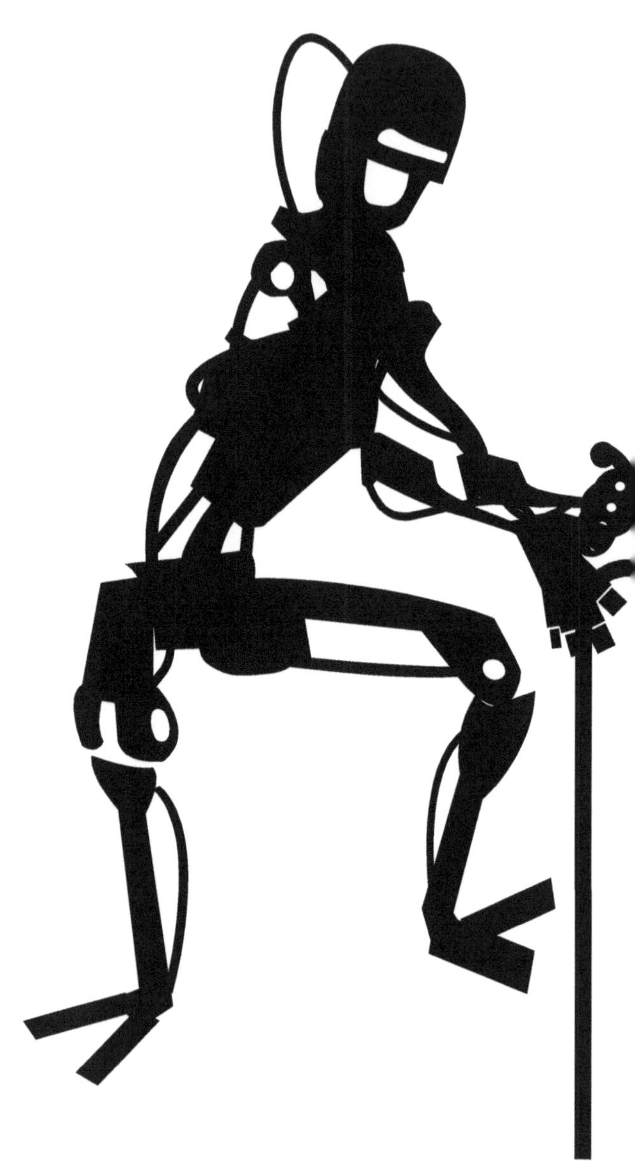

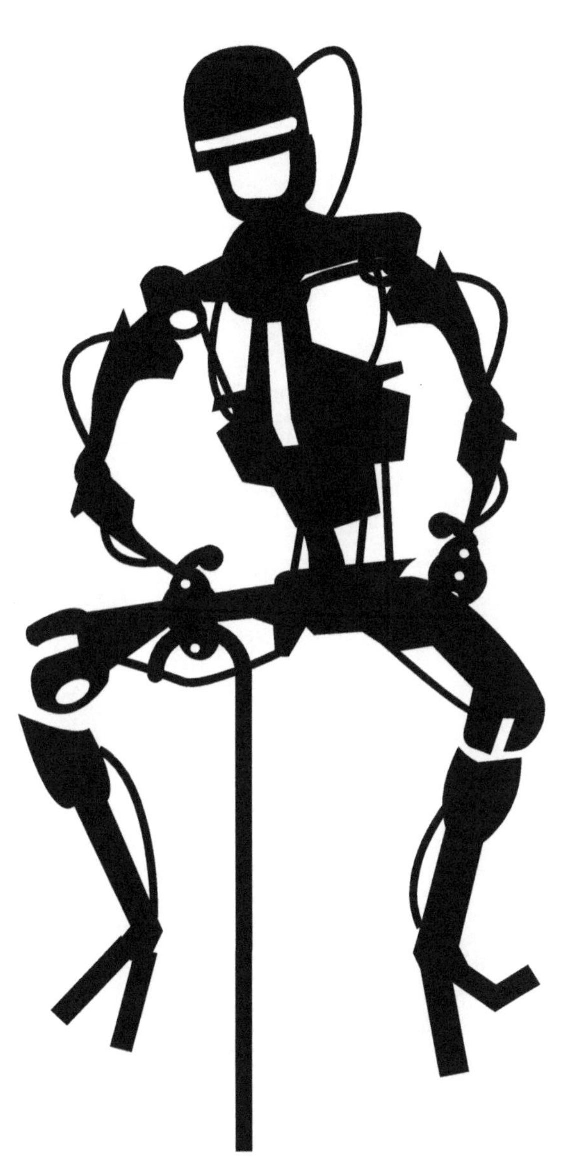

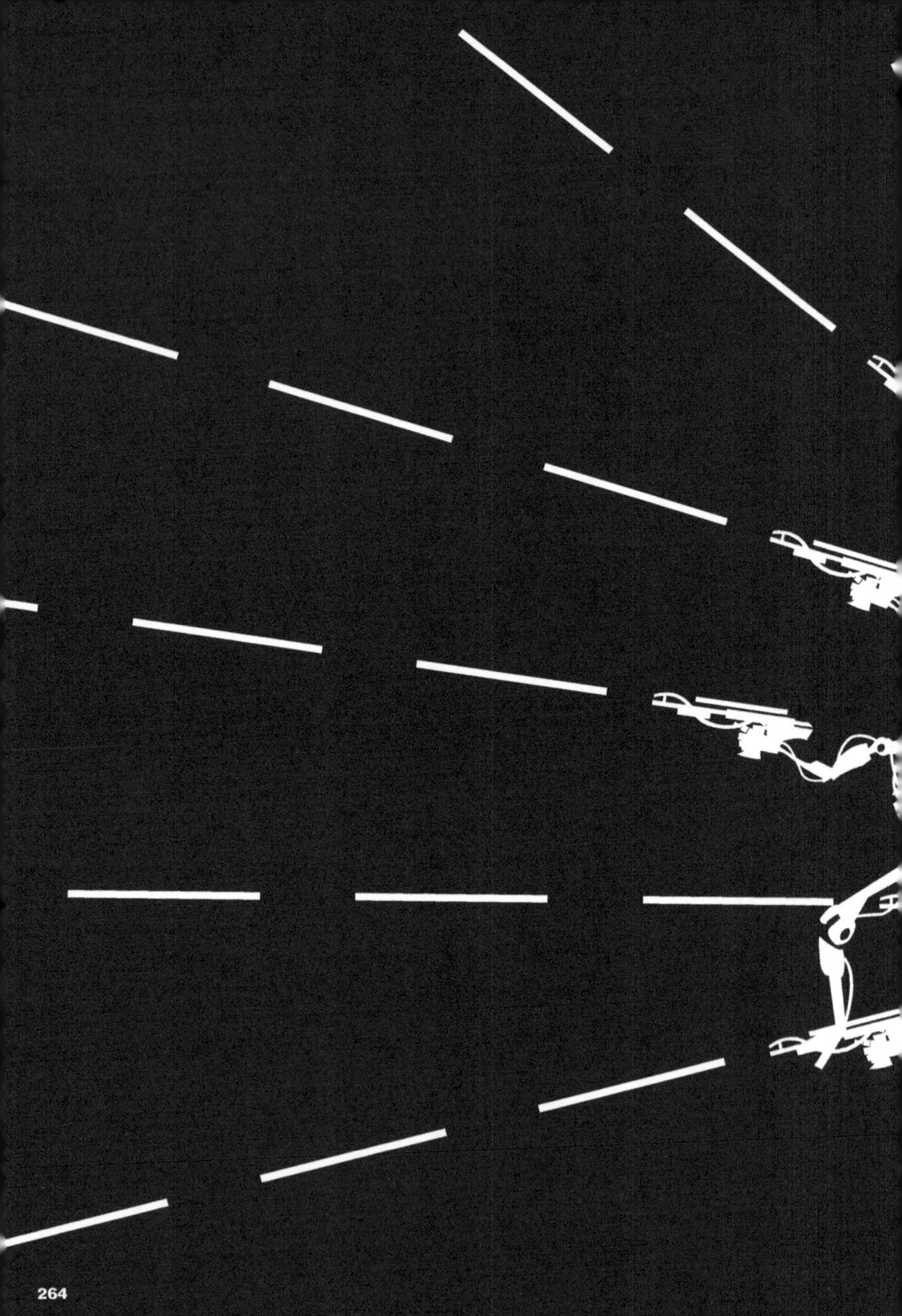

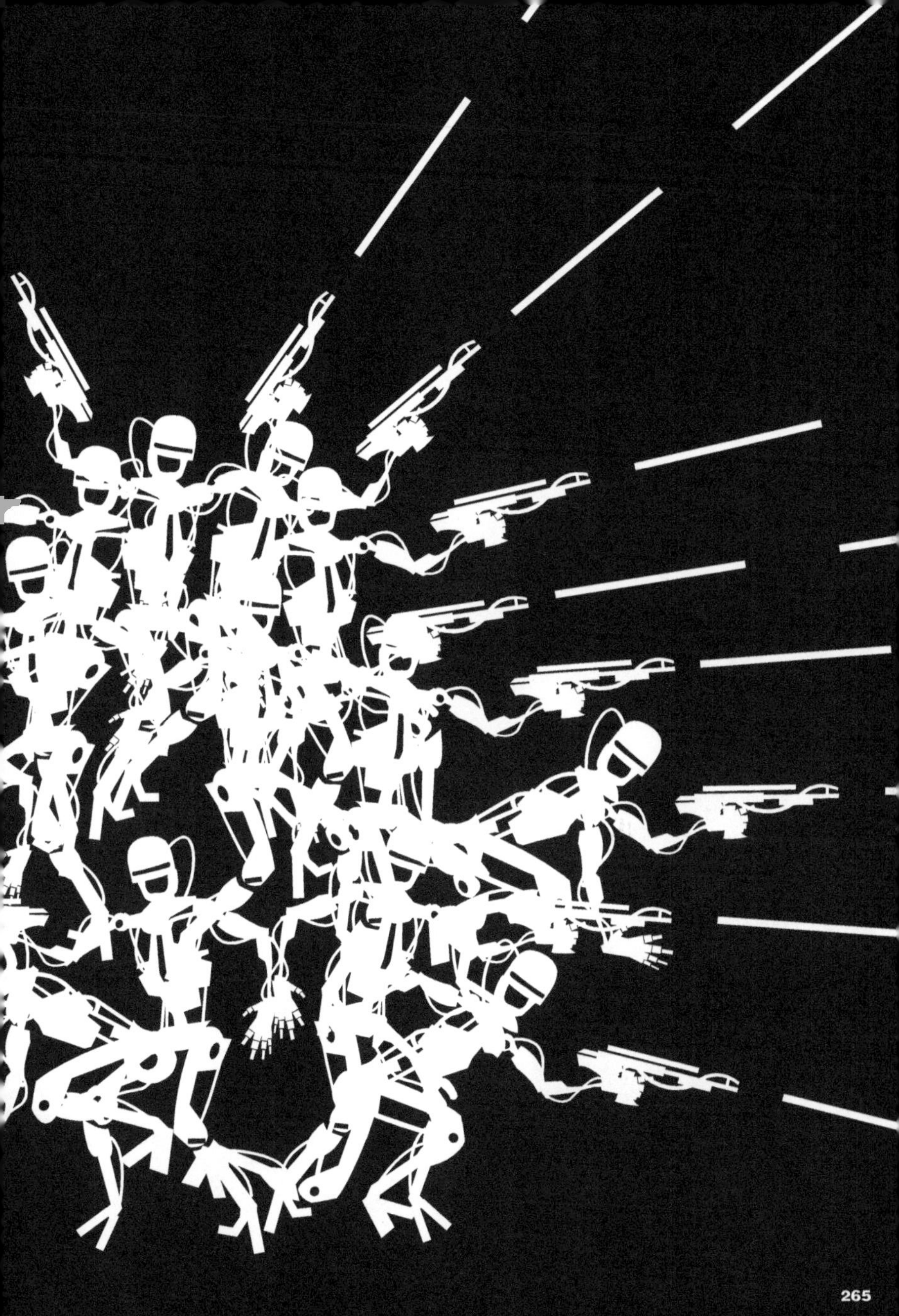

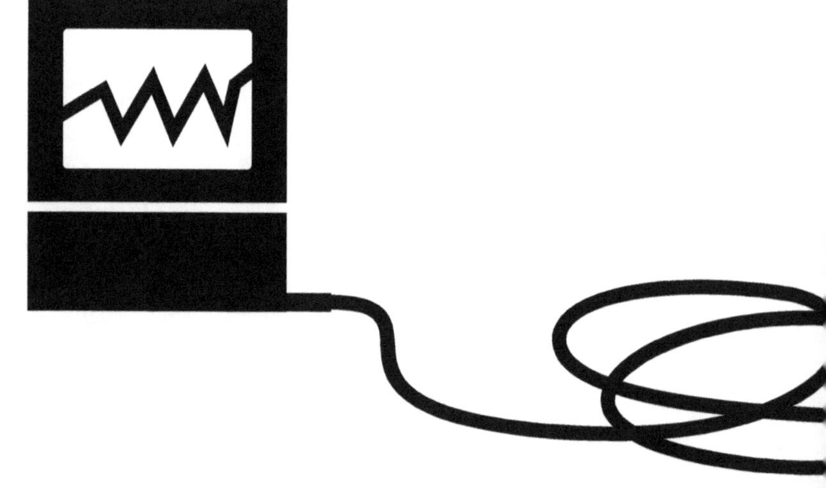

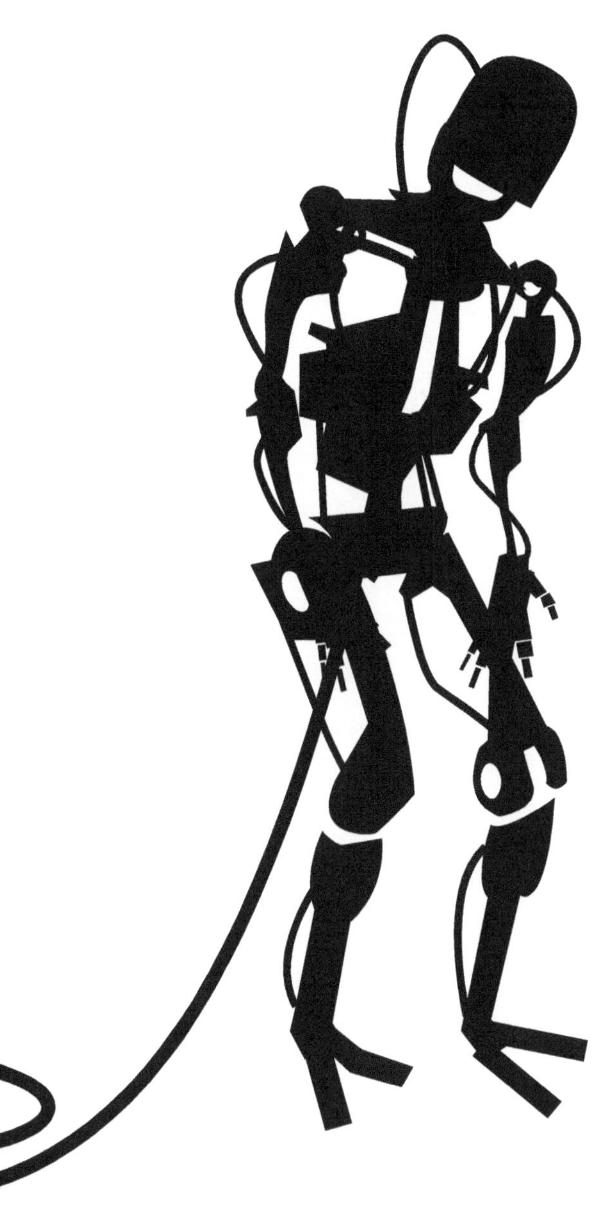

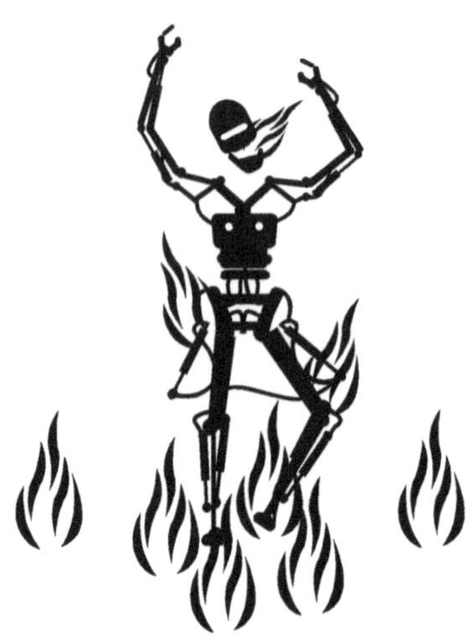

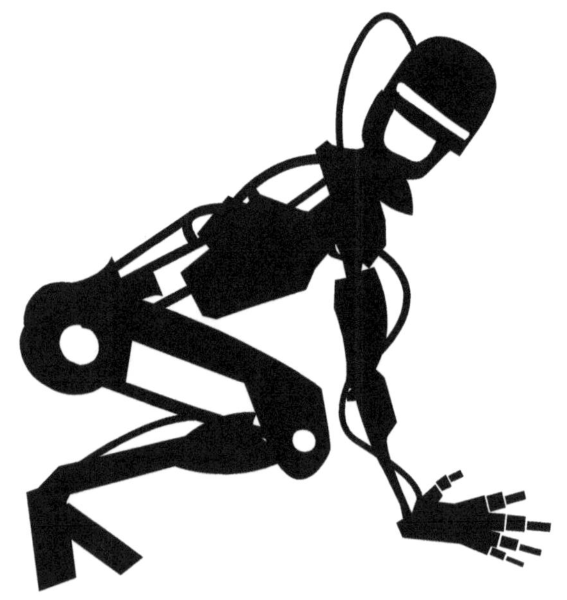

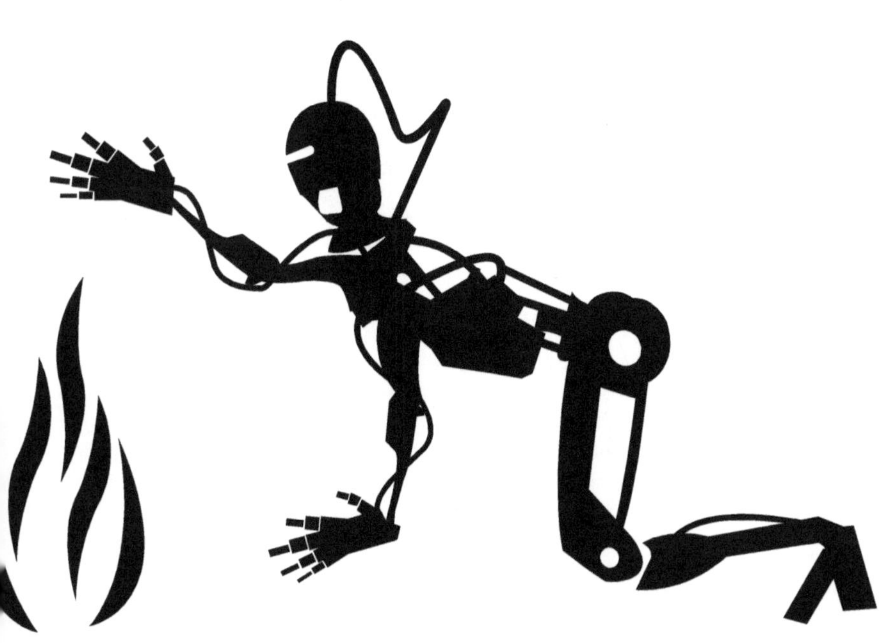

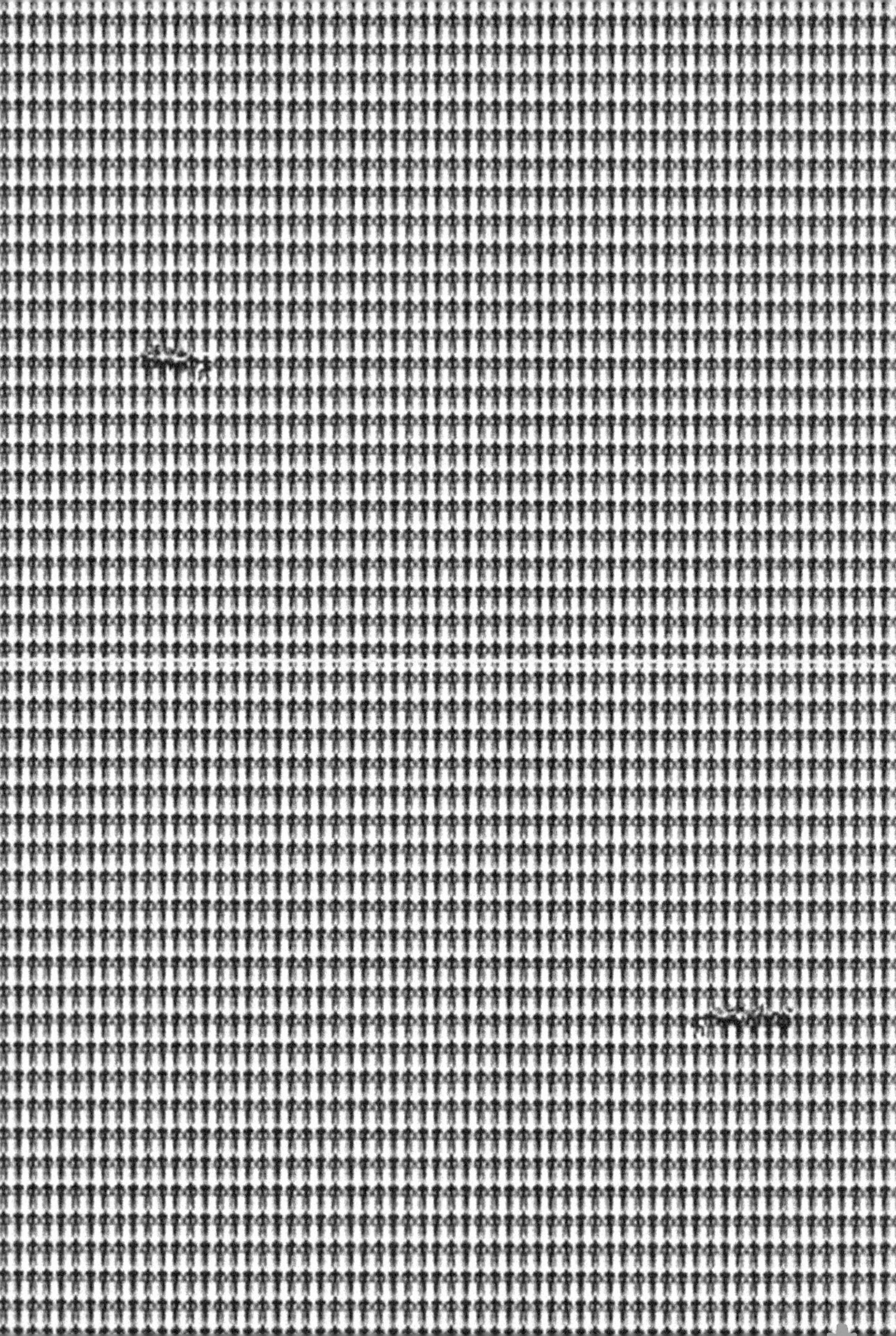

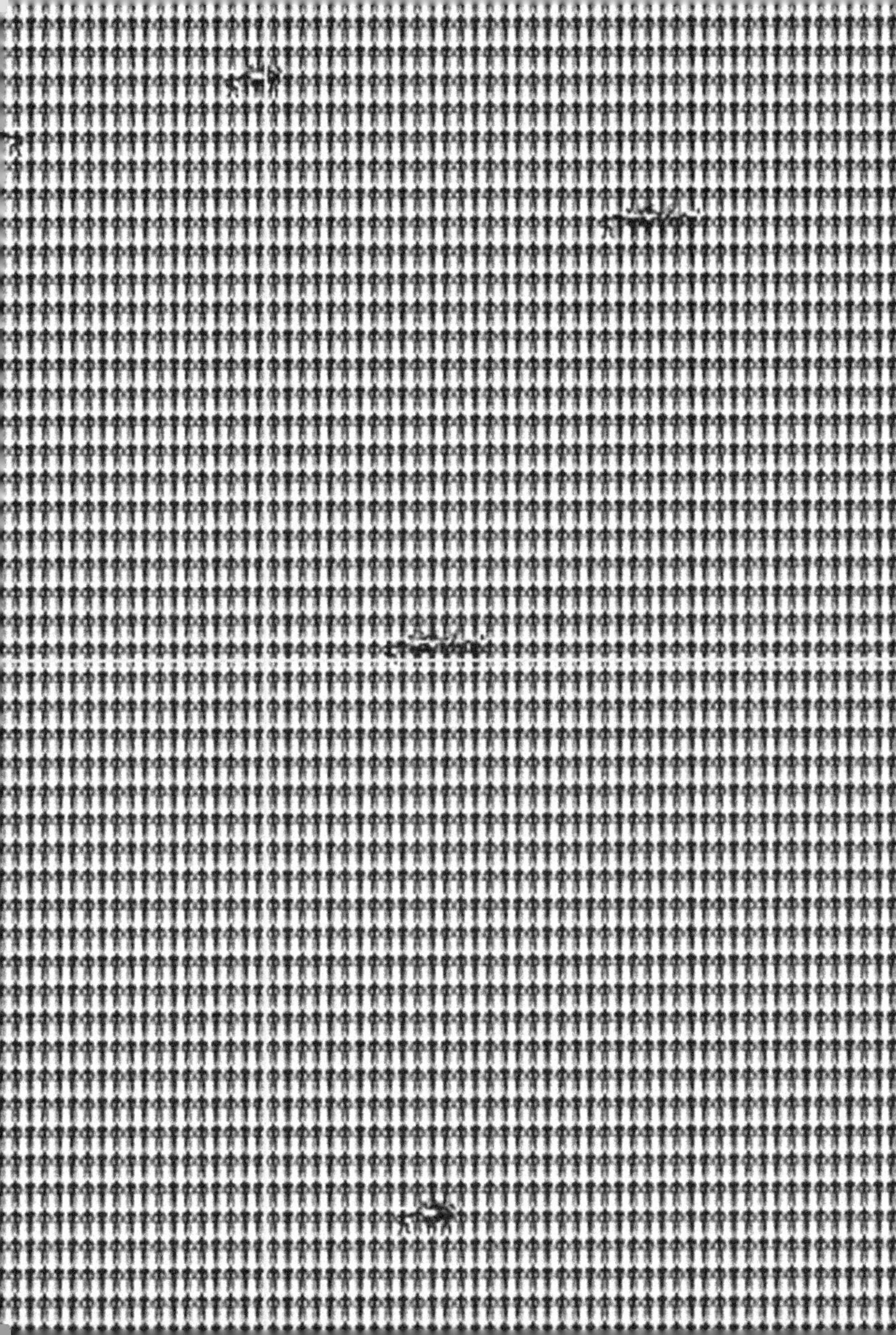

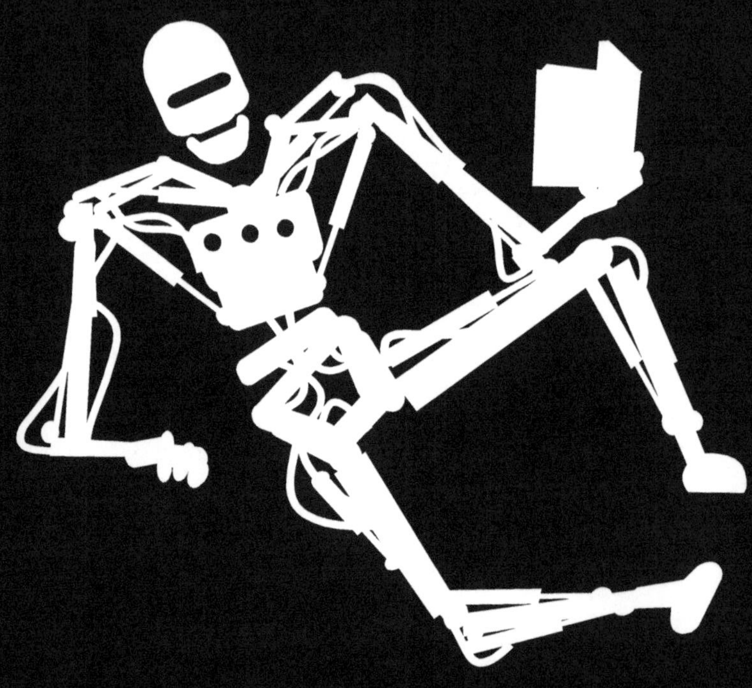

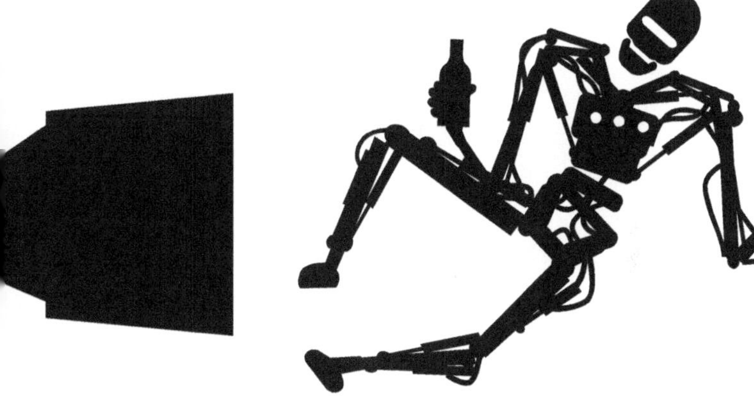

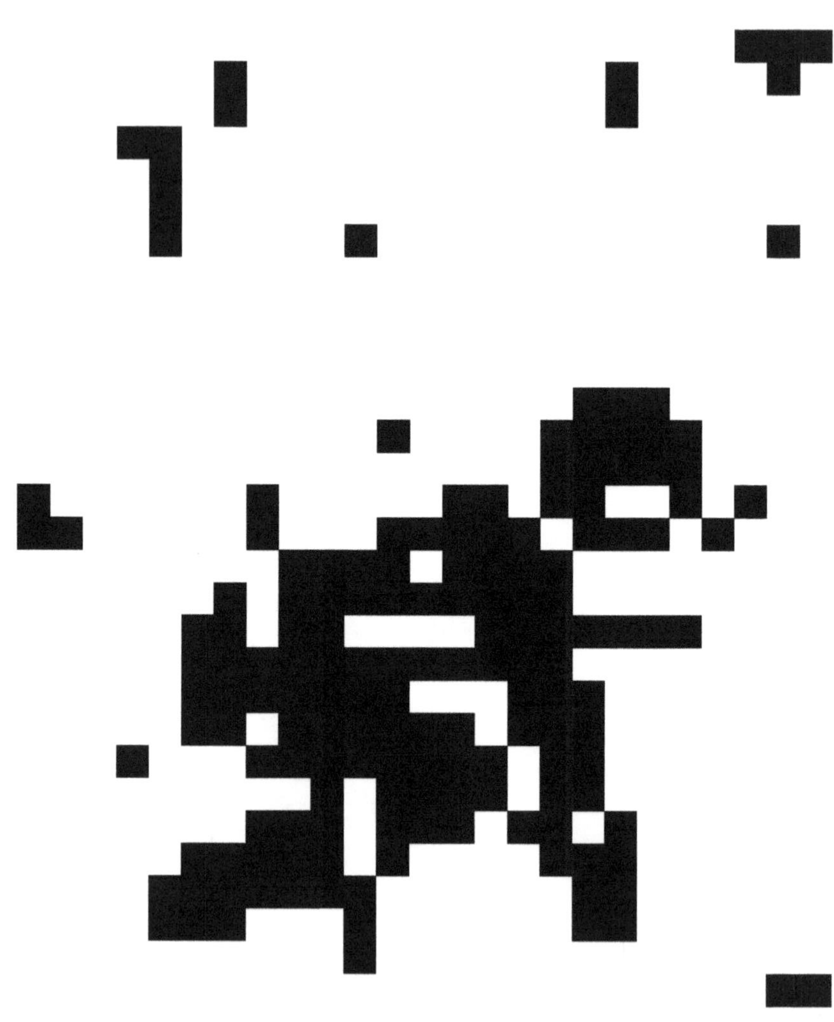

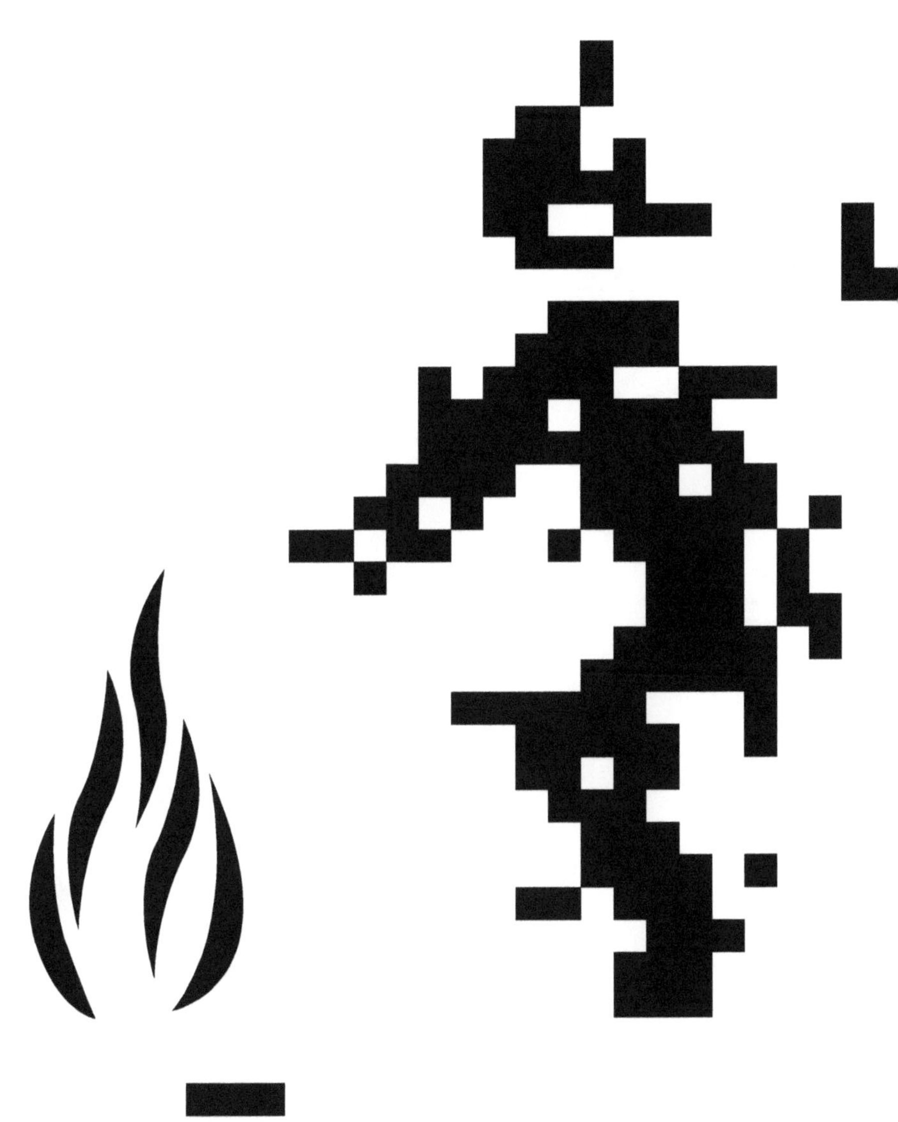

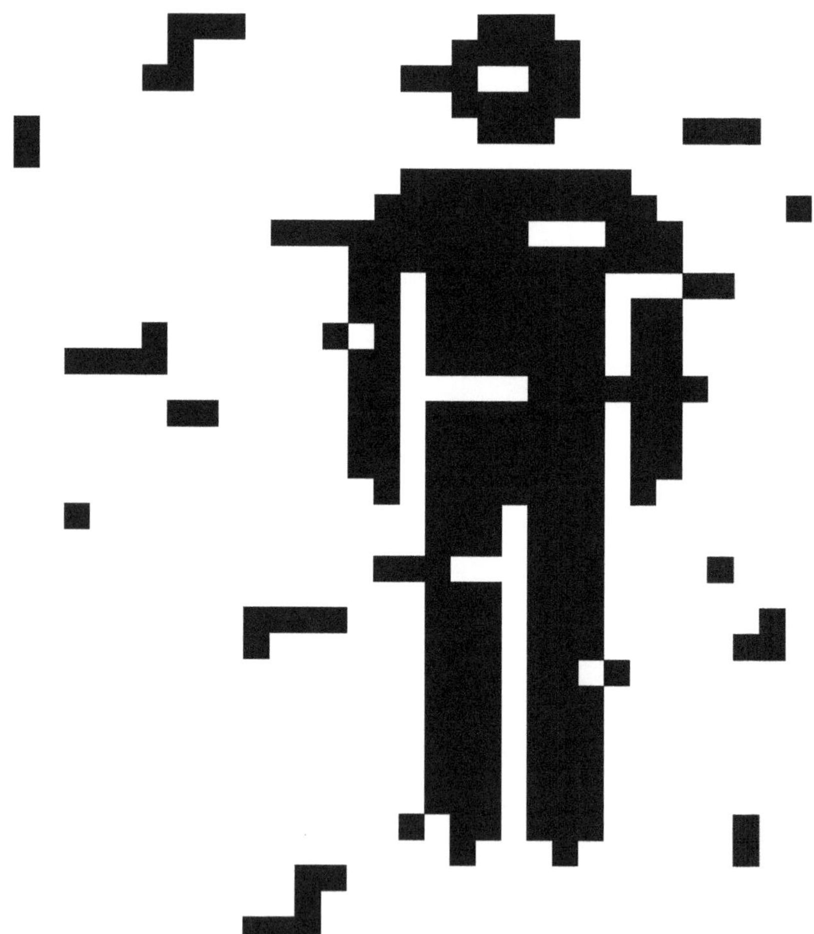

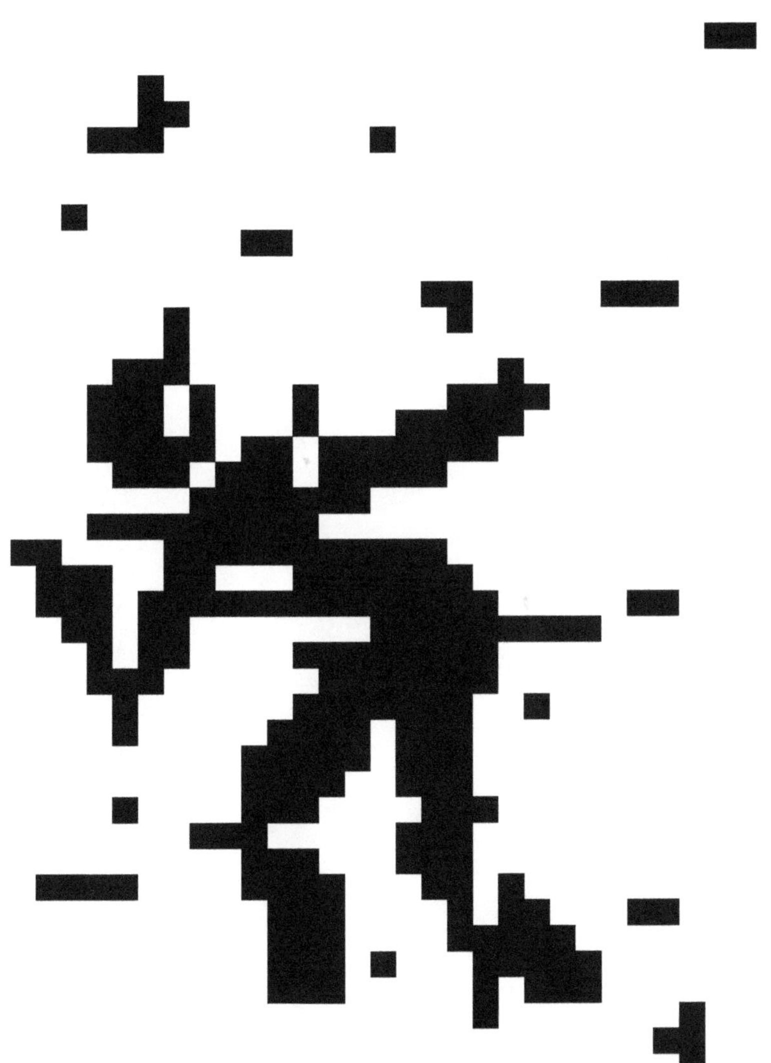

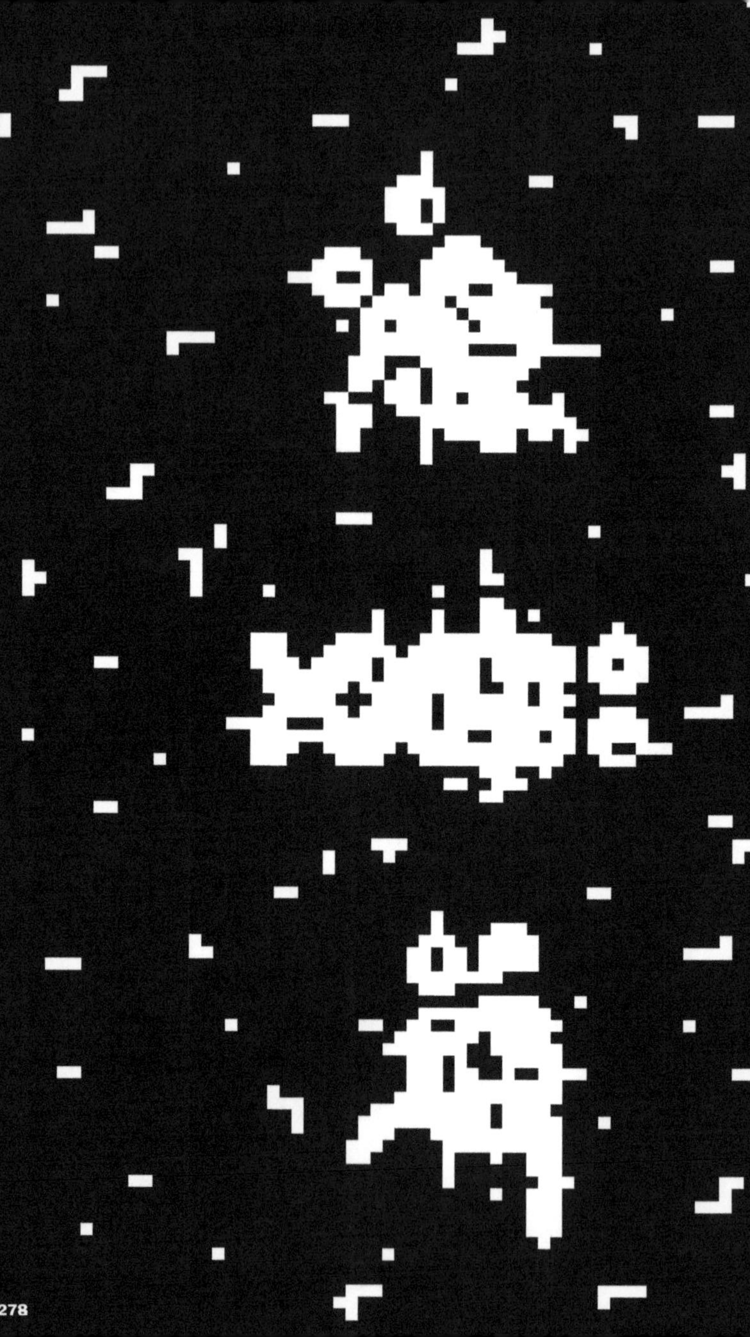

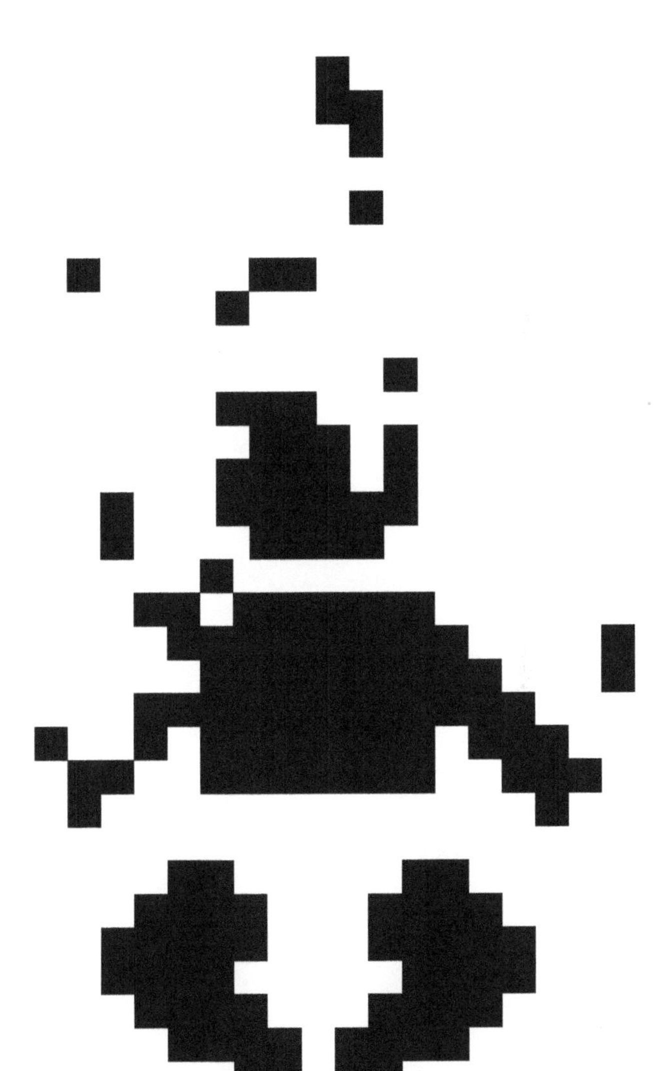

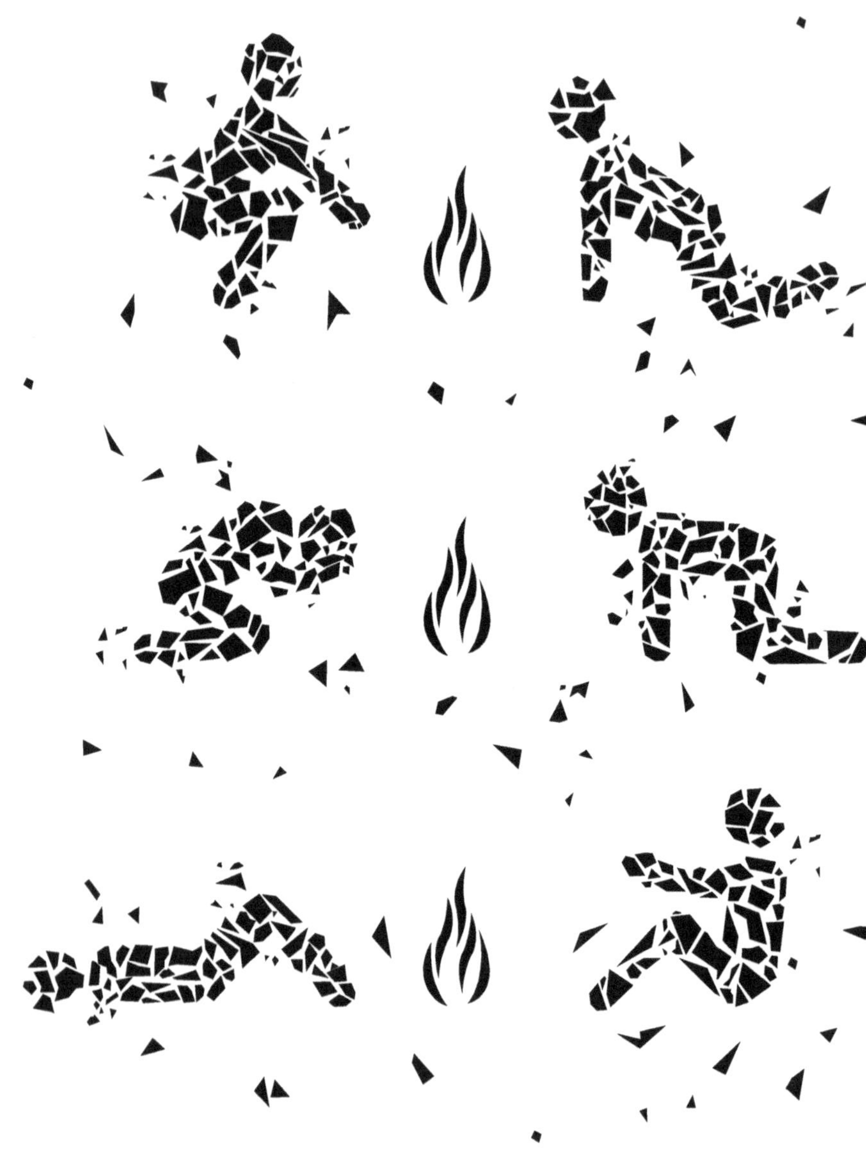

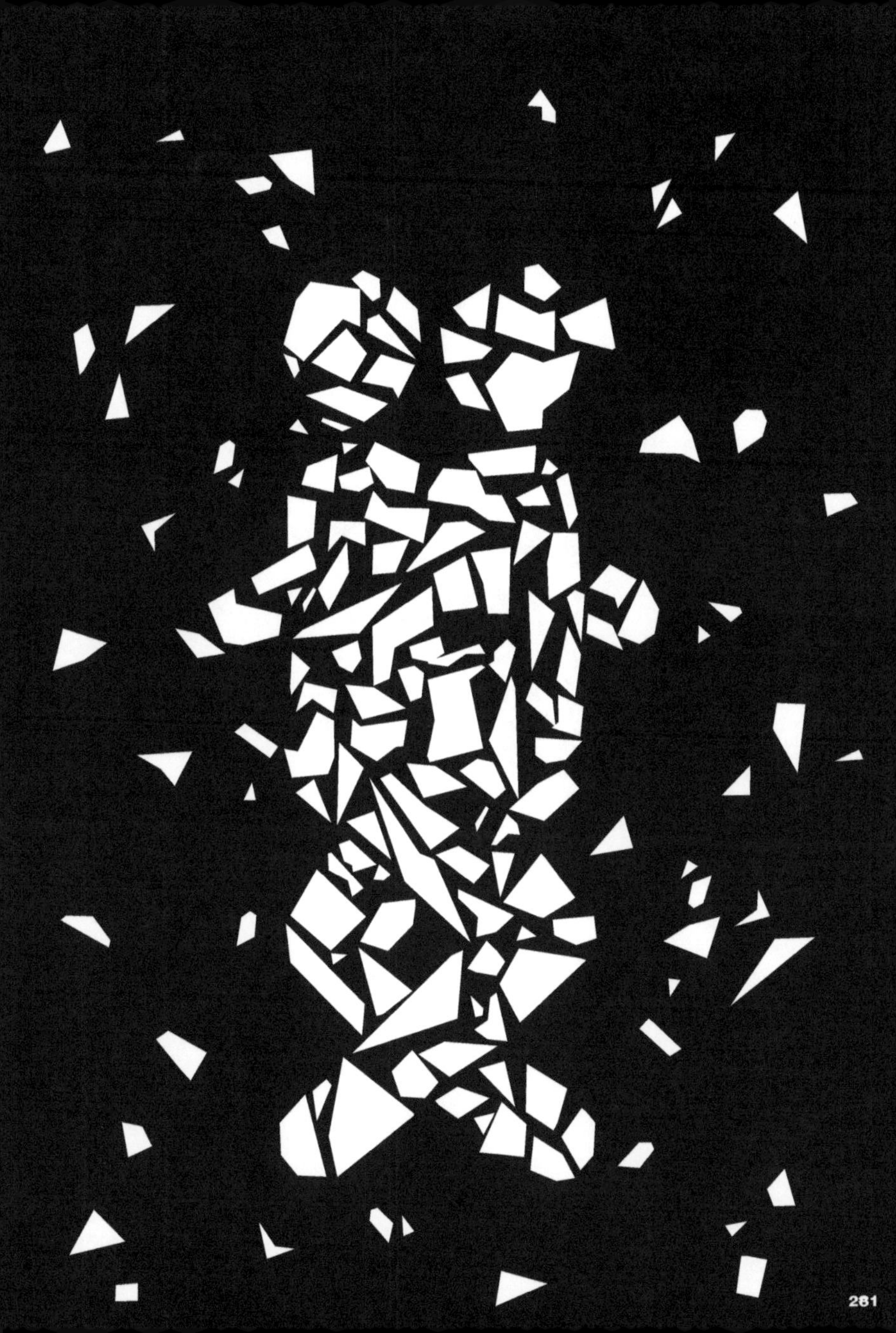

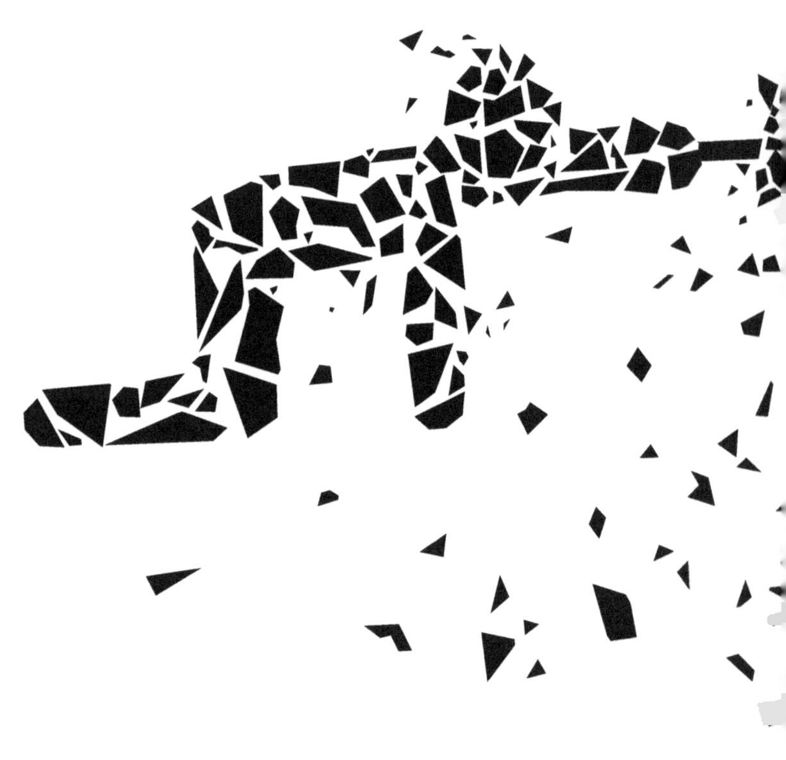

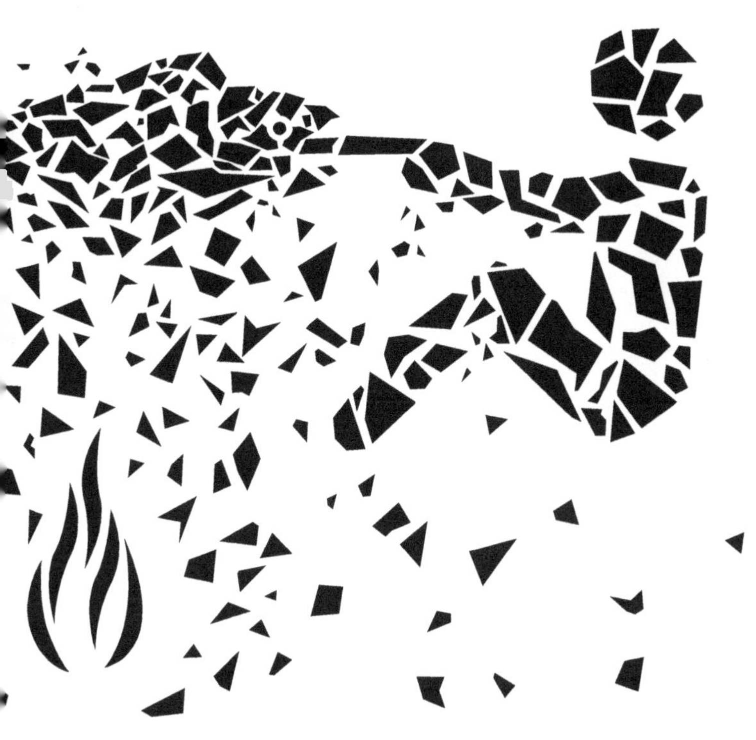

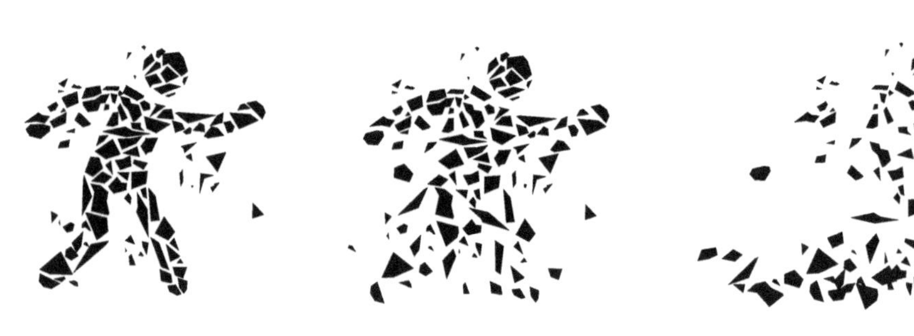

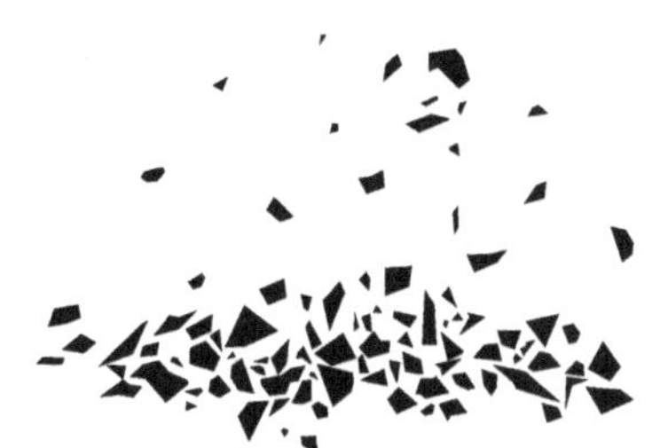

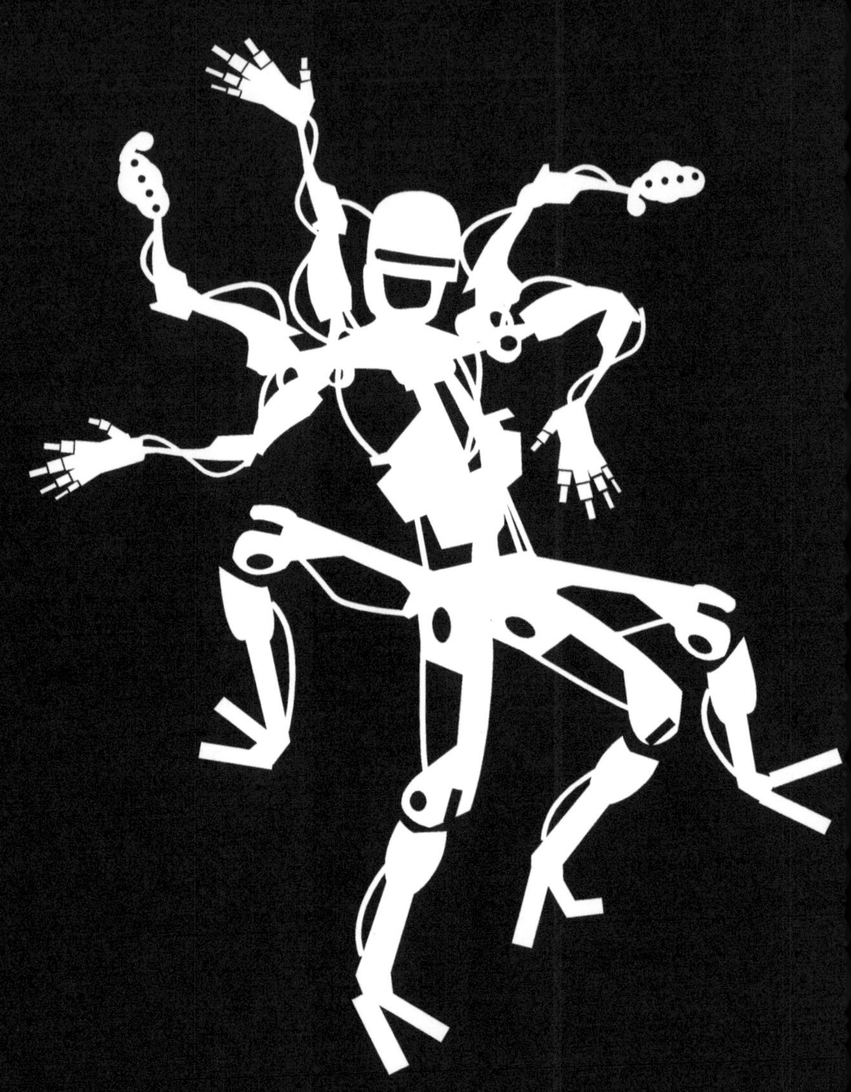

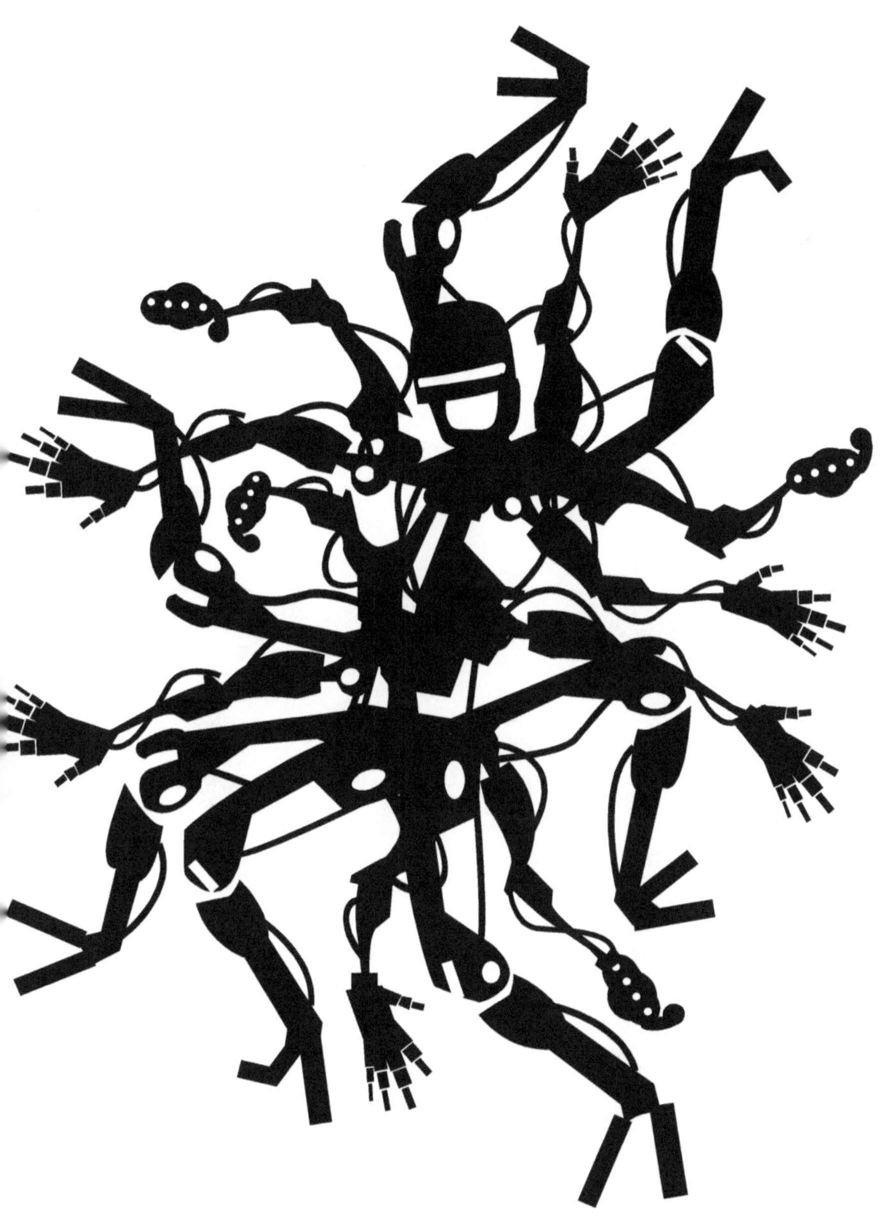

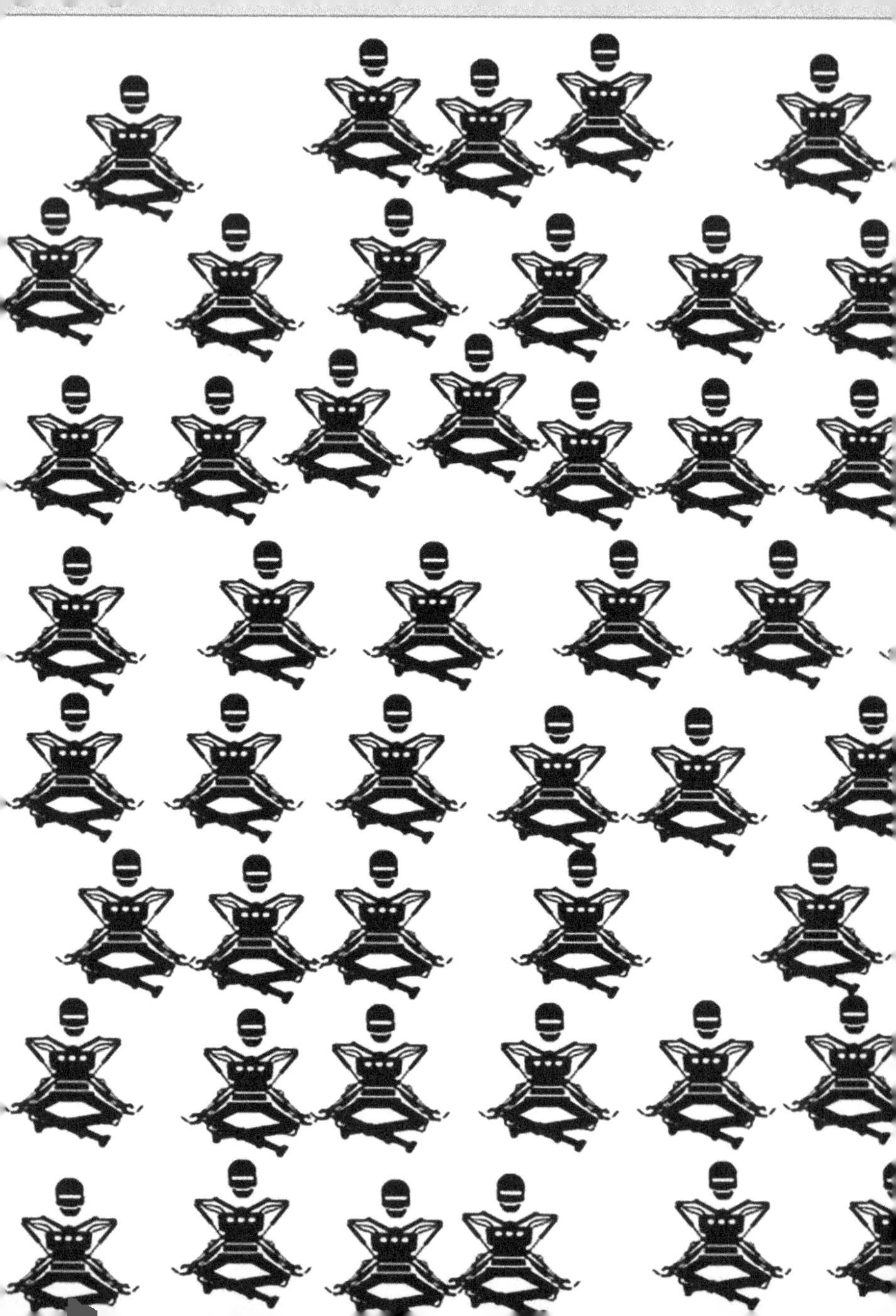

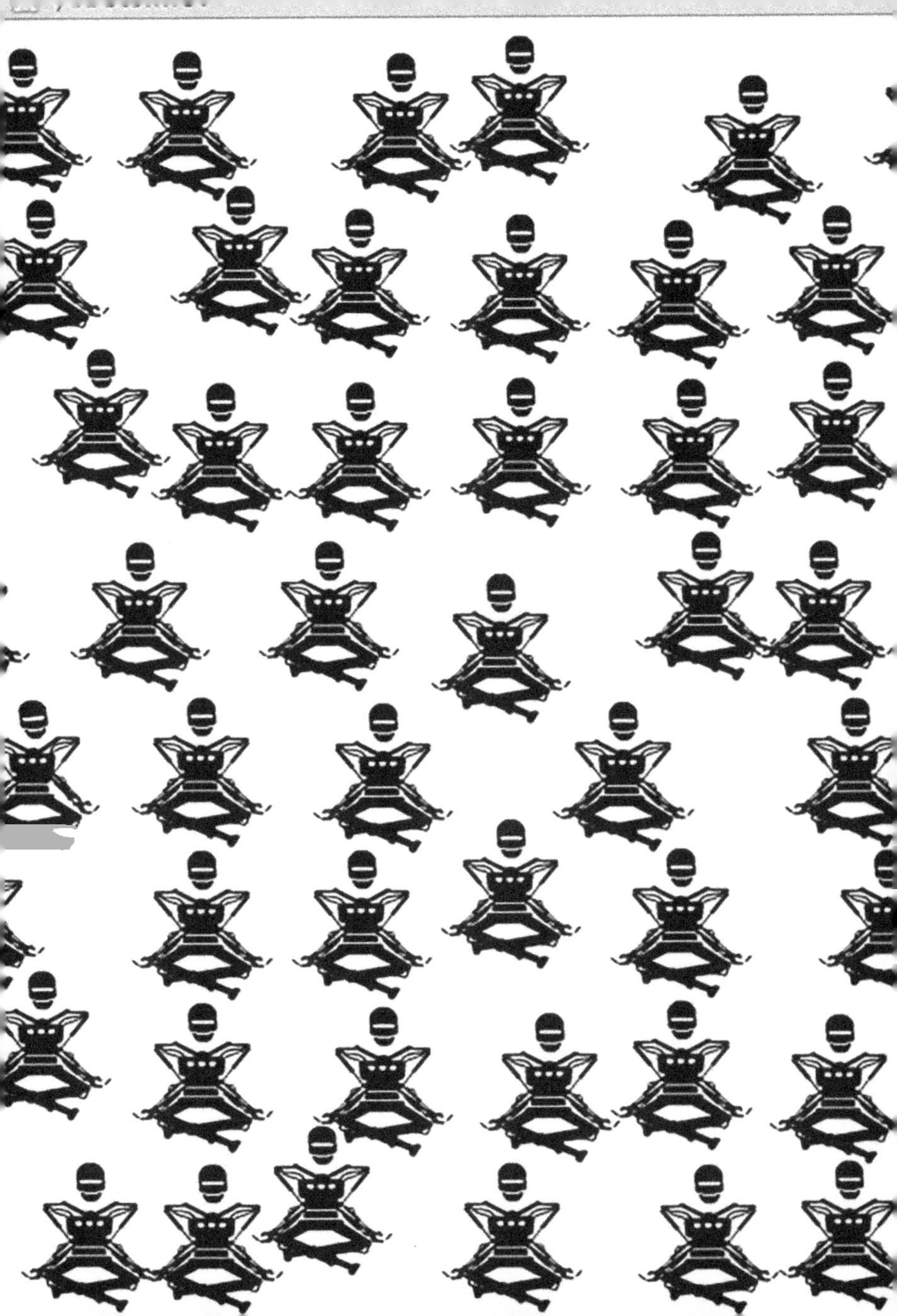

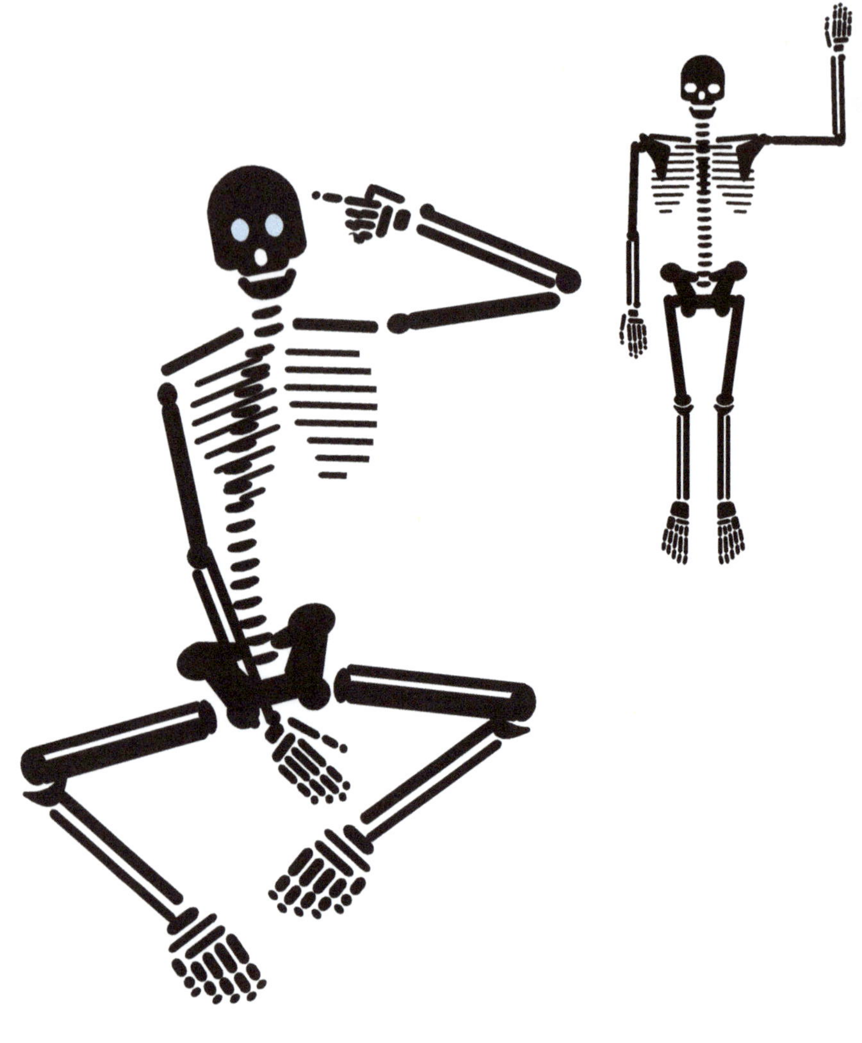

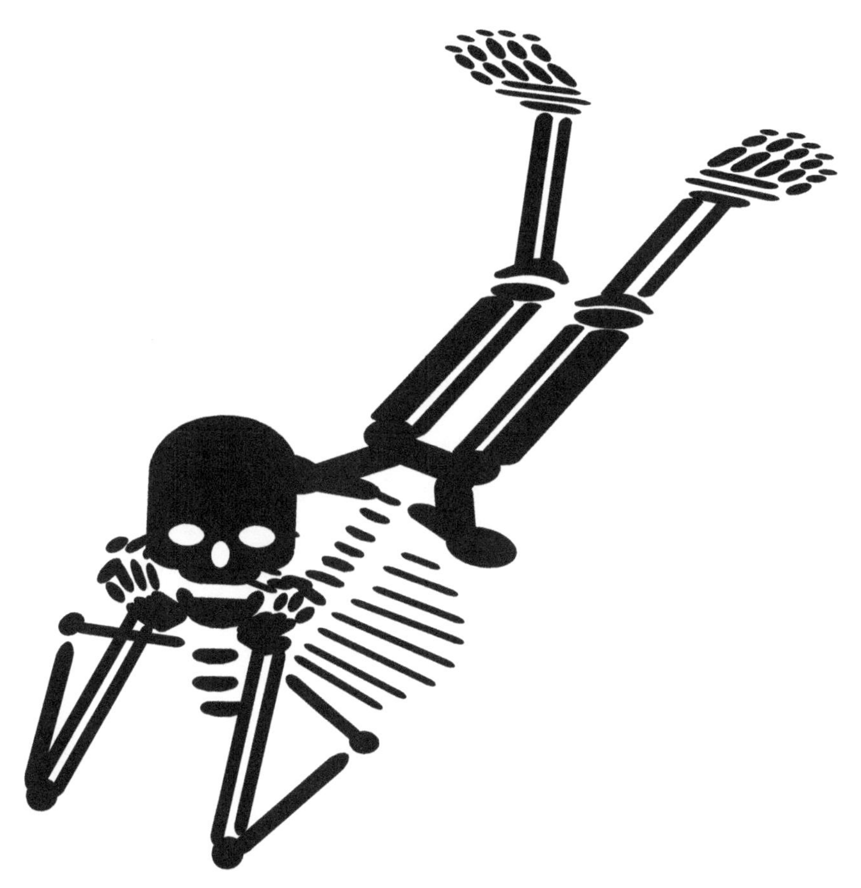

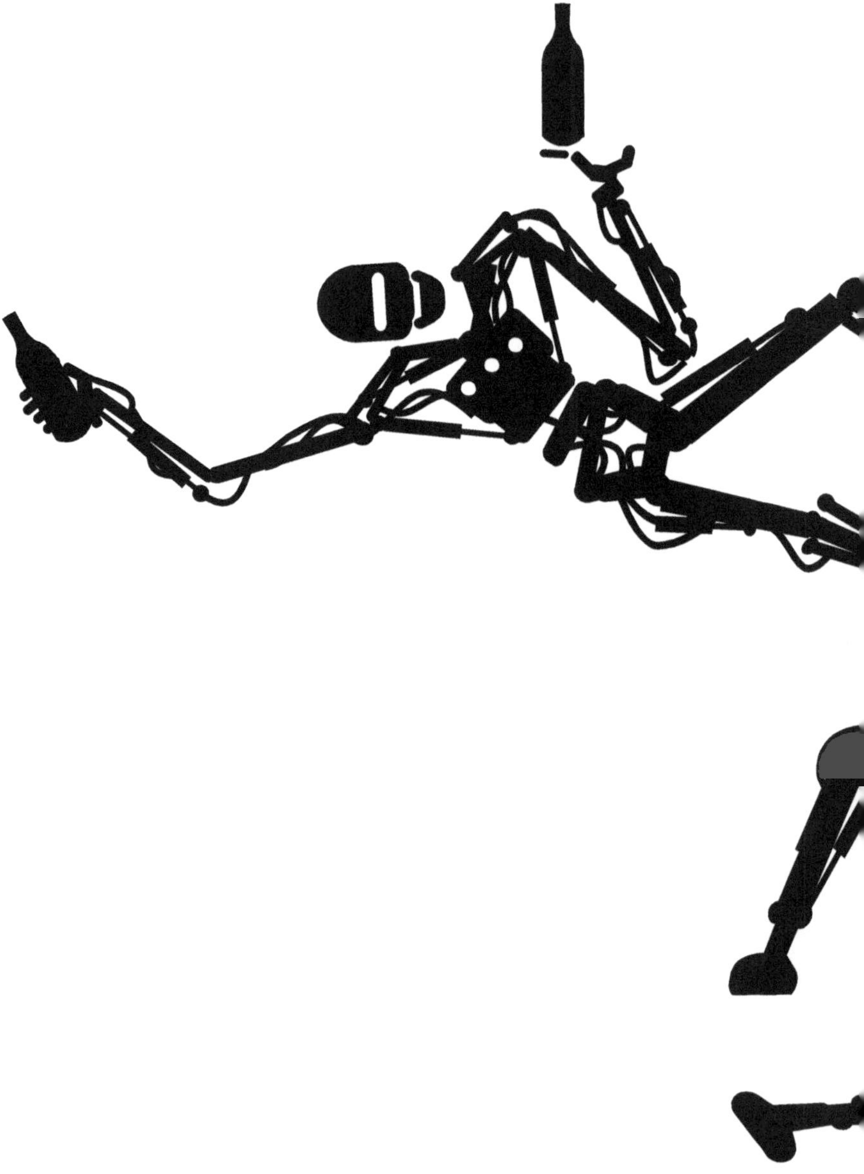

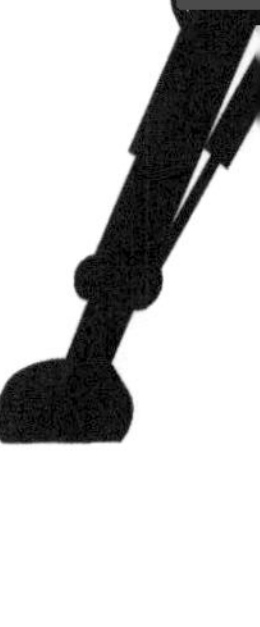
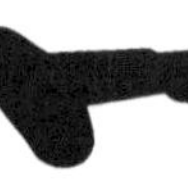

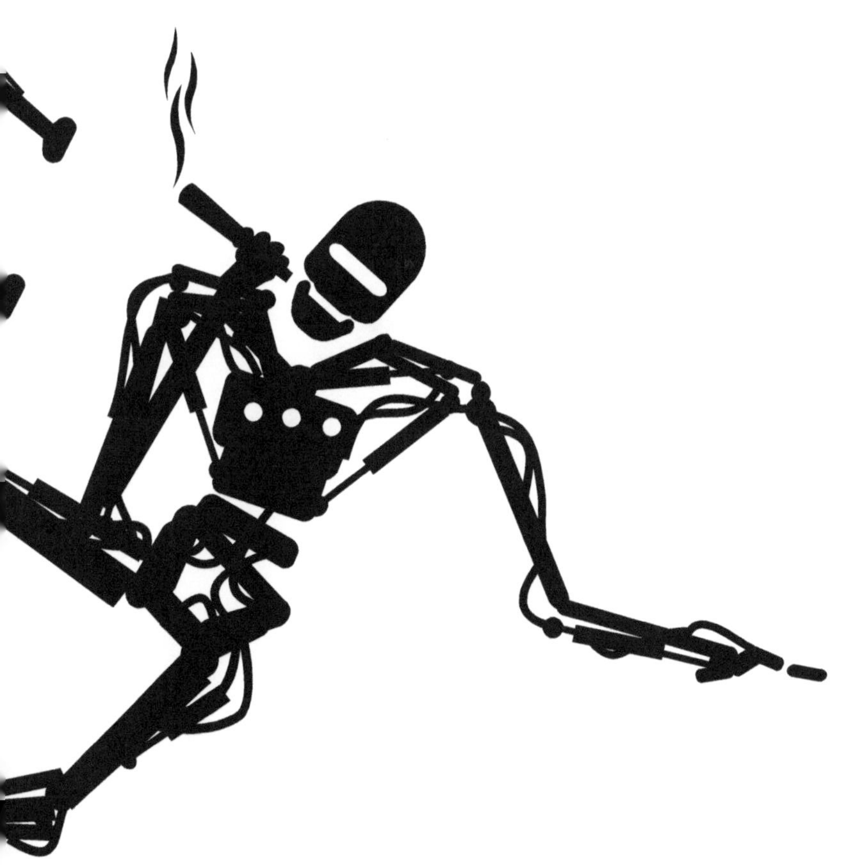

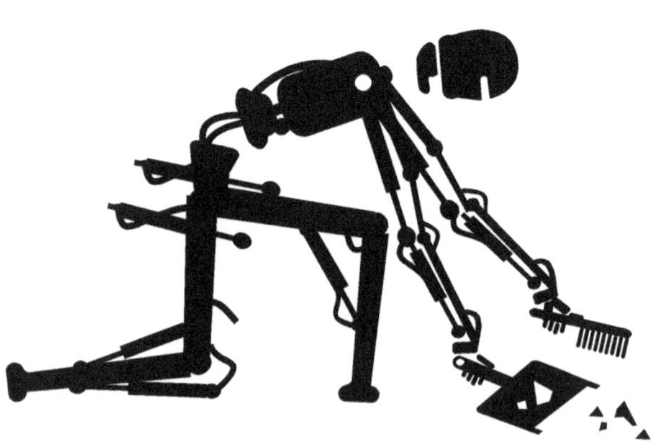

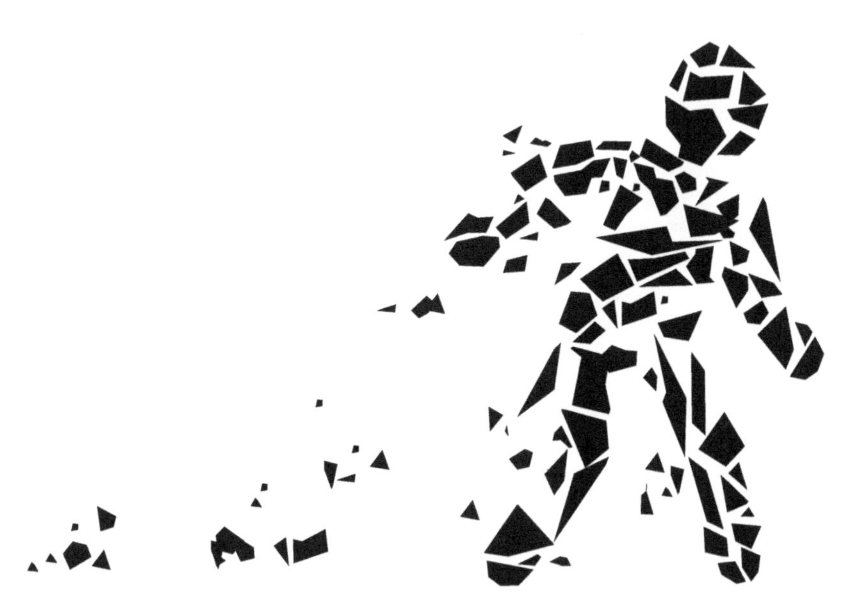

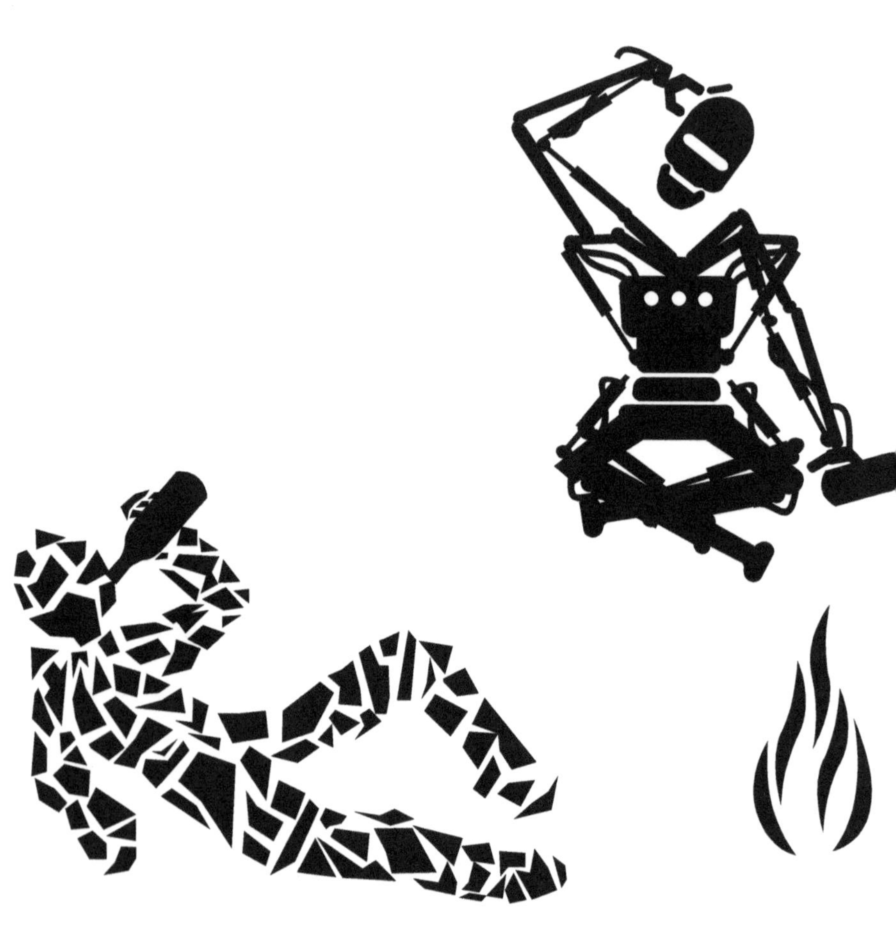

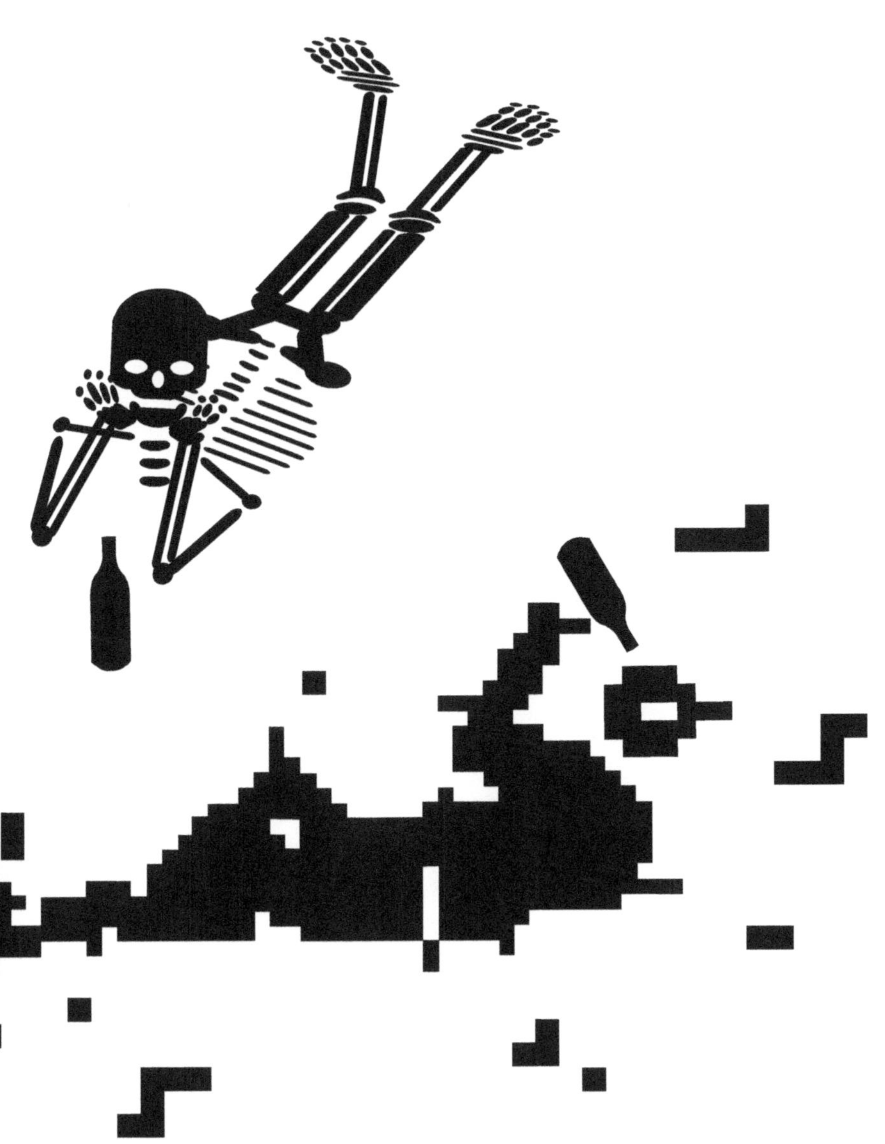

Pippo Lionni, was born in New York and has been living in Paris since the early eighties. His multicultural background and multidisciplinary education result in variety of activities and forms of expression such as big wall installations, projected animations and painting. He was awarded the distinction of « Chevalier de l'Ordre des Arts et des Lettres » by French Ministry of culture in 2001. In 1998, Pippo Lionni began work on Facts of Life. Over the next 10 years this body of work took on many art and design forms from installations in galleries and museums, to animations projected in institutions and in the public spaces. in 2009 he turned from art with a message to abstract painting. For more information see www.lionni.com

publications
Facts of Life 3, 100 pages - Verlag H. Schmidt GmbH & Co - 2002
Facts of Life 2, 140 pages - Verlag H. Schmidt GmbH & Co - 2001
Facts of Life 1, 100 pages - Verlag H. Schmidt GmbH & Co - 2000
Facts of Life 1, 100 pages - Verlag H. Schmidt GmbH & Co - 1999